THE MATURIDI SCHOOL

from Abu Hanifa to al-Kawthari

THE MATURIDI SCHOOL

from Abu Hanifa to al-Kawthari

Gibril Fouad Haddad

BEACON BOOKS

First published in the UK by Beacon Books and Media Ltd, Earl Business Centre, Dowry Street, Oldham, OL8 2PF
www.beaconbooks.net

ISBN:	978-1-912356-72-0	Paperback
	978-1-912356-73-7	Hardback
	978-1-912356-74-4	Ebook

Cataloging-in-Publication Data
Haddad, Gibril Fouad, 1960-
The Maturidi School from Abu Hanifa to al-Kawthari.

1. Islam -- Doctrines -- Early works to 1800. 2. Islam -- Doctrines. 3. Islamic theology. 4. Islam -- Theology -- History. 5. God (Islam) -- History of doctrines. 6. God (Islam) -- Attributes. 7. Islamic sects. 8. Sunnites -- Doctrines. 9. Sunnites -- Doctrines -- History. 10. Māturīdī, Muḥammad ibn Muḥammad, -944 or 945 -- Influence. 11. Maturidites. 12. Asharites. 13. Muslim Scholars -- Biography. 14. Islam -- Bibliography. I. Haddad, Gibril Fouad, 1960- . II. Title.

Cover image: The monument featured on the front cover is the final resting place of Imam al-Maturidi. In 1947, the cemetery was razed to the ground. After decades of neglect, the current mausoleum was built and opened on the 17th of November 2000, commemorating 1130 years since the birth of the Imam.

بِسْمِ ٱللَّهِ ٱلرَّحْمَٰنِ ٱلرَّحِيمِ

In the Name of the One God,
the All-Beneficent, the Most Merciful

Contents

ABBREVIATIONS

AA	*al-Rawḍat al-bahiyya fīmā bayna al-Ashāʿira wal-Māturīdiyya* (Abū ʿAdhaba)
AM	*al-ʿĀlim wal-mutaʿallim* (Abū Ḥanīfa)
ʿAqd	*ʿAqāʾid al-Nasafī* (Burhān al-Dīn Nasafī)
Badʾ	*Badʾ al-amālī fī uṣūl al-dīn* (Ūshī)
Baḥr	*Baḥr al-kalām* (Maymūn Nasafī)
Bar	*Barīqa Maḥmūdiyya fī sharḥ ṭarīqa Muḥammadiyya* (Khādimī)
Bid	*al-Bidāya min al-kifāya fīl-hidāya* (Ṣābūnī)
FAk	*al-Fiqh al-akbar* (Abū Ḥanīfa)
FAb	*al-Fiqh al-absaṭ* (Abū Ḥanīfa)
Güm	*Jāmiʿ al-mutūn fīl-ṣifāt wal-ʿaqāʾid al-Māturīdiyya* (Gümüşhanevi)
HUD	*al-Hādī fī uṣūl al-dīn* (Khabbāzī)
Ifāda	*al-Ifādat al-Madaniyya fīl-irādat al-juzʾiyya* (Abū al-Ḥasan al-Sindī)
IKB	*Masāʾil al-ikhtilāf bayna al-Ashāʿira wal-Māturīdiyya* (Ibn Kamāl Bāshā)
ʿIqd	*al-ʿIqd al-jawharī fīl-farq bayn al-kasbayn* (Khālid Baghdādī)
Ish	*Ishārāt al-marām min ʿibārāt al-imām* (Bayāḍī)
Iʿtmd	*al-Iʿtimād fīl-iʿtiqād* (ʿAbd Allāh Nasafī)
Iʿtqd	*al-Iʿtiqād: ʿAqīdatun marwiyya ʿan Abī Ḥanīfa* (Ustuwāʾī)
Lubāb	*Lubāb al-kalām* (Usmandī)
MfA	*Masāʾil fīl-ʿaqīda* (Abū al-Layth Samarqandī)
Minḥ	*Minaḥ al-rawḍ al-azhar* (Qārī)
MinḥS	*Minaḥ al-rawḍ al-azhar Supplements* (Qārī)
Minḥz	*Minaḥ al-rawḍ al-azhar – Alfāẓ al-kufr* (Badr al-Rashīd)
Mumz	*Mumayyizāt madhhab al-Māturīdiyya* (Isbīrī Qādīzāde)
Musyr	*al-Musāyara fī ʿilm al-kalām wal-ʿaqāʾid al-tawḥīdiyya* (Ibn al-Humām)
Muʿtq	*al-Muʿtaqad al-muntaqad* (Badāyūnī)
Naẓm	*Naẓm al-farāʾid fīl-ikhtilāf fīl-ʿaqāʾid* (Shaykhī Zādah)

Qawl	*al-Qawl al-faṣl sharḥ al-Fiqh al-akbar* (Bahā' al-Dīn Shaykh Zādah)
RJ	*Rawḍat al-jannāt* (Aqḥiṣārī)
Ruk	*al-ʿAqīdat al-rukniyya* (Rukn al-Dīn Samarqandī)
Sawd	*al-Sawād al-aʿẓam fīl-kalām* (Ibn al-Ḥakīm al-Samarqandī)
Tabṣ	*Tabṣirat al-adilla* (Maymūn Nasafī)
Taft	*Sharḥ al-ʿaqā'id al-nasafiyya* (Taftāzānī)
Talkh	*Talkhīṣ al-adilla li-qawāʿid al-tawḥīd* (Ṣaffār)
TamL	*al-Tamhīd li-qawāʿid al-tawḥīd* (Lāmishī)
TamN	*al-Tamhīd li-qawāʿid al-tawḥīd* (Maymūn Nasafī)
Tawḥ	*Kitāb al-Tawḥīd* (Māturīdī)
UṣGh	*Uṣūl al-dīn* (Ghaznawī)
UṣPz	*Uṣūl al-dīn* (Abū al-Yusr Pazdawī)
Zubad	*Kitāb zubad al-ʿaqā'id al-Nasafiyya* (al-Ṣaʿīdī)

﴿ قُلْ هَٰذِهِۦ سَبِيلِىٓ أَدْعُوٓا۟ إِلَى ٱللَّهِ ۚ عَلَىٰ بَصِيرَةٍ أَنَا۠ وَمَنِ ٱتَّبَعَنِى ۖ
وَسُبْحَٰنَ ٱللَّهِ وَمَآ أَنَا۠ مِنَ ٱلْمُشْرِكِينَ ١٠٨ ﴾

سورة يوسف على نبينا وعليه الصلاة والسلام

Introduction

This work is a survey of the salient themes and comparative translation of the bullet points of the most important Māturīdī authorities and their doctrinal textbooks with a synoptic (i.e. presenting a condensed overview) bio-bibliography of Māturīdī scholars and scholarship in descending order of antiquity. It highlights their resolutions (*taqrīrāt*) as the defining parameters of Sunnism and can serve both as an introductory synopsis of the great themes of Maturidism and as a tool for the study of the school's theology from its early founders to our time.

The doctrinal creed of the largest denomination of Muslims that came to be known as 'The Adherents to the Sunna and the Congregation' found staunch defenders in the school of the 'Arch-master of guidance' (*Imām al-hudā*) and 'Standard-bearer of guidance' (*'Alam al-hudā*) of Samarqand, Abū Manṣūr al-Māturīdī (d. 333/945),[1] who codified the theology of 'the Greatest Leader' (*al-imām al-a'ẓam*) Abū Ḥanīfa (80–150/699–767) that dominated the central Asian region of Transoxiana (present-day Uzbekistan and parts of Turkmenistan, Tajikistan, and Kazakhstan). As the chief clearing-house of Sunni *kalām* and Sunnicentric heresiology together with Ash'arism, Maturidism catalogues, on the one hand, the spectrum of Sunni and non-Sunni doctrines and, on the other, all creeds other than Islam. The purpose was not intellectual

1 See, on his life, the works of al-Ghālī (1989), Kutlu (2003), al-Maghribī (2009), Rudolph (2015), Chaker (2016), Sālim (2017) and Damanhūrī (2018) listed in the section on contemporary literature at the end of this book.

research on 'religions' but rather the production of knowledge and certainty regarding Sunni Islamic identity and orthodox ('doctrinally sound') Muslim belief and practice. Māturīdī theology thus defined itself in contrast both with Sunna-contrariant doctrines and Islam-contrariant ones, furthermore doing so on the *kalām* dialectic-theological bases which form the definitional foundations of *tawḥīd* to which people were summoned by Prophets 'with full insight' (*'alā baṣīra*, Sūrat Yūsuf 12:108).

Salient Themes of Maturidism

Imitative belief (*īmān al-muqallid*), speculative study (*naẓar*), and acquired knowledge (*ma'rifa*)

This is an issue discussed in Māturīdī literature under the heading of 'the faith of the imitator (*muqallid*).' Imām al-Māturīdī began *al-Tawḥīd* by stating that mere *taqlīd* was null as an avenue to knowledge of Allah—as did al-Ashʿarī—and the Samarqand masters deemed rational investigation (*naẓar al-ʿaql*) obligatory (Usmandī, *Lubāb* pp. 42–43 *wujūb al-naẓar fī maʿrifat Allāh*, his *Badhl al-naẓar fil uṣūl*, and Abū al-Yusr Pazdawī, *Uṣūl al-dīn*). At the same time his School emphasized the fact that an imitative believer is still a believer whom Allah has promised Paradise, contrary to the Muʿtazila who alone claimed that imitative belief was unbelief (per Ūshī, *Badʾ*, 'the faith of the imitator is taken in consideration'; Lāmishī, *Tamhīd*, 'the faith of an imitator in belief who is convinced but ignorant of the proofs is valid, contrary to the Muʿtazila'; and Ibn al-Subkī, *Jamʿ al-jawāmiʿ*, *Masʾala: al-taqlīd fī uṣūl al-dīn*, stating that only the Muʿtazila, specifically Abū ʿAlī al-Jubbāʾī, held that the imitator's faith is invalid). This was discussed by Abū al-Yusr Pazdawī, *Uṣūl al-dīn*, ch. 39, 'the imitative believer is a believer by consensus'; Maymūn Nasafī in the chapter 'On the faith of the imitator' in *Tabṣirat al-adilla* (1:27); Ghaznawī in *Uṣūl al-Dīn*, 11.5: 'The imitator's faith is valid'; and Bahāʾ al-Dīn Zādah at the beginning of *al-Qawl al-faṣl* (p. 17), his commentary on Abū Ḥanīfa's *Fiqh al-akbar* (*q.v.*) among others. Ashʿarīs also consider the imitator a believer but, at the same time, viewed *naẓar* as individually compulsory and its neglect a sin (per Imām al-Ashʿarī as cited by Abū Manṣūr al-Baghdādī in Nasafī's *Tabṣira* 1:29; cf. Lāmishī, *Tamhīd*, pp. 138–140; Imām al-Ḥaramayn in *al-Irshād*, '*naẓar* conducive to the *maʿārif* [of Allah] is obligatory' and Ibn al-Tilimsānī's recapitulation at the beginning of his commentary on al-Rāzī's *Maʿālim uṣūl al-dīn*). They defined *naẓar* as 'knowledge of every article of belief with its proof, even if undetailed, as an individual obligation' (Bājūrī on *Jawharat al-tawḥīd*). The report that al-Ashʿarī and Ibn al-Bāqillānī said the imitator's belief is invalid was adduced by some Māturīdīs and even certain Ashʿarīs (e.g. Abū Manṣūr al-Baghdādī and al-ʿIzz b. Jamāʿa), but was declared false and inauthentic by Abū al-Qāsim al-Qushayrī and Abū Muḥammad al-Juwaynī (see Badr al-Dīn al-Zarkashī, *al-Baḥr al-muḥīṭ fī uṣūl al-fiqh, Taqlīd, wa-qad ishtaharat hādhihi al-maqālatu ʿani al-Ashʿarī*, al-Maḥallī's *Sharḥ Jamʿ*

al-jawāmiʿ, Ijtihād, al-taqlīd fī uṣūl al-dīn, ʿwa-ʿani al-Ashʿarī annahu lā yaṣiḥḥu īmān al-muqallid, Ibn al-Subkī as already cited, and Saʿīd Fawda's clarifications in his edition of ʿAlāʾ al-Dīn al-Bukhārī's *Risāla fil-iʿtiqād*).

Kasb as a Māturīdī concept and not only an Ashʿarī one

A synoptic survey allows the extraction of general thematic guidelines. Of the many themes that emerge from the present study, some can be said to typify the Māturīdī school exclusively and others can be said to be shared with Ashʿarīs,[2] while notions can be corrected or refined. For example, it can be inferred from the frequent use of the concept of 'acquisition' (*kasb*) among Māturīdī masters such as Maymūn Nasafī in *Baḥr al-kalām*, al-Khādimī, al-Khabbāzī, Ibn al-Humām, al-Qārī and al-Badāyūnī, that the remark of al-Subkī (*q.v.*) in his *Nūniyya* that Māturīdīs prefer to call *kasb* 'choice' (*ikhtiyār*) does not apply invariably. The very title of Mawlānā Khālid al-Baghdādī's (d. 1827) epistle *al-ʿIqd al-jawharī fil-farq bayna al-kasb al-Māturīdī wal-Ashʿarī* presupposes the common usage of the term in both schools, although its concept might differ across them as demonstrated in detail by al-Nābulusī and Mawlānā Khālid in their monographs on that question as well as Abū ʿAdhaba in the *Rawḍa* (sixth issue of the terminological differences).

The Māturīdī differentiation between divine contentment (*riḍā*) and divine will (*irāda*)

Equally open to nuance is al-Subkī's assertion (which, in fairness, he qualifies) that 'what is narrated from Abū Ḥanīfa is that divine good pleasure (*riḍā*) and divine will (*irāda*) are one,' since al-Māturīdī, Maymūn al-Nasafī in the *Tamhīd*, al-Ūshī, Ibn al-Humām, al-Bayāḍī, al-Khādimī, Abū ʿAdhaba and Shaykhī Zādah explicitly differentiate between them, while Maymūn al-Nasafī (*Tamhīd*) and al-Usmandī do so implicitly, through the affirmation that

2 Others yet can be said to be shared across all the three schools held by al-Saffārīnī to represent *Ahl al-Sunna*, the third being the so-called Atharī school, a euphemism for Hanbalis who might be either Ashʿarī/Māturīdī-leaning or literalists.

'sins are by virtue of the will of Allah and His decision.' Al-Qārī contributed a luminous page on the two distinct contexts of the divine will corresponding respectively to will as creation and existentiation (*irāda qadariyya kawniyya khalqiyya*) on the one hand and, on the other, will as a tasking will (*irāda amriyya*). An example of the first context is the verse *So whomsoever the One God wants* (yurīdu) *to guide, He opens up his chest to self-resignation, and whomsoever He wants to lead astray, He makes his chest narrow and constricted, as if he were climbing up the sky* (al-Anʿām 6:125) and an example of the second is the verse *Allah wants* (yurīdu) *ease for you and He does not want hardship for you* (al-Baqara 2:185).[3]

Synonymity of *irāda* and *mashī'a* (will); near-synonymity with *ikhtiyār* (choice)

On the other hand, *irāda* and *mashī'a* are synonymous (Maymūn Nasafī, *Tamhīd*) as also suggested by the expression *al-shā'ī al-murīd* in the *'Aqā'id al-Nasafī*, except that *mashī'a* is used to express 'complete will followed by act without delay' (*al-irādat al-tāmma al-latī lā yatakhallaf 'anhā al-fi'l*), while *irāda* is applicable to both 'integral' and 'partial' will. Thus, the first is what is meant from the divine perspective, while the latter is what is meant from the creature's perspective.[4] Both *irāda* and *mashī'a* are near in meaning to *ikhtiyār* as well (Badāyūnī, *Muʿtaqad*). Al-Nābulusī wrote extensively on all the five themes of this and the preceding two paragraphs (*al-Kawkab al-sārī, al-Qawl al-sadīd, Taḥqīq al-intiṣār,* and *Taḥrīk silsilat al-widād*).

Māturīdīs mostly reject the possibility that Allah can task servants beyond capacity

Also among the famous Māturīdī positions in opposition to Ashʿarī is the explicit rejection of the possibility of Allah 'tasking His servants beyond their capacity' (*al-taklīf bi-mā lā yuṭāq*) in the texts of al-Māturīdī's *al-Tawḥīd*,

3 al-Qārī, *Sharḥ al-Fiqh al-akbar*, Nafā'is ed. p. 61 = *Minaḥ*, p. 80.

4 al-Qārī, *Minaḥ*, p. 78.

al-Pazdawī's *Uṣūl al-dīn*, Maymūn al-Nasafī's *Baḥr al-kalām*, Usmandī's *Lubāb al-kalām*, Ṣābūnī's *Bidāya*, Khabbāzī's *Hādī*, al-Samarqandī's *Rukniyya*, ʿAbd Allāh al-Nasafī's *Iʿtimād*, al-Taftāzānī's *Sharḥ al-ʿaqā'id*, al-Qārī's supplements to *Minaḥ al-rawḍ al-azhar*, and Shaykhī Zādah's *Naẓm al-farā'id*, with the notable dissent of Ibn al-Humām in the *Musāyara*, where he took the Ashʿarī position.

The difference between the two schools is terminological rather than actual. Both schools rejected the Muʿtazilī claim of *istiṭāʿa* or autonomous ability as existing in servants before, during, and after an act except as 'haleness of means, instruments and limbs' (*salāmat al-asbāb wal-ālāt wal-jawāriḥ*). In the sense of one's 'acquisition' or 'choice' (*kasb, ikhtiyār*), both schools mostly viewed *istiṭāʿa* as strictly concomitant with the servant's act, neither preceding nor following it. In their reasoning, such acquisition (i.e. a creature's appropriation of moral responsibility) could never take place except at the time of the act exclusively, since '*istiṭāʿa* is a means (*sabab*) for acquisition, and the means can no more temporally precede the mediated (*musabbab*) than the cause (*ʿilla*) can precede the caused (*maʿlūl*).' Since only Allah is *the arch-effective agent of His will* (*faʿʿālun li-mā yurīd*, Hūd 11:107, al-Burūj 85:16), then the relation between what is perceived to be the means/cause (*sabab/ʿilla*) and what is the mediated/caused (*musabbab/maʿlūl*) can only be one of conjunction (*iqtirān*), not one of efficacy or influence (*ta'thīr*), or engendering or existentiating (*ījād*). This credal stance (i) is in logical congruence with the rejection of a 'nature' (*ṭabīʿa*) inherent in things as an autonomous causal agent and (ii) affirms the theological conclusion that all causation (*ta'thīriyya*), in actuality, is 'vertical' and never 'horizontal.'[5] The Ashʿarīs took the above reasoning to its logical conclusion that, at the time of the Divine command and until its implementation by the servant's act, literal ability is missing and

5 Ibn Fūrak, *Maqālāt al-shaykh Abī al-Ḥasan al-Ashʿarī imām Ahl al-Sunna*, ed. Aḥmad ʿAbd al-Raḥīm al-Sāyiḥ (Cairo: Maktabat al-Thaqāfat al-Dīniyya, 1425/2005), p. 111; cf. al-Ashʿarī, *al-Lumaʿ fil-radd ʿalā ahl al-zaygh wal-bidaʿ*. With his *Risāla fī istiḥsān al-khawḍ fī ʿilm al-kalām*, ed. Muḥammad Ḥusayn al-Ḍawī (Beirut: Dār al-Kutub al-ʿIlmiyya, 1421/2000), pp. 58–61; Abū Ḥafṣ al-Nasafī, *al-ʿAqā'id*, ed. al-Jābī, p. 23; Abū al-Muʿīn al-Nasafī, *Tabṣira*, Salamé ed. ['by consensus in that sense'] 2:541–543; Abū al-Layth al-Samarqandī, *Sharḥ al-Fiqh al-akbar*, Dā'irat al-Maʿārif al-Niẓāmiyya ed., p. 8; Būṭī, *Kubrā al-yaqīniyyāt al-kawniyya*, 8th ed. (Beirut: Dār al-Fikr al-Muʿāṣir; Damascus: Dār al-Fikr, 1982), pp. 155–169.

continues to be missing until the act takes place. Hence their rule that 'legal responsibilities in their entirety befall in contravention of [independent] ability' (*al-takālīf kulluhā wāqiʿa ʿalā khilāf al-istiṭāʿa*) as stated by Imām al-Ḥaramayn and elucidated by al-Āmidī in the opening of the third *aṣl* of his *Iḥkām*.[6]

Nevertheless, Ashʿarīs and Māturīdīs all posited that there were two possible scenarios whereby one can be ordered to do something one was unable to do: (i) physical inability, in which case legal responsibility (*taklīf*) was cancelled; here, the legally responsible person (*mukallaf*) is psychologically aware of his physical inability and thus cannot conceive of fulfilling the command, and so the inability is not wilful; (ii) wilful avoidance and opposition, as with those like Abū Jahl and Abū Lahab who were commanded to believe although Allah knew they would not, and who *will be plunged in a flaming fire* (al-Masad 111:3); here, the *mukallaf* is psychologically aware of his ability and thus can conceive of fulfilling the command, so that any inability is wilful. The latter wilful inability, moreover, is the general status of all disbelievers. It also shows that ability for disbelief differs from ability for belief, and that the inner reality of this matter remains hidden, lest volition (*ikhtiyār*) turn to coercion (*jabr*) although, ontologically, both scenarios derive directly from the divine will and power.[7]

6 Ibn al-Juwaynī, *al-Burhān fī uṣūl al-fiqh*, ed. ʿAbd al-ʿAẓīm al-Dīb, 2nd ed., 2 vols. (Cairo: Dār al-Anṣār, 1400/1980), 1:102–105; al-Āmidī, *al-Iḥkām fī uṣūl al-aḥkām*, ed. ʿAbd al-Razzāq ʿAfīfī, 4 vols. (Riyadh: Dār al-Ṣumayʿī, 1424/2003), 1:179–192.

7 Ibn Fūrak, *Maqālāt*, pp. 110–113; cf. al-Ashʿarī, *Lumaʿ*, pp. 62–63 and *al-Ibāna ʿan uṣūl al-diyāna*, ed. Bashīr Muḥammad ʿUyūn, 3rd ed. (Damascus: Maktabat Dār al-Bayān, 1416–1996), pp. 134–135; Abū al-Muʿīn al-Nasafī, *Tabṣira*, Salamé ed. 2:544–545; al-Taftāzānī, *Sharḥ al-ʿAqāʾid al-nasafiyya*, pp. 145–150; al-Bunānī, *Ḥāshiya* on al-Maḥallī's *Sharḥ* on al-Subkī's *Jamʿ al-jawāmiʿ* entitled *Ḥāshiyat al-ʿallāma al-Bunnānī* [sic] *ʿalā sharḥ al-Jalāl Shams al-Dīn Muḥammad b. Aḥmad al-Maḥallī ʿalā matn Jamʿ al-jawāmiʿ lil-imām Tāj al-Dīn ʿAbd al-Wahhāb Ibn al-Subkī*, 2 vols. [Cairo: s.n.], 1285/1868; rept. Beirut: Dār al-Fikr, 1982/1402, 1:206 (section entitled *Masʾala: yajūz al-taklīf bil-muḥāl muṭlaqan*); al-Haytamī, *al-Fatḥ al-mubīn bi-sharḥ al-Arbaʿīn*, with Ḥasan b. ʿAlī al-Mudābighī's *Ḥāshiya*, ed. Muḥammad Ḥasan Ismāʿīl (Beirut: Dār al-Kutub al-ʿIlmiyya, 2007), pp. 180–181 (discussion of *qaḍāʾ* in the commentary on the second of the Forty Hadiths) and *al-Minaḥ al-Makkiyya fī sharḥ al-Hamziyya*, ed. Bassām Muḥammad Bārūd, 3 vols. (Abū Dhabī: al-Mujammaʿ al-Thaqāfī and Beirut: Dār al-Ḥāwī, 1418/1998), 2:822 'by consensus.'

The Māturīdī view that *īmān* (faith/belief) neither increases nor decreases

Time and again in the Māturīdī creeds the position that '*īmān*'—since it means the very same as *islām* (submission)—'neither increases nor decreases' is reaffirmed.[8] We have established elsewhere that the majority Sunni position is that it does, and we have documented the majority's differentiation between *islām* and *īmān* in that respect.[9] One of the authoritative texts of Ashʿarī doctrine, however, does take the Māturīdī position that 'belief... neither increases nor decreases; however, it must be stated: *I am a believer if Allah wills (in shā' Allāh).*'[10]

The Orientalist construct of Māturīdīs as near to Muʿtazilīs

Trite as Goldziher's observation of Māturīdīs as 'a shade closer to the Muʿtazilites than Ashʿarites are'[11] may be, Wensinck's claims—endorsed by Cerić—that Abū Ḥanīfa's theology does not even address the issues brought up by the Muʿtazila and that their refutation is a later development are an outright blunder.[12] Such a construct is untenable in light of the sustained refutation of Muʿtazilism that emerges from the Māturīdī creeds beginning with both versions of the *Fiqh al-akbar* as illustrated by Pazdawī, Abū al-Layth, al-Maghnīsāwī, al-Bayāḍī, al-Qārī and other commentators on these and other

8 Cf. Usmandī, *Lubāb*, ch. 53; Khabbāzī, *Hādī*, ch. 4.12; Samarqandī, *Rukniyya*, ch. 96; ʿAbd Allāh al-Nasafī, *Iʿtimād*, ch. 35; Taftāzānī, *Sharḥ al-ʿaqā'id*, ch. 31; Qārī, *Minaḥ*, Supplements, no. 26; Bayāḍī, *Ishārāt*, position no. 40; Khādimī, *Barīqa*, difference no. 19; Badāyūnī, *Muʿtaqad*, ch. 6.9; Ṣaʿīdī, *Zubad*, ch. 36; and note 51 below. Etc.

9 See Gibril Fouad Haddad, *The Four Imams and Their Schools: Abū Ḥanīfa, Mālik, al-Shāfiʿi, Aḥmad b. Ḥanbal* (London: Muslim Academic Trust, 2007), pp. 40–46 and Ibn Ḥajar's extensive commentary on the hadith of Jibrīl translated in full in Haddad, *Sunna Notes III: The Binding Proof of the Sunna* (Birmingham: al-Qur'an wal-Sunna Association, 2010), pp. 149–202.

10 Ibn al-Ḥājib, *'Aqīda*, in al-Kūmī, *Taḥrīr al-maṭālib li-mā taḍammanathu 'Aqīdat Ibn al-Ḥājib*, ed. Nizār Ḥammādī (Beirut: Mu'assasat al-Maʿārif, 1428/2008), p. 31.

11 Ignaz Goldziher, *Introduction to Islamic Theology and Law*, transl. Andras and Ruth Hamori (Princeton: Princeton University Press, p. 95.

12 Cerić, *Roots*, p. 12.

texts attributed to Abū Ḥanīfa.[13] More nuanced are Kawtharī's remarks that 'Ash'arīs are the median between the Mu'tazila and the Ḥashawiyya while Māturīdīs are the median between Ash'arīs and the Mu'tazila.'[14] Yet this is not to say that such mediateness is invariably true. Al-Subkī stated, for example, that on some issues Imām al-Ḥaramayn and al-Ghazālī were 'as close as it gets' to Mu'tazilism,[15] while al-Suyūṭī lamented al-Bayḍāwī's 'Zamakhsharian copy-isms' (*mashyat qalam mimmā fil-Kashshāf*), which he denounced as 'definitely not our *madhhab*.'[16] Nor is al-Razī's assertion, in his *Tafsīr*, that 'reason' can be the *rasūl* meant in the verse *We never punish until We first send forth a messenger* (al-Isrā' 17:15)[17] or Ibn Abī Sharīf's assertion that 'The sacred law

13 See Balqāsim al-Ghālī, *Abū Manṣūr al-Māturīdī: ḥayātuh wa-ārā'uh al-'aqadiyya* (Tunis: Dār al-Turkī lil-Nashr, 1989), pp. 218–221; al-Maghribī, *Imām Ahl al-Sunna*, pp. 401–422; Christian Lange, 'Sin, Expiation and Non-rationality in Ḥanafī and Shāfi'ī *Fiqh*,' in *Islamic Law in Theory*, ed. A. Kevin Reinhart and Robert Gleave (Leiden and Boston: Brill, 2014), pp. 160–163 and Wilfred Madelung's review of Hans Daiber's translation of Abū al-Layth al-Samarqandī's commentary on the *Fiqh al-absaṭ*, in *Journal of the Royal Asiatic Society*, Third Series, Vol. 6, No. 3 (Nov. 1996), pp. 420–421. This aspect is confirmed even by rabidly anti-Māturīdī writers such as Muḥammad Khumayyis in his *Uṣūl al-dīn 'inda al-imām Abī Ḥanīfa* (Riyadh: Dār al-Ṣumay'ī, 1996), p. 194 and Aḥmad 'Awaḍ Allāh al-Ḥarbī, *al-Māturīdiyya dirāsatan wa-taqwīman* (Riyadh: Dār al-'Āṣima, 1413/1993), pp. 502–507. Note: Lange (p. 163) misinterprets the passage he cites from Abū al-Mu'īn al-Nasafī's *Baḥr al-kalām* (Farfūr ed. p. 163) by misconstruing al-Nasafī's expression *lā yartafi' bil-tawba* ('the offense is not wiped out by repentance') to mean there is no repentance possible whatsoever ('Abū al-Mu'in states categorically that there is no repentance for grave sins if these sins are committed knowingly'), which is Mu'tazilism and Khārijism and not what the text implies at all, which is that the repayable onus of the offense remains even after repentance (i.e., until the *ḥadd* is applied, because such sins are *ḥadd* offenses: *kal-zinā wal-liwāṭa wa-shurb al-khamr*, while *kadhib, ghība* and *buhtān* require amends towards their victims). This is made abundantly clear by the next line in al-Nasafī's text allowing repentance for graver offenses than the above, namely quitting prayer, the remittance of *zakāt*, and fasting, by simply 'making up for all of them' (*bi-qaḍā' al-fawā'it*), although the quitter had done so knowingly.

14 al-Kawtharī, introduction to Ibn 'Asākir's *Tabyīn kadhib al-muftarī*, in *Muqaddimāt al-imām al-Kawtharī* (Damascus and Beirut: Dār al-Thurayyā, 1418/1997), pp. 50–51.

15 al-Subkī, *Ṭabaqāt*, 3:386; cf. al-Jābī, *al-Masā'il*, p. 70.

16 Haddad, *Lights of Revelation*, p. 564 n., citing al-Suyūṭī, *Nawāhid al-abkār wa-shawārid al-afkār*, ed. Aḥmad Ḥājj Muḥ. 'Uthmān et al., unpublished Ph.D. dissertations, 6 vols. in 4 (Mecca: Jāmi'at Umm al-Qurā, 1423–1426/2002–2005), under al-Baqara 2:48 (on the repetition of the word *hudā*).

17 الْعَقْلُ هُوَ رَسُولُ اللَّه إِلَى الْخَلْقِ، بَلْ هُوَ الرَّسُولُ الَّذِي لَوْلَاهُ لَمَا تَقَرَّرَتْ رِسَالَةُ أَحَدٍ مِنَ الْأَنْبِيَاءِ، فَالْعَقْلُ هُوَ الرَّسُولُ الْأَصْلِيُّ

is only established through reason' (Badāyūnī 2.4.9). Such examples might therefore be adduced to construe at least some Ashʿarīs as contenders for the position of mediateness.

The Wahhābī construct of Māturīdīs as 'denying all' but a handful of divine attributes

Another over-simplification or outright falsehood is that of the denial by Māturīdīs and Ashʿarīs of all but six, seven, eight, twelve or twenty attributes,[18] which is put to rest by Rukn al-Dīn al-Samarqandī's explicit affirmation that 'Allah has attributes and names beyond count from pre-existence to eternity' (لله تعالى صفات وأسماء لا تحصى من الأزل إلى الأبد); al-Badāyūni's statement that 'affirmation of the attributes (*ithbāt al-ṣifāt*) is the *madhhab* of all *Ahl al-Sunna*'; and al-Kumushkhānawī's detailed listing of 220 transcendental (*tanzīhiyya*) attributes and his statement that the attributes of acts are beyond count. Any six, seven, eight, twelve, sixteen or twenty attributes are singled out only for emphasis or obligatoriness of specific belief.[19] More than that, 'all attributes of act go back to the essential attribute of existentiation' *takwīn*—as pointed out by al-Khādimī, which al-Kumushkhānawī also calls *takhlīq*—among the positions taken by most Māturīdīs as opposed to Ashʿarīs. At the same time, Rukn al-Dīn says, 'There is no contradiction nor reduplication among the attributes of Allah or His names,' and 'There is no overlapping (*tadākhul*) among the beautiful Names and Attributes of Allah and it must not be said that one is preferable to another.' Many other gross misrepresentations of Māturīdī and Ashʿarī positions can be found in Wahhābī literature.[20]

18 Muḥammad Khumayyis in his tract *Ḥiwār maʿa Ashʿarī* (Riyadh: Maktabat al-Maʿārif, 1426/2005) p. 23, states: "al-Maqrīzī said… 'And among the most important opinions of the Ashʿarīs is the negation of the Attributes except seven, which they affirm through reason,' [footnote:] See al-Maqrīzī's *Khiṭaṭ* (2:359–385) and *Shadharāt al-dhahab* (2:303)." In reality there is no such statement in either book.

19 Cf. Wahbī Sulaymān Ghāwjī al-Albānī, *Arkān al-īmān*, 2nd ed. (Beirut: Mu'assasat al-Īmān, 1420/1999), pp. 39–91.

20 See Aḥmad ʿAwaḍ Allāh al-Ḥarbī, *al-Māturīdiyya dirāsatan wa-taqwīman* (Riyadh: Dār al-ʿĀṣima, 1413/1993); Muḥammad Khumayyis, *Manhaj al-Māturīdiyya fil-ʿaqīda* (Riyadh: Dār al-Waṭan, 1413/1993), refuted by Saʿīd Fawda, *al-Naqd wal-taqwīm: wa-huwa naqd li-kitāb Manhaj al-Māturīdiyya fil-ʿaqā'id* (Amman: Dār al-Rāzī, 1425/2004); Shams

The Māturīdī condemnation of the philosophers (*falāsifa*)

In the *Barīqa maḥmūdiyya* al-Khādimī also often points out the congruence of the positions of Muʿtazilīs with those of the philosophers. He lists 62 positions of the *falāsifa* in which they contradict Sunni beliefs, which he concludes with al-Ghazālī's recapitulation in *al-Munqidh min al-ḍalāl* in which the latter said, 'The totality of the errors of the philosophers boil down to 20 headings, 17 of which call for anathema (*tabdīʿ*) while three of them constitute outright unbelief, namely the denial of bodily resurrection, the denial of Allah's knowledge of particulars, and their claim that the universe exists without beginning.'[21] Al-Badāyūnī (*q.v.*) goes further in *al-Muʿtaqad al-muntaqad*, in the section on *Nubuwwāt*, where he shows that although philosophers do affirm Prophethood, such affirmation revolves around heretical beliefs, 'including the claims that sending Prophets is obligatory for Allah and He has no choice in it; that Prophethood is acquired; and that it is not sent down through the agency of the angel of revelation; in addition to the denial of bodily resurrection, paradise, and hell, whereby they committed unbelief.'[22]

al-Dīn al-Afghānī, *ʿAdāʾ al-Māturīdiyya lil-ʿaqīdat al-salafiyya* (al-Ṭāʾif: Maktabat al-Ṣiddīq, 1413/1993), refuted by Saʿīd Fawda, *Tahāfut al-Taymiyya radd kitāb ʿAdāʾ al-Māturīdiyya* (1431/2010) in 109 p.; Muḥammad al-Khumayyis, *al-Māturīdiyya rabībat al-Kullābiyya* (Riyadh: Maktabat al-Maʿārif, 1426/2005); Khālid ʿAlī al-Ghamidī, *Naqḍ ʿaqāʾid al-Ashāʿira wal-Māturīdiyya* (Riyadh: Dār Aṭlas al-Khaḍrāʾ, 1430/2009). Both the books of al-Ḥarbī and al-Afghānī were originally Master's theses, the first under the direction of ʿAbd al-Raḥmān Nāṣir Barāk and the latter under that of (i) Ṣāliḥ ʿAbd Allāh al-ʿAbbūd, the foremost contemporary commentator and teacher of the works of Aḥmad b. Taymiyya and Muḥammad b. ʿAbd al-Wahhāb in Saudi Arabia, and (ii) Safar al-Ḥawālī, the author of the 55-page *Manhaj al-Ashāʿira fil-ʿaqīda* (Cairo: Maktabat al-ʿIlm, 1995) which was refuted by Ṣalāḥ al-Dīn Aḥmad al-Idlibī, *ʿAqāʾid al-Ashāʿira fī ḥiwārin hādiʾ maʿa shubuhāt al-munāwiʾīn* (Cairo: Dār al-Salām, 1429/2008).

21 *Barīqa maḥmūdiyya*, Istanbul ed., 1:317–318.

22 *Muʿtaqad*, pp. 97–98.

The Muʿtazilī and Deobandi position that Allah is described as 'having power to lie'

Equally condemned was the Muʿtazilī view that 'Allah can be described as having power to lie' (*yajūz an yūṣaf bil-qudrati ʿalā al-kadhib*) whereas the Māturidī position is that injustice and lying are precluded from Him. The Muʿtazilī position resurfaced and was recirculated by the Indian Shāh Ismāʿīl b. ʿAbd al-Ghanī al-Dihlawī (1193–1246/1779–1830) and his Deobandi continuators, principally Rashīd Aḥmad Gangūhī (1244–1323/1829–1905), as a supposedly Ashʿarī position. It is more reminiscent of a pagan Greek/Roman and Christian theology akin to Ibn Ḥazm's blunderous statement that 'Allah is able to take for Himself a son' (cf. Badāyūnī, *Muʿtaqad* 2.3.8.2). Likewise the antithesis of the same—the claim that 'Allah is powerless' to do foolish things, lie etc., is found in a handwritten gloss on a manuscript of Ibn Taymiyya's *Minhāj al-Sunna* misconstruing the Māturidī position that 'foolishness, lying and injustice are precluded from Him, *in the sense that [they affirm] He has no power to do that*' (*qālū: ... yamtaniʿ lahu taʿālā al-safah wal-kadhib wal-ẓulm, bi-maʿnā annahu taʿālā lā yaqdiru ʿalayh*) in order to pigeonhole them into the same doctrinal camp as Shīʿīs, Muʿtazilīs and Qadarīs.[23] In reality neither position (power to lie/powerlessness to lie) is anywhere recorded as an Ashʿarī or a Māturīdī position. Rather, 'it is impermissible that Allah be described as having power to commit injustice or to lie' (*Rukniyya*; Qārī, supplements to the *Minaḥ*; Laqānī, *Sharḥ al-Jawhara*), and 'what is unsuitable/not right' (Bayāḍī, *Ishārāt*). Moreover, 'Divine power (*qudra*) does not pertain to necessities nor to impossibilities' (Badāyūnī). In addition, the position that 'Allah has power to lie' was denounced as Muʿtazilism by early and late Māturīdī authorities as shown in Table 1.

23 Ibn Taymiyya, *Minhāj al-Sunna al-nabawiyya*, ed. Muḥammad Rashād Sālim, 9 vols. ([Riyadh:] Jāmiʿat al-Imām Muḥammad ibn Saʿūd,1406/1986), 2:293 n.

Table 1. Māturīdī condemnations of the claim that 'Allah can lie' as Mu'tazilism

al-Māturīdī in *al-Tawḥīd*, 2001 ed., pp. 295–301 ('Question on wisdom and foolishness')	وضربوا لتقدير فعله بفعل غيره مثلا بما لا يجوز أن يكون منه الكذب أو الجَوْر ... فثبت أن تقدير فعله على فعل الحكماء في الشاهد لازم، إلا أنهم دفعوا عنه الإرتفاع بالفعل والإنحطاط بترك فعل ما.
Rukn al-Islām Ibrāhīm b. Ismāʿīl al-Ṣaffār (d. 534/1139) in *Talkhīṣ al-adilla*, pp. 395, 397	لا يجوز أن يذكر في معنى اسم من أسماء الله تعالى ما يوجب نقصاً في ذاته... فلا يُقال هو قادرٌ على الظُّلْم، ولا يُقال غيرُ قادر؛ لأنّ هذا الوصف عنه مستحيل.
Nūr al-Dīn Aḥmad b. Maḥmūd al-Ṣābūnī (d. 580/1184) in *al-Bidāya*, p. 84	الظلم والسفه والكذب هل هي مقدورةٌ لله تعالى أم لا؟ فعندنا هي مستحيلة، لا يوصف الله تعالى بالقدرة عليها، خلافاً للمعتزلة، فإنّهم قالوا: يَقدِرُ ولا يفعل.
Jalāl al-Dīn ʿUmar b. Muḥammad Khabbāzī (d. 691/1292) in *al-Hādī*, p. 259	إنّ الله تعالى لا يوصف بالقدرة على الظلم والكذب؛ وعند الجمهور من المعتزلة: يقدر، ولا يفعل.
Rukn al-Dīn ʿUbayd Allāh b. Muḥammad al-Samarqandī (d. 701/1301 in *al-ʿAqīdat al-rukniyya*, p. 75	لا يجوز أن يوصف الله بالقدرة على الظلم والكذب، لأنّهما من المُحالات؛ وعند المعتزلة أنّه قادرٌ عليهما ولكن لا يفعل.
Ḥāfiẓ al-Dīn ʿAbd Allāh al-Nasafī (d. 710/1310), *ʿUmdat al-ʿaqāʾid*, p. 25	وعندنا لا يجوز، ولا يوصف الله تعالى بالقدرة على الظلم والسفه والكذب، لأنّ المُحال لا يدخل تحت القدرة؛ وعند المعتزلة: يَقدِر ولا يفعل.
The same Ḥāfiẓ al-Dīn al-Nasafī in *al-Iʿtimād*, p. 425	ولا يوصف الله تعالى بالقدرة على الظلم والسفه والكذب، لأنّ المُحال لا يدخل تحت القدرة؛ إذ المحال: ما يمتنع وقوعه؛ والمقدور: ما يمكن وقوعه؛ والجمع بينهما محال. وعند المعتزلة: يَقدِر ولا يفعل. والنظّام معنا.
Mullā ʿAlī al-Qārī (d. 1014/1605), *Minaḥ al-rawḍ al-azhar*, p. 392	لا يوصف الله تعالى بالقدرة على الظلم، لأنّ المُحال لا يدخل تحت القدرة؛ وعند المعتزلة أنّه يَقدِر ولكن لا يفعل.

Shaykhī Zādah (d. 1078?/1667?) in *Naẓm al-farā'id*, pp. 29 (no. 19) and 33 (no. 22)	احتج مشايخ الحنفية بأن الخلف في الوعيد تبديل للقول ... وبأنه يلزم جواز الكذب على الله في وعيده، وقد قام الإجماع على تنزّه خبره منه... لو جاز الكذب وخلف الوعد من الله تعالى لارتفعت الشرائع.
al-Bayāḍī (1044–1098/1634–1687) in *Ishārāt al-marām*	ويستحيل عقلاً اتّصافُه تعالى بالجَور وما لا ينبغي.
Koca Ragıp Pasha (1110–1176/1699–1763) in *Safinat al-rāghib*[1]	والمُحال لا يدخل تحت القدرة، فلا يجوز أن يوصف الله بالقدرة على الظلم والكذب؛ وعند المعتزلة: يقدر، ولا يفعل.
al-Badāyūnī (1213–1279/1798–1862) in *al-Mu'taqad al-muntaqad*	وكذا يستحيل الكذب وسائر سِمات النّقص عليه تعالى، والنّجدية [أي الديوبندية] قد فارقوا أهل الإسلام في هذا المقام.

1 Muḥammad Rāghib Bāshā, *Safinat al-rāghib wa-dafinat al-maṭālib* (Bulāq: Dār al-Ṭibā'at al-'Āmira, 1255/1839), p. 464

Ibn al-Humām in the *Musāyara* faulted Ḥāfiẓ al-Dīn al-Nasafī for saying in *al-'Umda* that the attribution of the power to lie to Allah was the Mu'tazilī position and asserted that he should have attributed it to the Ash'arīs instead. This was apparently endorsed by some later scholars (such as al-Bayāḍī and Shaykhī Zādah) but was an error on the part of Ibn al-Humām for several reasons. *First,* Ḥāfiẓ al-Dīn reasserts his statement in his own commentary on the *'Umda* entitled *al-I'timād* and adds that al-Naẓẓām, a major Mu'tazilī authority, dissents with them and is one with the Māturīdīs on that point, which shows this is well-researched and far from being a slip of the pen or an 'alteration' as speculated by Ibn al-Humām. *Second,* Ḥāfiẓ al-Dīn al-Nasafī's report is very much the Mu'tazilī position as expounded verbatim by Qāḍī 'Abd al-Jabbār al-Mu'tazilī in his *Sharḥ al-uṣūl al-khamsa*, namely that 'He—may He be exalted—is described as able to do what would be ugly if He indeed did it' (إنه تعالى موصوفٌ بالقدرة على ما لو فعله لكان قبيحا), including lying, 'because if He is able to be truthful then it is necessary that He is able to lie' (وكذلك الحال في القديم تعالى: إذا قدر على الصدق، وجب قدرته على الكذب).[24] *Third,* Ḥāfiẓ al-Dīn's statement is the standard Māturīdī understanding as shown before him by al-Māturīdī,

24 'Abd al-Jabbār b. Aḥmad, *Sharḥ al-uṣūl al-khamsa*, ed. 'Abd al-Karīm 'Uthmān, 3rd ed. (Cairo: Maktabat Wahba, 1416/1996), p. 313–314, cf. p. 303.

al-Ṣaffār, al-Ṣābūnī, al-Khabbāzī, and Rukn al-Dīn al-Samarqandī; and by al-Qārī, Shaykh Zādah, al-Bayāḍī, Muḥammad Rāghib Bashā and al-Badāyūnī after him. *Fourth,* one of the foremost Ashʿarī exegetes of the Qurʾān, Qadi al-Bayḍāwī (d. 708?/1308?) in his *Anwār al-tanzīl,* under al-Baqara 2:80, states that the verse forms proof that 'for Allah to contravene His own report is an impossibility' (*al-khulf fī khabarih muḥāl*). Al-Qūnawī in his supercommentary (*Ḥāshiyat al-Qūnawī ʿalā Tafsīr al-Bayḍāwī*) said (3:452): 'Because to contravene His own report is to lie, of which Allah is obligatorily declared exempt by consensus' i.e. of *Ahl al-Sunna*.

Another major Ashʿarī, Ibrāhīm al-Laqānī (bef. 960–1041/bef. 1553–1632) in his large commentary on his own poem *Jawharat al-tawḥīd* entitled *ʿUmdat al-murīd* discusses the Ashʿarī position as the impossibility of lying for Allah from three perspectives, and the Muʿtazilī position likewise from two (Burhān al-Dīn Abū al-Imdād Ibrāhīm b. Ibrāhīm b. Ḥasan b. ʿAlī al-Laqānī, *ʿUmdat al-murīd: Sharḥ Jawharat al-tawḥīd, wa-huwa al-Sharḥ al-kabīr lil-nāẓim*, ed. ʿAbd al-Mannān Aḥmad al-Idrīsī et al., 4 vols., Amman: Dār al-Nūr al-Mubīn, 2016, 2:957–962, see also *mā yastaḥīl ʿalā Allāh* 2:596–597 and *mā yajūz ʿalā Allāh* 2:603). Another major Ashʿarī and one of the foremost scholars of his time, Wajīh al-Dīn ʿAbd al-Raḥmān b. ʿAbd Allāh b. Aḥmad Balfaqīh (1089–1162/1678–1749) states in the first section of his long poem رشفات شرب أهل الكمال ونسمات قرب أهل الوصال:

يَخْرُجُ مِنْ كُلِّ عَنَا وَبُونِ *** وَغَيمِ كُلِّ حَادِثٍ وَدُونِ
إِلَى عُلُومِ عَالِمٍ مَصُونِ *** عَنْ خُلْفِ تَحْقِيقٍ أَوِ اخْتِلالِ

He shall come out from all exhaustion and estrangement,
and from the fog of every created 'other,'
To the sciences of an All-Knowing Who is exempt
of any breach of averment or untruth.[25]

25 ʿAbd al-Raḥmān b. ʿAbd Allāh Balfaqīh, *Majmūʿ al-aʿmāl al-kāmila li-muʾallafāt wa-fatāwā wa-rasāʾil al-Imām al-ʿallāma al-Ḥabīb ʿAbd al-Raḥmān b. ʿAbd Allāh Balfaqīh*, ed. ʿAlī b. Ḥasan Balfaqīh, 2 vols. (Tarīm: Dār al-Turāth, 1436/2015) 2:409.

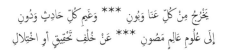

Māturīdīs and the sub-genre of 'blasphemous expressions' (*alfāẓ al-kufr*)[26]

Although the declaration of belief has simple parameters, expressions of unbelief abound and Māturīdīs specialized in identifying such expressions according to time and place over the centuries. An early example of this literature is Abū al-Layth al-Samarqandī's list of seventy expressions in *Bāb alfāẓ al-kufr* at the very end of his *Khizānat al-fiqh wa-'uyūn al-masā'il.*[27] Badī' al-Dīn Aḥmad b. Abī Bakr al-Qazwīnī[28] (d. 620/1223) built upon Abū al-Layth's list with his 10-folio *al-Kalimāt al-mukaffira al-latī tajrī 'alā lisān al-'āmma.* The *Rukniyya* has a section (§100) examining the immediate apostasy brought about by the mere intention to apostatize even years down the line. Badr al-Rashīd Muḥammad b. Ismā'īl b. Maḥmūd (d. 768/1367) followed with *Alfāẓ al-kufr*, which he prefaced with a list of about two dozen books of Ḥanafī *fiqh* and fatwa from which he said he gathered the material for his book. Mullā 'Alī al-Qārī reproduced in full and commented it at the end of *Minaḥ al-rawḍ al-azhar*, his commentary on the *Fiqh al-akbar*. The latter list includes *istithnā'* in rebuttal of Ash'arīs. The obscure Tāj al-Dīn Abū al-Ma'ālī Mas'ūd b. Aḥmad b. 'Abd al-'Azīz's detailed *Kalimāt tajrī 'alā alsinat al-'āmma wa-ghayrihim tūjib al-kufr 'alā qā'ilihā* (ms. copied in 774/1373) cites 260 scenarios including probable but not certain blasphemy (*yukhshā 'alayh al-kufr*). The Ottoman scholar Yūsuf b. Junayd al-Tawqādī, known as Akhī Yūsuf (d. 902/1497) authored *Hadiyyat al-mahdiyyīn* (Waqf Ikhlāṣ ed. 1423/2002) on blasphemous expressions which he ordered according to the topical headings of jurisprudence for the most part. The ascetic *mutakallim* Qāsim b. Ṣalāḥ al-Dīn al-Khānī al-Ḥalabī's (1028–1109/1619–1698) *Risāla fī bayān al-ridda* discusses about 90 examples of blasphemous expressions gathered from the books of the Sunni schools. Al-Kumushkhānawī also included a section on blasphemous expressions in his *Jāmi' al-mutūn* (*q.v.*).

26 See also Gibril Fouad Haddad, art. 'Apostasy' in *Integrated Encyclopedia of the Qur'ān* (Sherwood Park and Karachi: CIS-SQS, 2013), 1:232–233, section on apostasy literature.

27 Abū al-Layth al-Samarqandī, *Khizānat al-fiqh wa-'uyūn al-masā'il*, ed. Ṣalāḥ al-Dīn al-Nāhī (Baghdad: Sharikat al-Ṭab' al-Ahliyya, 1385/1965), pp. 434–441.

28 On him see Ibn Abī al-Wafā' al-Qurashī, *al-Jawāhir al-muḍī'a fī ṭabaqāt al-Ḥanafiyya*, ed. 'Abd al-Fattāḥ Muḥammad al-Ḥilw, 2nd ed., 5 vols. (Giza: Dār Hajar, 1413/1993), 1:133.

All of the above were Ḥanafī Māturīdī works and were recently republished (with the exception of Abū al-Layth's, al-Qazwīnī's, and Kumushkhānawī's) in a single volume which also includes the compendium *al-I'lām bi-qawāṭi' al-Islām* by the Shāfi'ī-Ash'arī jurist Ibn Ḥajar al-Haytamī.[29] Another, 200-page Māturīdī work on the same subject was penned by a Deobandi, Muḥammad Anwar Shāh al-Kashmīrī (1292–1352/1875–1933), entitled *Ikfār al-mulḥidīn fī ḍarūriyyāt al-dīn*,[30] of which a great part bears on the condemnation of Mirzā Ghulām Aḥmad Qadyānī, the founder of the Qadyānī and Aḥmadiyya sects. A Saudi contemporary, Bakr Abū Zayd, gathered up 'about 800 phrases' qualifying as blasphemies which he arranged alphabetically in his 1989 *Mu'jam al-manāhī al-lafẓiyya*, and which in its third edition seven years later had grown to 'about 1,500 phrases.'

The heart's *taṣdīq* as the core of faith for both Māturīdīs and Ash'arīs

One of the most remarkable and least understood Māturīdī/Ash'arī congruences is that confirmation (*al-taṣdīq*) is the irreducible core of faith *stricto sensu* (or might even be synonymous with *īmān*) and is located in the heart. This important position is inferred, on the Māturīdī side, from Abū Ḥanīfa's *al-'Ālim wal-muta'allim*, al-Māturīdī's *Tawḥīd*, al-Khabbāzī's *Hādī*, the *Masā'il fil-'aqīda* attributed to Abū al-Layth al-Samarqandī, Maymūn al-Nasafī in the *Tamhīd*, Ibn al-Humām in the *Musāyara*, and al-Aqḥiṣārī in *Rawḍāt al-jannāt*. Al-Khabbāzī asserts that faith is confirmation in the heart according to Abū Ḥanīfa, al-Māturīdī and the soundest of two positions related from al-Ash'arī, with affirmation being only a precondition for the legal status of being deemed a Muslim. The *'Ālim wal-muta'allim* conveys the explicit statement of the teacher that 'Whoever believes in his heart and does not speak with his tongue is a believer in the sight of Allah.' Similarly al-Aqḥiṣārī says, 'Know that *īmān*,... in the sacred law, is defined as a confirmation by the heart (*taṣdīq qalbī*).... Its upshot is that it is an act of the heart, so that it is wholly

29 *al-Jāmi' fī alfāẓ al-kufr*, ed. Muḥammad b. 'Abd al-Raḥmān al-Khumayyis (Kuwait: Dār Īlāf al-Duwaliyya, 1420/1999).

30 al-Kashmīrī, *Majmū' fīh thalāth rasā'il lil-Kashmīrī*, ed. Muḥammad Raḥmat Allāh Ḥāfiẓ al-Nadwī, 3 vols. in 1 (Beirut: Dār al-Bashā'ir al-Islāmiyya, 1431/2010), 3rd volume.

indispensable (*lā yaḥtamil al-suqūṭ*), contrary to affirmation, which is not, as in the case of coercion.'[31] This is indeed the gist of the preponderant (*rājiḥ*) Ashʿarī position regarding the identification of belief *in the heart* as the single irreducible core of belief: 'It was said that it [=*īmān*] was confirmation (*al-taṣdīq*) with the heart only; this is the preferred position among the masses of the Ashʿarīs.'[32] Nevertheless affirmation 'might be indispensable'—as proposed by al-Rāghib al-Aṣfahānī, al-Rāzī, and, after both of them, al-Bayḍāwī in their respective *tafsīrs*. Al-Bayḍāwī states:

> *Īmān*, lexically, expresses confirmation (*taṣdīq*).... In the legal sense, it is the confirmation of what is absolutely necessary to know as part of the religion of Muḥammad—upon him blessings and peace—such as pure monotheism, prophethood, resurrection and requital. It is the sum of three things: firm belief (*iʿtiqād*) in the truth, affirmation (*taqrīr*) of it, and acting upon its exigencies according to the vast majority of hadith scholars, the Muʿtazila and the Khawārij. Thus, whoever comes short of belief is a hypocrite; whoever comes short of affirmation, an unbeliever; and whoever comes short of deeds, a transgressor by agreement. *What indicates that it is confirmation alone* is that Allah Most High has annexed *īmān* to the heart and said, *As for such, He has written faith upon their hearts* (al-Mujādila 58:22), etc.... Then comes the difference of opinion whether pure confirmation with the heart is enough—for that is the purpose—or is it indispensable to also have affirmation for those able to provide it? The truth might be the latter; for Allah Most High has blamed the obdurate more than He has blamed the negligent ignoramus. One who holds the opposite view may deem the blame directed at denial, not at lack of affirmation for someone able to provide it.[33]

In comment of the above passage Qūnawī (a Māturīdī) said:

> [Fakhr al-Islām Abū al-Ḥasan ʿAlī b. Muḥammad b. al-Ḥusayn] al-Pazdawī (d. 482/1089) in the *Kashf* [*al-Asrār*] said that affirmation expresses the

31 al-Aqḥiṣārī, *Rawḍāt al-jannāt*, first *rawḍa*, in Badeen, *Sunnitische Theologie*, pp. 35–36.

32 Ibn al-Humām, *al-Musāyara fī ʿilm al-kalām wal-ʿaqāʾid al-tawḥīdiyya al-munjiya fil-ākhira*, ed. Muḥammad Muḥyī al-Dīn ʿAbd al-Ḥamīd (Cairo: al-Maṭbaʿat al-Maḥmūdiyya al-Tijāriyya fī Miṣr, 1348/1929), p. 172.

33 al-Bayḍāwī, *Anwār al-tanzīl wa-asrār al-taʾwīl*, *sub* verse *those who believe in the unseen* (2:3), see Gibril Fouad Haddad, *The Lights of Revelation and the Secrets of Interpretation:* Ḥizb *One of the Commentary on the Qurʾān by al-Bayḍāwī* (London: Beacon Books, 2016), pp. 259–262.

heart's content and signals confirmation. Hence it is a 'potentially dispensable pillar' (*rukn yaḥtamil al-suqūṭ*).... He [Bayḍāwī] did not categorically assert it [i.e., the indispensability of affirmation], for three reasons: conflicting evidence; rebuttal of the most literal evidence with the objection he is about to mention; and the fact that the preponderant Ashʿarī position is that affirmation is not an integral of *īmān* (*ʿadam kawn al-iqrār ruknan huwa al-rājiḥ ʿinda al-Ashāʿira*).[34]

Ashʿarīs who were also from *Ahl al-Ḥadīth* such as al-Bayhaqī, al-Qushayrī and, most vehemently, al-Suyūṭī in his supercommentary on al-Bayḍāwī entitled *Nawāhid al-abkār*, followed the *contra* position that affirmation was categorically indispensable and part of the irreducible core of belief.[35] Al-Khabbāzī himself acknowledges that 'many of our [Māturīdī] colleagues said *īmān* is both confirmation and affirmation.'[36]

Works of Ashʿarī-Māturīdī systematic comparative theology

I have included in this bio-bibliography the foremost works of Māturīdī-Ashʿarī systematic comparative theology. Some of these are, from the Māturīdī perspective, Shaykh Zādah's *Naẓm al-farāʾid*; al-Bayāḍī's *Ishārāt al-marām*; Ibn al-Humām's *Musāyara*; Ibn Kamāl Bāshā's *Masāʾil al-ikhtilāf*; Khādimī's *Barīqa maḥmūdiyya*; and, from the Ashʿarī perspective, al-Subkī's *Nūniyya*; Abū ʿAdhaba's *al-Rawḍat al-bahiyya*, al-Nābulusī's *Taḥqīq al-intiṣār fī ittifāq al-Ashʿarī wal-Māturīdī ʿalā khalq al-ikhtiyār*; Mawlānā Khālid al-Baghdādī's *al-ʿIqd al-jawharī*, already referred to; and al-Hātifī al-Fārūqī's (fl. ca. 1265/1849) *al-Risāla al-wajīza*.[37] Al-Nābulusī's contributions straddle the two schools as he leaned to Ashʿarism more because it was closer to sufism in

34 *Ibid.*, p. 262 n., citing ʿIṣām al-Dīn Ismāʿīl b. Muḥammad b. Muṣṭafā al-Qūnawī, *Ḥāshiyat al-Qūnawī ʿalā Tafsīr al-Bayḍāwī*, ed. ʿAbd Allāh ʿUmar, 20 vols. (Beirut: Dār al-Kutub al-ʿIlmiyya, 1422/2001), 1:455–457.

35 Haddad, *The Lights of Revelation*, pp. 260–261 n.

36 al-Khabbāzī, *Kitāb al-hādī*, p. 261.

37 *al-Risāla al-wajīza fī bayān al-farq bayna al-Ashʿariyya wal-Māturīdiyya*, Cairo, al-Maktabat al-Azhariyya, MS 324025. Another copy of it is preserved in Vatican Library, MS 1/1422. A critical edition was published in Egypt (based only on the Egyptian copy), see Marzūq, ʿImād Ḥasan, *al-Farq bayna al-Ashʿariyya wal-Māturīdiyya* (Cairo: Maktabat Bustān al-Maʿrifa, 2009). This footnote is slightly adapted from Haida, *Debates*, p. 199 n. 755.

his view. The detailed modern edition and study of al-Ūshī's *Bad' al-amālī* by Muḥammad Aḥmad Kan'ān also qualifies as a comparative encyclopedia.[38]

Spurious attributions/ascriptions in Māturīdī scholarship

Certain attributions were established or at least flagged as spurious ascriptions in past and recent Māturīdī scholarship. The following list recapitulates and expands on such misattributions, although not exhaustively:

(1) A small text entitled *al-ʿAqīda* or *Risāla fil-ʿaqā'id* was attributed to al-Māturīdī by Ḥājjī Khalīfa, al-Bayāḍī and Brockelmann and, according to Mustafa Cerić, was copied and commented by Taqī al-Dīn al-Subkī (683–756/1284–1355) under the title *al-Sayf al-mashhūr fī ʿaqīdat Abī Manṣūr* (*q.v.*),[39] while Hans Daiber and Rudolph Ulrich date it as subsequent to Abū al-Layth al-Samarqandī's *Sharh al-fiqh al-absaṭ*, the latter describing it as 'summariz[ing] in 43 articles the main teachings adhered to by... the Transoxianan Hanafites... a compilation of teachings heavily indebted to the *Sharḥ al-fiqh al-akbar* [i.e., *absaṭ*].'[40] Daiber and Rudolph's dating makes sense but Cerić apparently confuses this treatise with the *Nūniyya* on the comparative stances of Ashʿarīs and Māturīdīs, authored and commented not by Taqī al-Dīn but by his son Tāj al-Dīn al-Subkī, known as Ibn al-Subkī (727–771/1327–1370) (*q.v.*).

(2) As is now agreed upon, the *Sharḥ al-fiqh al-akbar* attributed to Abū Manṣūr al-Māturīdī on the cover of its 1321/1904 edition at Dā'irat al-Maʿārif al-Niẓāmiyya was not authored by him but by Abū al-Layth Naṣr b. Muḥammad al-Samarqandī (d. 373/983) or someone later, and its more exact title should be *Sharḥ al-fiqh al-absaṭ* since it deals with the catechetically-formatted version narrated from Abū Ḥanīfa by Abū Muṭīʿ al-Balkhī, all as detailed below under Abū Ḥanīfa and al-Māturīdī.

38 Muḥammad Aḥmad Kanʿān, *Jāmiʿ al-la'ālī sharḥ Bad' al-amālī fī ʿilm al-ʿaqā'id* (Beirut: Dār al-Bashā'ir al-Islāmiyya, 1429/2008).

39 Cerić, *Roots*, pp. 48–49.

40 Rudolph, *al-Māturīdī*, pp. 329, 342, referencing Pseudo-Māturīdī, *Risāla fil-ʿaqā'id*, ed. Y.Z. Yörükan, *Ankara Üniversitesi Ilahiyat Fakültesi Yayınlarından* 5 (1953), pp. 7–22 = *Kitāb al-Uṣūl*, Ms Gotha 100, fols. 1a–15b.

(3) Another *Sharḥ al-fiqh al-akbar* was misattributed to Fakhr al-Islām ʿAlī al-Pazdawī (the brother of Abū al-Yusr) on the cover of its 1279/1862 edition, whereas it is in fact a text by Abū al-Muntahā Shihāb al-Dīn Aḥmad b. Muḥammad al-Maghnīsāwī (d. 1000/1592) as mentioned in the very preamble of the text (*fa-yaqūlu Abū al-Muntahā*), and he then cites Fakhr al-Islām al-Pazdawī in passing.

(4) The *ʿAqāʾid al-nasafiyya* is famously attributed to the jurist and exegete Najm al-Dīn Abū Ḥafṣ ʿUmar b. Muḥammad al-Nasafī (461–537/1068–1142) but the Moroccan transmissologist Muḥammad b. Sulaymān al-Rūdānī pointed out that it was in fact the work of the well-known theologian and exegete Burhān al-Dīn Abū al-Faḍl Muḥammad b. Muḥammad al-Nasafī (600–687/1203–1288),[41] often described (unlike Najm al-Dīn) as *ṣāḥib al-muʾallafāt al-kalāmiyya*. The error was popularized by al-Taftāzānī and spread thereafter by several subsequent scholars such as Ibn Abī Sharīf, Ḥājjī Khalīfa and others, followed by the Orientalists one and all including Cureton, Wensinck, Watt, Cerić, Rudolph and Lange. The pedagographical (*athbāt*) and biographical sources list several scholarly Nasafīs: the *ḥāfiẓ* Abū al-Riḍā Muḥammad b. ʿAlī b. Yaḥyā b. Yūsuf known as Ibn Hubayra al-Nasafī (d. 517/1123); the pre-eminent exegete and jurist Najm al-Dīn Abū Ḥafṣ ʿUmar b. Muḥammad b. Aḥmad b. Ismāʿīl al-Nasafī (461–537/1068–1142) (*q.v.*); his son the jurist and admonisher Abū al-Layth Aḥmad b. ʿUmar al-Nasafī (d. 552/1157); Burhān al-Dīn Abū al-Faḍl Muḥammad b. Muḥammad b. Muḥammad al-Nasafī (600–687/1203–1288), the author of an epitome of al-Rāzī's *Mafātīḥ al-ghayb* entitled *al-Wāḍiḥ*, *Baḥr al-kalām*, the *Muqaddima* on juridical differences, and the *ʿAqāʾid* 'among many other works in *kalām*' (al-Rūdānī); Ḥāfiẓ al-Dīn Muḥammad b. Muḥammad b. Naṣr al-Bukhārī

41 As stated in al-Rūdānī (d. 1094/1683), *Ṣilat al-khalaf bi-mawṣūl al-salaf*, ed. Muḥammad Ḥajjī (Beirut: Dār al-Gharb al-Islāmī, 1408/1988), p. 190; Ibn ʿĀbidīn (1198–1252/1784–1836), *Thabat Ibn ʿĀbidīn al-musammā ʿUqūd al-laʾālī fil-asānīd al-ʿawālī*, ed. Muḥammad Ibrāhīm al-Ḥusayn (Beirut: Dār al-Bashāʾir al-Islāmiyya, 1431/2001), p. 431; al-Laknawī (1264–1304/1848–1887), *al-Fawāʾid al-bahiyya fī tarājim al-Ḥanafiyya*, ed. Aḥmad al-Zuʿbī (Beirut: Dār al-Arqam, 1418/1998), p. 319; Ibn al-Islām ʿUbayd Allāh al-Sindī (1872–1944), *al-Tamhīd li-taʿrīf aʾimmat al-tajdīd*, ed. Abū Saʿīd Ghulām Muṣṭafā al-Qāsimī al-Sindī (Jāmshūrū (Pakistan): Lajnat Iḥyāʾ al-Adab al-Sindī, 1976), p. 289; and ʿUmar al-Nushūqātī, *al-Taḥrīr al-farīd li-ʿawālī al-asānīd: Thabat asānīd al-ʿallāmat al-shaykh Muḥammad Ṣāliḥ al-Furfūrī* (Damascus: Dār al-Farfūr, 1422/2002), pp. 107–108.

al-Nasafī al-Kabīr (d. 693/1294); Ḥāfiẓ al-Dīn Abū al-Barakāt ʿAbd Allāh b. Aḥmad b. Maḥmud al-Nasafī (d. 710/1310) the author of *Madārik al-Tanzīl*; and others including Abū al-Yusr al-Pazdawī who is also known as Ṣadr al-Dīn and Ṣadr al-Islām al-Nasafī.[42]

(5) Al-Rūdānī also stated that *Baḥr al-kalām* was by the same Burhān al-Dīn al-Nasafī rather than Abū al-Muʿīn Maymūn al-Nasafī as commonly believed.[43] This assertion is unlikely to be correct in light of the multitude of extant manuscripts—about three dozens—all presumably attributing the work to Abū al-Muʿīn.

(6) Shaykh Zādah's *Naẓm al-farā'id*, a work on the differences between the two schools of the Māturīdīs and the Ashʿarīs listing them as forty 'singularities' (*farā'id*), was attributed to Shaykh Zādah ʿAbd al-Raḥīm b. ʿAlī b. al-Mu'ayyad al-Amāsī (d. 944/1537) by our contemporaries such as al-Jābī, al-Ḥimyarī, Rudolph and others, an impossibility since the work refers to such as al-Qārī (d. 1014/1605) and Ibrāhīm al-Laqānī (d. 1041/1632). It could be the work of a later Ottoman scholar from Gallipoli, ʿAbd al-Raḥmān b. Muḥammad b. Sulaymān al-Dāmād, known as Shaykhī Zādah (d. 1078/1667) but this is also open to question since he cites (cf. *Farīda*s 23 and 27) al-Bayāḍī's (1044–1098/1634–1687) (*q.v.*) *Ishārāt al-marām*.

(7) An oft-studied doctrinological poem entitled *ʿAqīdat al-Shaybānī* is sometimes cited among the Māturīdī texts, a compound error as the author is not Muḥammad b. al-Ḥasan al-Shaybānī (131–189/749–805) as erroneously claimed in the University of Tokyo cataloguing of its manuscript and a 1984 Master's study at the University of Muḥammad Ibn Saʿūd,[44] but the much later Muḥammad b. Aḥmad b. Abī Bakr al-Rabaʿī al-Shaybānī al-Aswānī al-Shāfiʿī (d. 777/1375), and the text has a clear Ashʿarī orientation.[45] Nor is this text known in the Ḥanafī and Māturīdī sources.

42 See al-Rūdānī, *Ṣilat al-khalaf*, p. 191; Ibn ʿĀbidīn, *Thabat*, pp. 431–432; Ibn al-Islām, *Tamhīd*, *s.v.*; and ʿĀdil Nuwayhid, *Muʿjam al-mufassirīn*, *s.v.*

43 al-Rūdānī, *Ṣilat al-khalaf*, p. 191.

44 Muḥammad al-Suḥaym, ed., Ibn Qāḍī ʿAjlūn, *Badīʿ al-maʿānī fī sharḥ ʿAqīdat al-Shaybānī*, unpub. diss. (Riyadh: Jāmiʿat al-Imām Muḥammad ibn Saʿūd, 1404–1405/1985), p. 3 and passim.

45 See ʿIṣām Muḥammad ʿAbd al-Mawlā, ed., ʿAlwān b. ʿAṭiyya al-Hamawī (d. 936/1530), *Bayān al-maʿānī fī sharḥ ʿAqīdat al-Shaybānī*, unpub. diss. (Sūhāj, Egypt: Jāmiʿat Sūhāj, 1435–1436/2014–2015), pp. 26–30 and passim.

(8) Another widespread text is the *'Aqīdat Abī al-Layth al-Samarqandī* edited by Juynboll, which has no suggestion of Māturīdī doctrine and seems unknown to Ḥanafī and Māturīdī sources, although very popular in Southeast Asia.[46]

(9) A Māturīdī commentary on al-Ūshī's (d. 569/1174) *Bad' al-amālī* by Muḥammad b. Abī Bakr al-Rāzī (who is unknown for anything other than this work), entitled *Hidāya min al-i'tiqād*, was thus identified and dated 751/1350 by Ḥajī Khalīfa but was grossly misattributed to Abū Bakr Aḥmad b. 'Alī al-Rāzī al-Jaṣṣāṣ (d. 370/981)—despite its numerous references to people born after his time—by a Wahhabi editor identifying himself as Abū 'Amr al-Ḥusaynī b. 'Umar b. 'Abd al-Raḥīm under the title *Sharḥ Bad' al-Amālī* (Beirut: Dār al-Kutub al-'Ilmiyya, 1422/2001).

Two Māturīdī Golden Ages

A tabular listing of the authorities and their works yields two Māturīdī 'golden ages' of celebrated texts, namely the sixth Hijrī century for detailed encyclopedic reference-works, and the 10th–14th centuries for a flourishing of detailed comparative Sunni *kalam* discussing both Ash'arī and Māturīdī positions (see Table 2).

46 See below, entry on Abū al-Layth al-Samarqandī.

Table 2. Chronology of mostly Māturīdī authors and doctrinal works (together with comparative Ash'ari-Māturīdī texts in bold) 2nd–14th centuries

Period	Authority	Work
2nd c.	Abū Ḥanīfa (80–150/ 699–767)	*(i) al-'Ālim wal-muta'allim* *(ii) al-Fiqh al-absaṭ* *(iii) al-Fiqh al-akbar* *(iv) Musnad Abī Ḥanīfa* *(v) Risālat Abī Ḥanīfa ilā 'Uthmān al-Battī* *(vi) Waṣiyyat Abī Ḥanīfa li-tilmīdhih Yūsuf al-Samtī*
4th c.	Abū Ja'far al-Ṭaḥāwī (229–321/844–933)	*al-'Aqīdat al-Ṭaḥāwiyya*
	Abū Manṣūr al-Māturīdī (d. 333/945)	*(i) Kitāb al-tawḥīd* *(ii) Ta'wīlāt Ahl al-Sunna (Tafsīr al-Māturīdī; Ta'wīlāt al-Qur'ān)*
	Abū Salama Muḥammad b. Muḥammad al-Samarqandī (d. bef. 340/951)	*Jumalun min uṣūl al-dīn*
	Ibn al-Ḥakīm al-Samarqandī (d. bet. 340 and 422/951 and 1031)	*al-Sawād al-a'ẓam*
	Abū al-Layth al-Samarqandī (d. 373/983)	*(i) Alfāẓ al-kufr* *(ii) Masā'il Abī al-Layth* *(iii) Sharḥ al-Fiqh al-absaṭ*
5th c.	Sa'īd al-Ustuwā'ī (343–432/ 954–1040)	*'Aqīdatun marwiyyatun 'an Abī Ḥanīfa*
	Abū Shakūr al-Sālimī (d. after 460/1068)	*al-Tamhīd fī bayān al-tawḥīd*
	Abū al-Yusr Pazdawī (421–493/1030–1100)	*Kitāb uṣūl al-dīn*

Period	Authority	Work
6th c.	Abū al-Mu'īn Maymūn al-Nasafī (438–508/1047–1115)	*(i) Baḥr al-kalām* *(ii) Sharḥ al-Ta'wīlāt* *(iii) Tabṣirat al-adilla* *(iv) al-Tamhīd li-qawā'id al-tawḥīd.*
	al-Ṣaffār (d. 534/1139)	*Talkhīṣ al adilla*
	[pseudo-]Nasafī, Najm al-Dīn 'Umar (461–537/1069–1142)	*al-'Aqā'id al-Nasafiyya* (in reality by Burhān al-Dīn al-Nasafī 600–687/1203–1288)
	'Alā' al-Dīn Usmandī (488–552/1095–1157)	*Lubāb al-kalām*
	Sirāj al-Dīn al-Ūshī (d. 575?/1180?)	*Bad' al-amālī fī uṣūl al-dīn*
	Nūr al-Dīn al-Ṣābūnī (d. 580/1184)	*(i) al-Kifāya fil-hidāya* *(ii) al-Bidāya min al-kifāya fil-hidāya fī uṣūl al-dīn*
	Jamāl al-Dīn Aḥmad al-Ghaznawī (d. 593/1197)	*Kitāb uṣūl al-dīn*
7th c.	al-Tūrabashtī (d. 661/1263)	*al-Mu'tamad fil-mu'taqad*
	Burhān al-Dīn al-Nasafī 600–687/1203–1288)	*al-'Aqā'id al-Nasafiyya*
	al-Khabbāzī (d. 691/1292)	*al-Hādī fī uṣūl al-dīn*
	Shams al-Dīn Muḥammad b. Ashraf al-Samarqandī (d. after 690/1291)	***(i) al-Ma'ārif fī sharḥ al-Ṣaḥā'if*** ***(ii) al-Ṣaḥā'if al-Ilāhiyya***
8th c.	Rukn al-Dīn Samarqandī (d. 701/1301)	*al-'Aqīdat al-Rukniyya fī sharḥ Lā ilāha illā Allāh Muḥammadun rasūl Allāh*
	Abū al-Barakāt Ḥafiẓ al-Dīn al-Nasafī (d. 710/1310)	*(i) al-I'timād fil-i'tiqād* [*Sharḥ al-'Umda*] *(ii) 'Umdat al-'aqā'id*

Period	Authority	Work
	Ḥusām al-Dīn al-Ḥusayn al-Sighnāqī (d. 710/1310)	*al-Tasdīd fī sharḥ al-Tamhīd*
	Najm al-Dīn al-Ṭarasūsī (721–758/1321–1357)	***Urjūza fī maʿrifat mā bayna al-Ashāʿira wal-Ḥanafiyya min al-khilāf fī uṣūl al-dīn***
	Tāj al-Dīn Ibn al-Subkī (727–771/1327–1370)	***(i) al-Qaṣīdat al-nūniyya fil-khilāf bayna al-Ashāʿira wal-Māturīdiyya (ii) al-Sayf al-mashhūr fī ʿaqīdat Abī Manṣūr***
	al-Taftāzānī (712–793/1320–1390)	*Sharḥ al-ʿAqāʾid al-Nasafiyya*
9th c.	**ʿIzz al-Dīn Ibn Jamāʿa (d. 819/1416)**	***Darj al-maʿālī sharḥ Badʾ al-amālī***
	Badr al-Dīn al-Maqdisī (760–836/1359–1433)	***Ghāyat al-marām fī sharḥ Baḥr al-kalām***
	ʿAlāʾ al-Dīn al-Bukhārī (779–841/1377/1438)	***Risāla fil-Iʿtiqād***
	Ibn al-Humām (790–861/1388–1457)	***al-Musāyara fī ʿilm al-kalām wal-ʿaqāʾid al-tawḥīdiyya***
10th c.	**Ibn Kamāl Bāshā (873–940/1469–1534)**	***Masāʾil al-ikhtilāf bayna al-Ashāʿira wal-Māturīdiyya***
	Nawʿī Efendi (940–1007/1533–1599)	***Risāla fil-farq bayna madhhab al-Ashāʿira wal-Māturīdiyya***
11th c.	al-Qārī (d. 1014/1605)	*(i) Ḍawʾ al-maʿālī ʿalā manẓūmat Badʾ al-amālī (ii) Minaḥ al-Rawḍ al-azhar sharḥ al-Fiqh al-akbar*
	Ḥasan Kāfī al-Aqḥiṣārī (951–1024/1544–1615)	*Rawḍāt al-jannāt fī uṣūl al-iʿtiqādāt*

Period	Authority	Work
	[Pseudo-]Shaykh Zādah al-Amāsī (d. 944/1537)	***Naẓm al-farā'id wa-jam' al-fawā'id fī bayān al-masā'il al-latī waqa'a fīhā al-ikhtilāf bayna al-Māturīdiyya wal-Ashā'ira fil-'aqā'id***, in reality by Dāmād Shaykhī Zādah (d. 1078/1667) or another.
	al-Shurunbulālī (994–1069/1586–1659)	*Marāqī al-sa'ādāt fī 'ilmāy al-tawḥīd wal-'ibādāt*
	al-Bayāḍī (1044–1098/1634–1687)	***Ishārāt al-marām min 'ibārāt al-imām***
12th c.	al-Isbīrī (fl. 1130/1718)	*Mumayyizāt madhhab al-Māturīdiyya 'an al-madhāhib al-ghayriyya*
	Abū al-Ḥasan al-Sindī (d. 1138/1727)	***al-Ifāḍat al-Madaniyya fil-irādat al-juz'iyya***
	al-Nābulusī (1050–1143/1640–1731)	***Taḥqīq al-intiṣār fī ittifāq al-Ash'arī wal-Māturīdī 'alā khalq al-ikhtiyār***
	al-Khādimī (1113–1176/1701–1763)	***Barīqa Maḥmūdiyya fī sharḥ ṭarīqa Muḥammadiyya***
	Abū 'Adhaba (fl. 1172/1758)	***al-Rawḍat al-bahiyya fī-mā bayna al-Ashā'ira wal-Māturīdiyya***
13th c.	**Khālid al-Baghdādī (1193–1242/1779–1827)**	***Risāla fī taḥqīq mas'alat al-irādat al-juz'iyya fil-farq bayna kasbay al-Māturīdī wal-Ash'arī***
	Al-Badāyūnī (1213–1279/1798–1862)	*al-Mu'taqad al-muntaqad*
14th c.	Qāwuqjī (1224–1305/1809–1888)	*(i) al-Durr al-ghālī 'alā bad' al-amālī* *(ii) al-I'timād fil-i'tiqād* *(iii) Kifāyat al-ṣibyān fī-mā yajib min 'aqā'id al-īmān wa-'amal al-arkān*

Period	Authority	Work
	Kumushkhānawī (Gümüşhanevi 1228–1311/1813–1893)	*Jāmiʿ al-mutūn fī ḥaqq anwāʿ al-ṣifāt al-ilāhiyya wal-ʿaqāʾid al-Māturīdiyya wa-alfāẓ al-kufr*
	al-Kawtharī **(1296–1371/1879–1952)**	***(i) al-Istibṣār fil-taḥadduth ʿan al-jabr wal-ikhtiyār*** ***(ii) Maqālāt al-Kawtharī***
	ʿAbd al-Mutaʿāl al-Ṣaʿīdī (1311–1386/1894–1966)	*Zubad al-ʿaqāʾid al-Nasafiyya*

Synoptic Bio-Bibliography

SECOND/EIGHTH CENTURY

Abū Ḥanīfa

Abū Ḥanīfa al-Nuʿmān b. Thābit. *al-ʿĀlim wal-mutaʿallim*. With *Risālat Abī Ḥanīfa ilā ʿUthmān al-Battī* and *al-Fiqh al-absaṭ*. Ed. Muḥammad Zāhid al-Kawtharī. Cairo: al-Anwār, 1368/1949.

———. *al-ʿĀlim wal-mutaʿallim*. Ed. Muḥammad Rawwās Qalʿajī and ʿAbd al-Wahhāb al-Hindī al-Nadwī. Aleppo: Maktabat al-Hādī, 1972.

———. *al-ʿĀlim wal-mutaʿallim*; *al-Fiqh al-absaṭ*; *al-Fiqh al-akbar*; *Risālat Abī Ḥanīfa*; *al-Waṣiyya*. Ed. Muḥammad Zāhid al-Kawtharī. Cairo: al-Maktabat al-Azhariyya lil-Turāth, 1421/2001.

An Iraqi of Persian origin, al-Nuʿmān b. Thābit b. Kāwūs b. Hurmuz b. Marzubān al-Taymī, Abū Ḥanīfa (80–150/699–767) is the first and earliest of the four *mujtahid* imams whose schools have survived to our time and the one who has acquired the greatest number of followers among the Sunni schools. He was dubbed 'the true *faqīh*' by Mālik, 'the imam' by Abū Dāwūd, *Faqīh al-milla* by al-Dhahabī, 'the imam among those who have reached the sky' by Ibn Ḥajar, and 'the greatest teacher' *(al-imām al-aʿẓam)* among Ḥanafīs. The hadith master Abū Muʿāwiya al-Ḍarīr (d. 195/811) said, 'Love of Abū Ḥanīfa is part of the Sunna,' however, Abū Ḥanīfa himself gave one of the pithiest definitions of Sunnism in Islam: 'The doctrine of *Ahl al-Sunna wal-Jamāʿa* consists in preferring the two Elders *(tafḍīl al-shaykhayn)* [Abū Bakr and ʿUmar], loving the two sons-in-law *(ḥubb al-khatanayn)* [ʿAlī and ʿUthmān], and [deeming lawful the] wiping on leather socks [in ablution] *(al-masḥ ʿalā al-khuffayn).*ʼ[47]

Al-ʿālim wal-mutaʿallim is a pedagogical dialogue on correct creed between a teacher and his student, authored by Abū Muqātil al-Samarqandī who features himself as the student and Abū Ḥanīfa as the teacher. Al-Kawtharī in his preamble to al-Bayāḍī's *Ishārāt al-marām* mentioned the chain of transmission to *al-ʿĀlim wal-mutaʿallim* as 'Abū al-Faḍl Aḥmad b. ʿAlī al-Bīkandī *al-ḥāfiẓ*, *ʿan* Ḥātim b. ʿAqīl, *ʿan* al-Fatḥ b. Abī ʿAlwān and Muḥammad b. Yazīd, *ʿān* al-Ḥasan b. Ṣāliḥ, *ʿan* Abī Muqātil Ḥafṣ b. Sālim al-Samarqandī, *ʿan* Abī Ḥanīfa;' he also cites it as narrated by Abū Manṣūr al-Māturīdī, from Abū Bakr Aḥmad b. Isḥāq al-Juzjānī, from Muḥammad b. Muqātil al-Rāzī, from Abū Muqātil.

———. *al-Fiqh al-absaṭ*. In the 1368/1949 and 1421/2001 editions of *al-ʿĀlim wal-mutaʿallim.*

The *Fiqh al-absaṭ* is originally known as *al-Fiqh al-akbar* but was named *absaṭ* (a synonym)[48] by later scholars to refer to the narration of Abū Muṭīʿ al-Ḥakam b. ʿAbd Allāh al-Balkhī (d. 199/814) from Abū Ḥanīfa in contradistinction to that of Ḥammād b. Abī Ḥanīfa (d. 176/793) from his father. It is a brief quasi-dialogical compilation of Abū Ḥanīfa's lessons and views on a variety of credal matters with a view to refuting non-Sunni sects on the divine will (*mashīʾa*),[49] the foreordained decree (*qadar*), belief, and pronouncing someone apostate (*takfīr*). Al-Kawtharī documents it as narrated by Abū Bakr al-Kāsānī (author of *Badāʾiʿ al-ṣanāʾiʿ*), from ʿAlāʾ al-Dīn

47 Narrated by Ibn ʿAbd al-Barr in *al-Intiqāʾ* through several different chains. The same statement is also related from Sufyān al-Thawrī by al-Lālakāʾī in *Iʿtiqād Ahl al-Sunna* despite Aḥmad al-Ghumārī's claim in *al-Burhān*, p. 82, who cites from Ibn Abī Khaythama through ʿAbd al-Razzāq a report that Sufyān al-Thawrī preferred ʿAlī to Abū Bakr and ʿUmar. This is not the position reported from the *Salaf*. Al-Qārī said in *Sharḥ al-Fiqh al-akbar*, Nafāʾis ed., p. 140: 'It is patent that to prefer ʿAlī to the Two Shaykhs contravenes the doctrine of *Ahl al-Sunna wal-Jamāʿa* according to what the totality of the *Salaf* follow.'

48 *Fiqh* or 'in-depth understanding' is defined by Ḥanafīs as 'the acquired knowledge of the self, its rights and liabilities' (*maʿrifat al-nafs mā lahā wa-mā ʿalayhā*) and as including both 'intellective in-depth understanding' (*al-fiqh al-ʿilmī*), also known as 'the greater *fiqh*' (*al-fiqh al-akbar*), and 'practical in-depth understanding' (*al-fiqh al-ʿamalī*), commonly referred to as *fiqh* itself. See on this the *Kashshāf iṣṭilāḥāt al-funūn* and other works on the classification of the Islamic sciences.

49 See Salient Themes, Synonymity of *irāda* and *mashīʾa*.

Muḥammad b. Aḥmad b. Abī Aḥmad al-Samarqandī (author of *Tuḥfat al-fuqahā'*), from Abū al-Mu'īn Maymūn al-Nasafī (the author of *Tabṣirat al-adilla*), from the prolific but unreliable *muḥaddith* and preacher al-Ḥusayn b. 'Alī al-Alma'ī al-Kāshgharī (d. 484/1091), from the jurist Abū Mālik Naṣrān b. Naṣr al-Khatlī (from Khatlān near Samarqand), from Abū al-Ḥasan 'Alī b. Aḥmad al-Fārisī al-Ghazzāl, from Nuṣayr b. Yaḥyā al-Balkhī (d. 268/882), from Abū Muṭī' al-Ḥakam b. 'Abd Allāh, from Abū Ḥanīfa. Among its commentaries in print are Abū al-Layth al-Samarqandī's (d. 373/983) *Sharḥ al-fiqh al-akbar* (i.e. *al-absaṭ*), misattributed to Abū Manṣūr al-Māturīdī in the Hyderabad Deccan edition 1321/1904; al-Bayāḍī's (*q.v.*) *Ishārāt al-marām min 'ibārāt al-imām*; the jurist 'Aṭā' b. 'Alī al-Jūzjānī's commentary as cited by Bayāḍī; and *Sharḥ Naẓm al-durar fī sarḥ al-Fiqh al-akbar bi-riwāyat Abī Muṭī' al-Balkhī* by 'Ubayd Allāh al-Muftī (Karachi: al-Majlis al-'Ilmī, 1405/1985). The *Fiqh al-absaṭ* was translated in full.[50]

———. *al-Fiqh al-akbar*. In the 1421/2001 edition of *al-'Ālim wal-muta'allim*.

Al-Kawtharī in his preamble to al-Bayāḍī's *Ishārāt al-marām* mentioned the chain of transmission to the *Fiqh al-akbar* as '*riwāyat* 'Alī b. Aḥmad al-Fārisī, *'an* Nuṣayr b. Yaḥyā, *'an* Abī Muqātil Ḥafṣ b. Sālim or Salam al-Samarqandī, *'an* 'Iṣām b. Yūsuf, *'an* Ḥammād b. Abī Ḥanīfa, *'an abīh*.' 'Abd al-Qāhir al-Baghdādī in *Uṣūl al-dīn* described the *Fiqh al-akbar* as a refutation of the Qadariyya sect while Muwaffaq al-Dīn al-Kardarī narrated in his *Manāqib Abī Ḥanīfa* that the latter had begun his career refuting the various sects of the Khawārij in Basra. The book received several editions; it also has commentaries by Fakhr al-Islām al-Pazdawī (more likely al-Maghnīsāwī, as already mentioned); Bahā' al-Dīn Zādah, 'Alī al-Qārī, and others, as well as English translations.[51]

50 In William Montgomery Watt, *Islamic Creeds: A Selection* (Edinburgh: Edinburgh University Press, 1994).

51 al-Pazdawī (attrib.), *Sharḥ al-Fiqh al-akbar*, ed. Baron Henry Edward John Stanley (London: n.p., 1279/1862, orig. kept at the British Library, rept. Mecca: Maktabat Makkat al-Mukarrama, 1986); Isḥāq al-Ḥakīm al-Rūmī (d. 950/1543), *Mukhtaṣar al-ḥikmat al-nabawiyya sharḥ al-Fiqh al-akbar*, ed. Bajazid Nicević (Beirut: Dār al-Kutub al-'Ilmiyya, 2015); Bahā' al-Dīn Zādah [Muḥyī al-Dīn Muḥammad b. Bahā' al-Dīn (d. 956/1549)], *al-Qawl al-faṣl sharḥ al-Fiqh al-akbar lil-imām Abī Ḥanīfa* (Istanbul: Hakîkat Kitabevi, 1990); *ibid.*, ed.

———. *Musnad Abī Ḥanīfa bi-tartīb al-Sindī.* With Mullā ʿAlī al-Qārī, *Sharḥ Musnad Abī Ḥanīfa.* Ed. ʿAbd al-Jalīl ʿAṭā. Damascus: Dār al-Nuʿmān, 1438/2017.

———. *Risālat Abī Ḥanīfa ilā ʿUthmān al-Battī.* In *Namādhij min rasāʾil al-aʾimmat al-salaf wa-adabihim al-ʿilmī.* Ed. ʿAbd al-Fattāḥ Abū Ghudda. Aleppo: Maktab al-Maṭbūʿāt al-Islāmiyya; Beirut: Dār al-Bashāʾir al-Islāmiyya, 1417/1996 and 1419/1999.

———. *Risālat Abī Ḥanīfa ilā ʿUthmān al-Battī.* In the 1368/1949 and 1421/2001 editions of *al-ʿĀlim wal-mutaʿallim.*

This is a brief epistle to the *mujtahid* of Basra, Abū ʿAmr ʿUthmān b. Muslim al-Battī (d. 143/760), narrated through Nuṣayr b. Yaḥyā, from Abū ʿAbd Allāh Muḥammad b. Samāʿa al-Tamīmī, from Abū Yūsuf, from Abū Ḥanīfa, in which the latter explains the principle whereby *īmān* has two, not three pillars in his view, namely, conviction in the heart and affirmation by the tongue, in refutation of those who imputed him with the label of *Murjiʾ*.[52] This text was translated in full.[53]

———. *Waṣiyyat Abī Ḥanīfa li-tilmīdhih Yūsuf al-Samtī.* With al-Zarnūjī's *Taʿlīm al-mutaʿallim.* Ed. ʿAbd al-Jalīl ʿAṭā. Damascus: Dār al-Nuʿmān lil-ʿUlūm, 1418/1998.

Rafiq al-Ajam, (Beirut, Dār al-Muntakhab al-ʿArabī, 1998); al-Qārī, *Sharḥ al-Fiqh al-akbar* (Beirut: Dār al-Kutub al-ʿIlmiyya, 1404/1984); ibid., *Sharḥ al-Fiqh al-akbar*, ed. Marwān Muḥammad al-Shaʿār (Beirut: Dār al-Nafāʾis, 1417/1997); ibid., *Minaḥ al-rawḍ al-azhar fī sharḥ al-Fiqh al-akbar*, ed. Wahbī Sulaymān Ghāwjī (Beirut: Dār al-Bashāʾir al-Islāmiyya, 1419/1998); al-Maghnīsāwī, *Sharḥ al-Fiqh al-akbar* in *al-Rasāʾil al-sabʿa fil-ʿaqāʾid* (Hyderabad Deccan: Dāʾirat al-Maʿārif al-Niẓāmiyya, 1321/1904); ibid., ʿAbd al-Karīm Tattān, *Sharḥ al-Fiqh al-akbar* in *Kutub al-ʿaqāʾid: Sharḥ al-Amālī, Sharḥ al-Fiqh al-akbar, ʿAqāʾid al-nūniyya, ʿAqāʾid al-Nasafī.* Istanbul: al-Maktabat al-Ḥanīfiyya, [1392/1972]. Translations by W.M. Watt (*Islamic Creeds*); Hamid Algar (*al-Bayān* magazine); Abdur-Rahman Yusuf (*Imām Abū Ḥanīfa's* al-Fiqh al-akbar *Explained*).

52 On the issues of Abū Ḥanīfa's Sunni *irjāʾ* and his views that ʿ*īmān* neither increases nor decreases' and that a Muslim should never add *in shāʾ Allāh* when saying 'I am a *muʾmin*' as it would constitute unbelief since *īmān* is identical with *islām*, see Haddad, *Four Imams*, pp. 42–47 and Ghāwjī al-Albānī, *Arkān al-īmān*, pp. 145–148.

53 In Haddad, *Four Imams*, pp. 69–74.

———. *Waṣiyyat al-Imām Abī Ḥanīfat al-Nuʿmān*. Ed. Muḥammad ʿUwayna. Beirut: Dār Ibn Ḥazm, 1418/1997.

The *Waṣiyya* is also known as *Risālat nuqirr* (The treatise 'We hold') after its first word.[54] Al-Bayāḍī in his bio-bibliography of Abū Ḥanīfa at the beginning of *Ishārāt al-marām* mentions that the complete text of the *Waṣiyya* was adduced by the Egyptian historian Ṣārim al-Dīn Ibrāhīm b. Muḥammad b. Duqmāq al-Miṣrī (750–809/1349/1406) in his *Naẓm al-jumān fī ṭabaqāt imāminā al-Nuʿmān*; the qadi Abū al-Faḍl Ibn al-Shiḥna Muḥammad b. Muḥammad b. Muḥammad al-Thaqafī al-Ḥalabī, (804–890/1402–1485)[55] at the beginning of his commentary on the *Hidāya* entitled *Nihāyat al-Nihāya fī taḥrīr taqrīr al-Hidāya*; the qadi Taqī al-Dīn b. ʿAbd al-Qādir al-Dārī al-Ghazzī al-Miṣrī (d. 1005/1597 or 1010/1602) in *al-Ṭabaqāt al-saniyya fī tarājim al-Ḥanafiyya*; and Akmal al-Dīn al-Bābartī (714–786/1314–1384) who wrote *Sharḥ Waṣiyyat al-Imām Abī Ḥanīfa* (Amman: Dār al-Fatḥ, 2009). ʿAṭā in the preface to his edition mentions the *Waṣiyya* was also adduced in full 'in *Manāqib Abī Ḥanīfa*.'[56] The *Waṣiyya* was reportedly transmitted from Abū Ḥanīfa by several students of his including his son Abū Ḥammād, Abū Yūsuf, Abū Muṭīʿ al-Balkhī, and Abū Muqātil Ḥafṣ b. Salam [not 'Muslim'] al-Samarqandī. From these four, the work was variously narrated by Ismāʿīl b. Ḥammād, Muḥammad b. Muqātil al-Rāzī, Muḥammad b. Samāʿa al-Tamīmī [not 'Taymī'], Nuṣayr b. Yaḥyā al-Balkhī, Shaddād b. Ḥakīm al-Balkhī, and Ṣāliḥ b. Muḥammad al-Tirmidhī. Al-Kawtharī said that al-Māturīdī narrated it (i) from Abū Bakr Aḥmad b. Isḥāq al-Jūzjānī and Abū Naṣr Aḥmad b. al-ʿIyāḍī, both of them from Abū Sulaymān Mūsā al-Jūzjānī, from Abū Yūsuf and Muḥammad b. al-Ḥasan; and (ii) from Nuṣayr b. Yaḥyā and Muḥammad b. Muqātil al-Rāzī, both of them from Abū Muṭīʿ al-Balkhī *and* Abū Muqātil,[57] from Abū Ḥanīfa.[58] The likeliest narration, however, appears to be that of Ṣāliḥ

54 See the edition published at the end of Ḥāfiẓ al-Dīn al-Nasafī, *Matn al-manār fī uṣūl al-fiqh* (Dar Saʿādat [=Istanbul]: Maṭbaʿat Aḥmad Kāmil, 1326/1908).

55 See on him https://www.arab-ency.com/ar/البحوث/ابن-الشحنة

56 There are at least three books entitled *Manāqib al-Imām al-aʿẓam Abī Ḥanīfa*: by al-Qudūrī (362–428/973–1037, unpublished), al-Muwaffaq b. Aḥmad al-Khwārizmī al-Makkī (d. 568/1173) (considered a Muʿtazilī), and al-Kardarī al-Bazzāzī (d. 827/1424).

57 Not 'from Abū Muqātil' (see note 266).

58 al-Bayāḍī, *Ishārāt al-marām min ʿibārāt al-imām*, ed. Yūsuf ʿAbd al-Razzāq (Cairo: Muṣṭafā Bābī al-Ḥalabī, 1368/1949), pp. 22–23.

b. Muḥammad al-Tirmidhī, from Ḥammād, from his father, as mentioned by Ibn Ṭūlūn and Ibn Ḥajar in their transmission catalogues.[59]

59 See Ibn Ṭūlūn, *al-Fihrist al-awsaṭ min al-marwiyyāt*, ed. ʿAbd Allāh al-Shabrāwī, 5 vols. (Damascus: Dār al-Nawādir, 1435/2015), 5:67–68 and Ibn Ḥajar, *al-Muʿjam al-mufahras aw tajrīd asānīd al-kutub al-mashhūra wal-ajzāʾ al-manthūra*, ed. Muḥammad Shakkūr al-Mayādinī (Beirut: Muʾassasat al-Risāla, 1418/1998), p. 269 no. 1121.

Fourth/Tenth Century

al-Ṭaḥāwī

al-Ṭaḥāwī Abū Ja'far. *al-'Aqīdat al-Ṭaḥāwiyya.* Ed. Muḥammad b. Ṣalāḥ al-Shawādifī. Riyadh: Madār al-Waṭan lil-Nashr, 1437/2016.

Abū Ja'far Aḥmad b. Muḥammad b. Salāma al-Azdī al-Ḥajrī al-Miṣrī al-Ṭaḥāwī (229–321/844–933) was the humble, self-effacing, scrupulous jurist and unrivalled master of the *madhhab* in hadith and its sciences, 'matched by none of those who followed' (Ibn Yūnus, al-Ṣafadī, al-Suyūṭī), 'unanimously agreed upon in his trustworthiness' (al-'Aynī, al-Sam'ānī, al-Dhahabī, al-Suyūṭī), 'the Master in all the Schools of *fiqh*' (Ibn 'Abd al-Barr), 'one of the established trustworthy giants among the hadith Masters' (Ibn Kathīr), who shared the same teachers in hadith as Muslim, al-Nasā'ī, Abū Dāwūd and Ibn Mājah, and 'whose *Sharḥ ma'ānī al-āthār* surpasses the *Sunan* in excellence' (al-Kawtharī).[60] In the history of Maturidism he is famous for his credal treatise *Bayān 'aqīdat fuqahā' al-milla Abī Ḥanīfa wa-Abī Yūsuf wa-Muḥammad ibn al-Ḥasan*, one of the most reliable concise early texts of Sunni doctrine, praised by Ibn al-Subkī as exemplifying al-Ash'arī's own creed and as mustering the agreement of all the Sunni schools. Its exact title is taken from its first words, *Exposition of the Creed of the People of the Sunna and the Congregation According to the Teachings of the Jurists of the Community, Abū Ḥanīfa, Abū Yūsuf and Muḥammad b. al-Ḥasan.* The above is the only scholarly edition of the *matn* itself as of yet. It has received several commentaries, notably by the very aged Damascene qadi Abū al-Faḍā'il Ismā'īl b. Ibrāhīm b. Aḥmad al-Shaybānī known as Ibn al-Mawṣilī (504–629/1110–1232) (published in

60 This claim, even if disputable, indicates the high rank of al-Ṭaḥāwī and his work.

2005), Abū Shujāʿ Najm al-Dīn Mankūbars b. Yalinqalj ʿAbd Allāh al-Nāṣirī[61] (d. 652/1254), Shujāʿ al-Dīn Hibat Allāh b. Aḥmad b. Muʿallā al-Turkistānī (671–733/1272–1333), Ibn al-Sarrāj Maḥmūd b. Aḥmad al-Qūnawī al-Dimashqī[62] (d. 771/1370), Abū Ḥafṣ Sirāj al-Dīn ʿUmar b. Isḥāq al-Hindī al-Ghaznawī (704 or 705–773/1304 or 1305–1372), Akmal al-Dīn Muḥammad b. Muḥammad b. Maḥmūd Bābirtī or Bābartī or Bābardī (714–786/1314–1384), the Bosnian Ḥasan Kāfī Afandī al-Aqḥiṣārī (951–1024/1544–1615) (*q.v.*), the Damascene ʿAbd al-Ghanī b. Ṭālib al-Ghunaymī al-Maydānī (1222–1298/1807–1881). One of the most widespread is by the Damascene Ibn Abī al-ʿIzz (*q.v.*), a follower of Ibn Taymiyya who is unknown but for this work and whom al-Zabīdī, al-Qārī, al-Kawtharī and others branded as heretical,[63] but who struck the keynote for many contemporary commentaries such as those by Muḥammad Nāṣir al-Albānī and the Saudi establishment on the one hand and, on the other, those by ʿAbd Allāh al-Hararī, Ḥasan ʿAlī al-Saqqāf and others, of which the reliable and authoritative one is Saʿīd ʿAbd al-Laṭīf Fawda's 1,500-page *al-Sharḥ al-kabīr ʿalā al-ʿAqīdat al-Ṭaḥāwiyya* (Beirut: Dār al-Dhakhā'ir, 2014). The *Ṭaḥāwiyya* has received several English translations.[64]

al-Māturīdī

al-Māturīdī, Abū Manṣūr Muḥammad b. Muḥammad. *Kitāb al-Tawḥīd.* Ed. Bekir Topaloğlu and Muhammad Aruçi. 2nd printing. Ankara: İSAM, İslâm Araştırmaları Merkezi Yayınları, 1426/2005; 2nd ed. Beirut: Dār Ṣādir; Istanbul: Maktabat al-Irshād, 1422/2001.

———. *Ta'wīlāt Ahl al-Sunna: Tafsīr al-Māturīdī.* Ed. Majdī Basallūm. 10 vols. Beirut: Dār al-Kutub al-ʿIlmiyya, 2005/1426.

61 *al-Nūr al-lāmiʿ wal-burhān al-sāṭiʿ.*

62 *al-Qalā'id fī sharḥ al-ʿaqā'id.*

63 See, among contemporary critiques, the book by ʿAbd al-ʿAzīz al-Ḥāḍirī in this bibliography.

64 Among them W.M. Watt, *Islamic Creeds*; Fahim Hoosen (*Al-Aqīda al-Ṭaḥāwiyya*); http://sunnah.org/aqida/aqida10.htm as of 5 December 2020; and Hamza Yusuf (*The Creed of Imam Al-Tahawi*).

———. *Ta'wīlāt al-Qur'ān*. Ed. Ertuğrul Boynukalin and Bekir Topaloğlu. 18 vols. Istanbul: Dār al-Mīzān, 2005–2011.

The foremost expositor of the credal doctrine of Abū Ḥanīfa, Abū Manṣūr Muḥammad b. Muḥammad b. Maḥmūd al-Samarqandī al-Māturīdī (d. 333/945) of Māturīd in Samarqand studied under Abū Naṣr al-ʿAyādī and Abū Bakr Aḥmad al-Jūzjānī. Among his senior students were ʿAlī b. Saʿīd Abū al-Ḥasan al-Rustughfānī,[65] Abū Muḥammad ʿAbd al-Karīm b. Mūsā b. ʿĪsā al-Pazdawī, and Abū al-Qāsim Isḥāq b. Muḥammad al-Ḥākim al-Samarqandī. He excelled in refuting the Muʿtazila in Transoxiana while his contemporary Abū al-Ḥasan al-Ashʿarī did the same in Basra and Baghdad. He died in Samarqand where he lived most of his life.

Al-Māturīdī is famous for two main works. One is a large commentary on the Qur'ān that still awaits serious study entitled *Ta'wilāt al-Qur'ān* (Interpretations of the Qur'ān), of which Ibn Abī al-Wafā' said, 'No book rivals it, indeed no book even comes near it among those who preceded him in this discipline.'[66] Ḥājjī Khalīfa cites it as *Ta'wilāt Ahl al-Sunna* and quotes al-Māturīdī's definition of the difference between 'explanation' *(tafsīr)* and 'interpretation' *(ta'wīl)* as follows: '*Tafsīr* is the categorical assertion *(al-qaṭʿ)* that the meaning of the term in question is *this* and the testimony before Allah Almighty that *this* is what He meant by the term in question, while *ta'wīl* is the preferment *(tarjīḥ)* of one of several possibilities without categorical assertion nor testimony.'[67] Al-Maturīdī's other famous great work is *al-Tawḥīd* (Monotheism), although the authenticity of the attribution of both works to him has been unsuccessfully challenged.[68] Also among the (mostly lost) works that he is said to have authored: *Bayān awhām al-Muʿtazila*; *Radd Awā'il al-adilla*, a refutation of the Muʿtazilī Abū al-Qāsim ʿAbd Allāh al-Kaʿbī's book entitled *Awā'il al-adilla*; *Radd al-tahdhīb fil-jadal*, another refutation of al-Kaʿbī;

65 He narrated from Abū Ḥanīfa the saying: *kullu mujtahidin muṣībun wal-ḥaqqu ʿinda Allāhi wāḥid* (every striving expert is correct even if the truth in the divine presence is one), while al-Māturīdī considered that the *mujtahid* is wrong in his *ijtihād* if his finding differs from the truth. Ibn Abī al-Wafā', *al-Jawāhir al-muḍiyya*, 3:360–361.

66 Ibn Abī al-Wafā', *al-Jawāhir al-muḍiyya*, 3:360.

67 In Ḥajjī Khalīfa, *Kashf al-ẓunūn*, 1:334–335.

68 See M. Sait Özervarlı, 'The Authenticity of the Manuscript of Māturīdī's *Kitāb al-Tawḥīd*: A Re-examination,' *İslâm Araştırmaları Dergisi* (Turkish Journal of Islamic Studies), Vol. 1 (1997), pp. 19–29 and Cerić, *Roots*, pp. 40–41, 47–48.

Radd al-uṣūl al-khamsa, a refutation of Abū Muḥammad al-Bāhilī's exposition of the Five Principles of the Muʿtazila; *Radd waʿīd al-fussāq*, a refutation of the Muʿtazilī and Khārijī doctrine that all grave sinners among the Muslims are doomed to eternal Hellfire (their 'Third principle'); *Radd al-imāma*, a refutation of the Shīʿī conception of the office of supreme leader or imām; *al-Radd ʿalā uṣūl al-Qarāmiṭa*, a refutation of Qarmatians, an Ismāʿīlī offshoot; *al-Jadal fī uṣūl al-fiqh* and *Maʾākhidh al-sharāʾiʿ*, both on legal theory; the lost *al-Maqālāt*, possibly a reference-book of heresiography like al-Ashʿarī's same-titled *Maqālāt al-islāmiyyīn*; and a *Risāla fī-mā lā yajūz al-waqf ʿalayh fil-Qurʾān*, in which he states there are 52 places in the Qurʾān where recitational pausing is forbidden on pains of committing apostasy.[69] Among the famous spurious attributions is that of a book entitled '*Sharḥ al-Fiqh al-akbar* by al-Māturīdī.' In reality the book is *Sharḥ al-Fiqh al-absaṭ* and the author is either Abū al-Layth al-Samarqandī (d. 373/983) or someone later.[70] The glaring absence of notices on Imām Abū Manṣūr al-Māturīdī in many of the latter-day biographical histories (al-Dhahabī's *Siyar* and *Tārīkh al-islām*, Ibn Khallikān and al-Ṣafadī) is a major omission in those works. The *Kitāb al-tawḥīd* comprises the following headings:

1. PREAMBLE
    - 1.1 The obligatoriness of acquiring knowledge of religion together with its evidence
    - 1.2 Hearing [from a Prophet] and reason being two principles whereby religion can be known
    - 1.3 The avenues of acquiring knowledge
    - 1.4 Eyewitnessing

69 See Cerić, *Roots*, pp. 43–44. Rudolph's arguments for its inauthenticity are unconvincing, *al-Māturīdī*, pp. 329–330. See, below, Najm al-Dīn al-Nasafī's work on the same subject entitled *Zallat al-qārī*.

70 It has two editions: *Sharḥ al-Fiqh al-Akbar li-Abī Manṣūr al-Samarqandī* in *al-Rasāʾil al-sabʿa fil-ʿaqāʾid* (Hyderabad Deccan: Dāʾirat al-Maʿārif al-Niẓāmiyya, 1321/1904), p. 1–28 thus reprinted with a reduplication of the misattribution in India, Egypt,Qatar and Lebanon; and Hans Daiber, *The Islamic Concept of Belief in the 4th/10th Century: Abū al-Layth al-Samarqandī's Commentary on Abū Ḥanīfah's* al-Fiqh al-Absaṭ (Tokyo: Tokyo University of Foreign Studies, 1995). See also Rudolph, *al-Māturīdī and the Development of Sunnī Theology*, pp. 325–328.

1.5 Reports
1.6 Mass-transmitted reports
1.7 Lone-transmitted reports
1.8 Investigation (*naẓar*)
1.9 Other rebuttals of those who deny the avenues of acquiring knowledge

2. TOPICS RELATED TO GODHEAD

2.1 The originated nature of the world and the necessity of its having a creator
2.2 The originated nature of concrete objects (*aʿyān*)
2.3 The accident or attribute
2.4 The Originator of the world is one (*wāḥid*)[71]
2.5 The negation of resemblance for Allah
2.6 Affirmation and resemblance
2.7 'Present witness as evidence for what is out of sight' (= as supposed proof for the eternity of the world)
2.8 Claims of those who hold the world is eternal
2.9 Claims of the dualists who hold the world is eternal
2.10 Applying the term 'body' (*jism*) to Allah
2.11 Applying the term 'thing' (*shay'*) to Allah[72]
2.12 On the attributes of Allah
2.13 Existentiation (*al-takwīn*)

71 As in the *Fiqh al-akbar*, 'One but not in the way of numbering... lest one be under the illusion that there should be anyone after Him,' al-Qārī, *Sharḥ al-Fiqh al-akbar*, Nafā'is ed., p. 48. 'He is *al-Wāḥid* in reality (*fil-ḥaqīqa*) while all other than Him in creation are compound units (*āḥād tarakkabat*); as for the discussion whether He is one in the way of numbering or not, it is not relevant to my purpose, which is the mention of the coinage and its denotation in usage.... One of the semanticists (*ahl al-maʿānī*) said the difference between *al-Wāḥid* and *al-Aḥad* is that *al-Wāḥid* denotes oneness of essence (*waḥdat al-dhāt*) only, while *al-Aḥad* denotes oneness of essence as well as meanings. Accordingly, it says in the revelation, *Qul Huwa Allāhu Aḥad* (al-Ikhlāṣ 112:1), by which He means the one Who is singled out (*munfarid*) in His oneness (*waḥdāniyya*) whether in His essence or His attributes.' al-Zajjāj (241–311/855–923), *Tafsīr al-asmā' al-ḥusnā*, ed. Aḥmad Yūsuf al-Daqqāq, 5th ed. (Damascus and Beirut: Dār al-Ma'mūn lil-Turāth, 1406/1986), pp. 57–57.

72 'A thing unlike things' (*shay' lā kal-ashyā'* and 'without body' (*bi-lā jism*): al-Qārī, *Sharḥ al-Fiqh al-akbar*, Nafā'is ed., pp. 16, 88–91.

2.14 Refutation of al-Kaʿbī's[73] views on the attributes of essence and of acts
2.15 The attribute of speech
2.16 That the acts of Allah are by choice
2.17 The rebuttal of the deniers of a Maker Who is all-wise and all-knowing
2.18 The names of Allah Almighty
2.19 Exposition of the Throne
2.20 Seeing Allah
2.21 Refutation of the Muʿtazila's claim that the non-existent is a thing
2.22 Giving attributes to and naming Allah does not necessitate resemblance
2.23 Why did Allah create creatures?
2.24 The wisdom behind command and prohibition
2.25 On the saying 'Whoever knows himself knows his Lord'
2.26 Applying the terms 'body' (*jism*) and 'thing' (*shay*) to Allah
2.27 The impermissibility of attributing place to Allah
2.28 On attributing quiddity (*māhiyya*), modality (*kayfiyya*) and proximity (*qurb*) to Allah
2.29 The wisdom behind the creation of noxious substances
2.30 The disparity of people on earth
2.31 Rebuttal of the dualists (*thanawiyya*)
2.32 Rebuttal of the naturalists (*ṭabāʾiʿiyya*)
2.33 The paths of pure monotheism
2.34 Views of Muḥammad b. Shabīb[74] on the Creator's existence and His attributes
2.35 Justification of knowledge through investigation
2.36 Muḥammad b. Shabīb's proof of the originated nature of bodies
2.37 Exposition of the inanity of the theses of the Dahriyya[75]
2.38 The claims of the Sumaniyya [Buddhists] and the exposition of their inanity

73 As mentioned above, al-Māturīdī also authored *Radd Awāʾil al-adilla*, a refutation of the Muʿtazilī Abū al-Qāsim ʿAbd Allāh al-Kaʿbī's book entitled *Awāʾil al-adilla*.

74 A disciple of the Muʿtazilī al-Naẓẓām.

75 Aeonists/'Perennialists' i.e. philosophers and Ismāʿīlīs.

2.39 The claims of the Sophists and the exposition of their inanity
2.40 The claims of the dualists and Manicheists and the exposition of their inanity
2.41 The claims of the Daysanists [Monophysites][76] and the exposition of their inanity
2.42 The claims of the Marcionites and the exposition of their inanity
2.43 The claims of the Zoroastrians and the exposition of their inanity

3. TOPICS RELATED TO PROPHETHOOD

3.1 Affirmation of prophetic messengership and exposition of humanity's need for it
3.2 Refutation of al-Warrāq's views on messengership
3.3 The affirmation of the messengership of Muḥammad—upon him blessings and peace
3.4 Ibn al-Rawandī's rebuttal of al-Warrāq
3.5 The views of Christians regarding the Christ and their refutation

4. TOPICS RELATED TO FOREORDAINED DESTINY

4.1 On wisdom and foolishness
4.2 The acts of creatures and their affirmation
4.3 Views of the sects on the acts of creatures
4.4 The claims of the Muʿtazila regarding the acts of creatures and the exposition of their inanity
4.5 The claims of al-Kaʿbī regarding the acts of creatures and the exposition of their inanity
4.6 The Prophetically-related evidence that acts are created
4.7 Power or ability to act
4.8 Is ability (*istiṭāʿa*) before the act or together with it?
4.9 On the applicability of power to opposites and the tasking beyond capacity
4.10 Exposition of the inanity of al-Kaʿbī's views on the above
4.11 On lifespans

76 'Monophysite. A heretic who believes that there is only one nature [viz., divine] in the person of Jesus Christ. The bodies of Christians now professing this belief are the Coptic, Armenian, Abyssinian, and Jacobite churches.' *OED*.

4.12 On sustenance
4.13 On will
4.14 Exposition of the inanity of al-Kaʿbī's views on the above
4.15 On foreordained destiny
4.16 Exposition of the inanity of al-Kaʿbī's views on the above
4.17 The blame of the Qadariyya also known as the Muʿtazila
4.18 Exposition of the inanity of al-Kaʿbī's views on the above

5. TOPICS RELATED TO GRAVE SINS AND GRAVE SINNERS

5.1 The status of sins and the appellation of those who commit them
5.2 The differences among Muslims concerning those who commit grave sins
5.3 Al-Kaʿbī's views on grave sins and the exposition of their inanity
5.4 The obligation to differentiate between the two types of sins with wisdom
5.5 The Muʿtazila and the appellation of *īmān*
5.6 Major sins and intercession

6. TOPICS RELATED TO *ĪMĀN* AND *ISLĀM*

6.1 On affirmation and confirmation in belief
6.2 Does belief consist in confirmation or in knowledge?
6.3 On postponement [*irjāʾ*]
6.4 The creation of faith
6.5 Saying *in shā Allāh* in the profession of faith
6.6 *Islām* and *īmān*

Al-Māturīdī refutes the doctrine of attributing locality to Allah in his book *al-Tawḥīd* in the following terms:

> The Muslims differ concerning the place of Allah Most High. Some have claimed that Allah is described as being 'established over the Throne' (*ʿalā al-ʿarshi mustawin*), and the Throne for them is a dais (*sarīr*) carried by the angels and surrounded by them [as in the verses]: *and eight will uphold the Throne of their Lord that day, above them* (69:17), *and you see the angels thronging round the Throne* (39:75), and *those who bear the Throne, and all who are round about it* (40:7). They adduced as a proof for that position His saying *the Merciful established Himself over the Throne* (20:5) and the

fact that people raise their hands toward the heaven in their supplications and whatever bounties they are hoping for. They also say that He moved there after not being there at first, on the basis of the verse *then He established Himself over the Throne* (57:4). Others say that He is in every place because He said *there is no secret conference of three but He is their fourth, nor of five but He is their sixth, nor of less than that or more but He is with them wheresoever they may be* (58:7), *We are nearer to him than his jugular vein* (50:16), *and We are nearer unto him than you are, but you see not* (56:85), and *He it is Who in the heaven is God, and in the earth God* (43:84). This group consider that to say that He is in one place at the exclusion of another necessitates a limit for Him, and that every limited object comes short of whatever is greater than it, which would constitute a disgraceful defect. Further, they consider that to be in one place necessitates need for that place together with the necessity of boundaries. ... Others deny the ascription of place to Allah, whether one place or every place, except in the metaphorical senses that He preserves them and causes them to exist. The sum of all this is that the predication of all things to Him; and His predication—may He be exalted!—to them is along the lines of His description in terms of exaltation (*ʿulūw*) and loftiness (*rifʿa*), and in terms of extolment (*taʿẓīm*) and majesty (*jalāl*), as in His saying: *the Sovereignty of the heavens and the earth* (2:107, 3:189, 5:17–18, 5:40 etc.), *Lord of the heavens and the earth* (13:16, 17:102, 18:14, 19:65, etc.), 'God of all creation' (*ilāh al-khalq*), *Lord of the worlds* (1:2, 5:28, 6:45, 6:162, 7:54, etc.), 'above everything' (*fawqa kulli shay'*) and so forth. As for the predication of specific objects to Him, it is along the lines of His being specifically attributed generosity (*karāma*), high rank (*manzila*) and immense favor (*tafḍīl*) for what is essentially meant to refer to Him, as in His sayings *Lo! Allah is with those who keep their duty unto Him* (16:128), *And the places of worship are only for Allah* (72:18), *The she-camel of Allah* (7:73, 11:64, 91:13), 'The House of Allah' (*bayt Allah*) and other similar instances. None of these examples is understood in the same way as the predication of created objects to one another.... The foundation of this issue is that Allah Almighty was when there was no place; then locations were set up while He remains exactly as He ever was. Therefore, He is as He ever was and He ever was as He is now. Exalted is He beyond any change or transition or movement or cessation! For all these are portents of contingency (*ḥadath*) by which the contingent nature of the world can be known, and the proofs of its eventual passing away.... Furthermore [concerning the claim that Allah is on the Throne], there is not, in the context of spatial elevation, any particular merit to sitting or standing, nor exaltation, nor any quality of magnificence and splendor. For example, someone standing higher than roofs or mountains does not deservedly acquire loftiness over someone who is below him spatially when their essence is identical. Therefore, it is not permissible to interpret the verse [20:5] in that sense when it is actually pointing to magnificence and majesty. For He has said *Verily, it is your Lord Who created the heavens and the earth* (7:54, 10:3, 21:56), thereby pointing to the extolment of the Throne, which is something created of light, or a substance the reality of which is beyond the knowledge of creatures. It was narrated that the Prophet, upon him blessings and peace, said in his description of the sun: 'Jibrīl brings it, in his hand, some of the light of the Throne with which he clothes it just as one of you wears his clothes, and does so every day that it rises'; he also mentioned that the moon receives a handful of the light of the Throne.[77] Therefore, the predication of *istiwā'* to the Throne is along two lines: first, its extolment in the light of all that He said concerning His authority in Lordship and over creatures; second, its specific mention as the greatest and loftiest of all objects in creation, in keeping with the customary predication of magnificent matters to magnificent objects, just as it is said: 'So-and-so has achieved sovereignty over such-and-such a country, and has established himself over such-and-such a region.' This is not to restrict the meaning of this sovereignty literally, but only to say that it is well-known that whoever owns sovereignty over this, then whatever lies below it is meant *a fortiori*.[78]

Abū Salama al-Samarqandī

Abū Salama al-Samarqandī Muḥammad b. Muḥammad. *Jumalun min uṣūl al-dīn*. Ed. Ilhām Qāsimī. Beirut: Dār al-Kutub al-ʿIlmiyya, 2015.

77 Something similar is narrated—without naming the angel—as part of a very long hadith from Ibn ʿAbbās by Abū al-Shaykh with a very weak chain in *al-ʿAẓama* (4:1163–1179). Another hadith states: "The Messenger of Allah told me that the sun, the moon, and the stars were created from the light of the Throne." Narrated from Anas by Abū al-Shaykh in *al-ʿAẓama* (4:1140). See also al-Suyūṭī's *al-Ḥabā'ik fī akhbār al-malā'ik*.

78 al-Māturīdī, *Kitāb al-Tawḥīd* (Beirut ed. pp. 131–134 = Ankara ed. pp. 104–108). Elsewhere al-Māturīdī says: "To suggest a place for Allah is idolatry." Quoted in Abū Ḥanīfa, *Kitāb al-Fiqh al-akbar bi-sharḥ al-Qārī* (Cairo: Dār al-Kutub al-ʿArabiyya al-Kubrā, 1327/1909) p. 16.

Nothing is known of Abū Salama Muḥammad b. Muḥammad al-Samarqandī (d. bef. 340/951) other than that he was a student of the major Ḥanafī authority Abū Aḥmad Naṣr b. Aḥmad al-Shahīd b. al-ʿAbbās b. Jabala al-ʿIyāḍī, whose father was al-Māturīdī's teacher. He is thus of the same generation as the latter. The only other detail mentioned by the *madhhab* historians is that Abū Salama authored *Jumalun min uṣūl al-dīn*.

Ibn al-Ḥakīm al-Samarqandī

Ibn al-Ḥakīm al-Samarqandī Abū al-Qāsim Isḥāq b. Muḥammad. *al-Sawād al-aʿẓam fil-kalām*. Princeton University. Ms. Garrett no. 345B. https://catalog.princeton.edu/catalog/6358523[79]

———. *al-Sawād al-aʿẓam fil-kalām*. [Istanbul]: Maṭbaʿat Ibrāhīm, 1304/1887. 39p. http://www.ilahiyatakademisi.com/kitaplar/sevadul.pdf

———. [*al-Sawād al-aʿẓam*. Persian.] *Tarjumah-'i al-Savād al-aʿẓam*. [Tehran]: Bunyād-i Farhang-i Īrān, [1969]. 250 p.

———. [*al-Sawād al-aʿẓam*. English.] *The Doctrines of the Māturīdite School with Special Reference to* As-Sawād al-Aʿẓam *of al-Ḥakīm al-Samarqandī*. Farouq ʿOmar ʿAbd-Allāh al-ʿOmar. Unpubl. diss. University of Edinburgh, 1974. Pp. 55–237. https://era.ed.ac.uk/handle/1842/8977

———. [*al-Sawād al-aʿẓam*. Turkish.] *Tarik-i müstakim=Doğru yol: Sevad-ı Azam tercümesi*. Transl. Şahver Çelikoğlu. Istanbul: Haşmet matbaası, 1980. 200p.

Abū al-Qāsim Isḥāq b. Muḥammad b. Ismāʿil b. Ibrāhīm b. Zayd, known as Ibn al-Ḥakīm or al-Ḥakīm al-Samarqandī (d. bet. 340 and 422/951 and 1031), was a Hanafi qadi and colleague of Abū Manṣūr al-Māturīdī, both of them students of Abū Naṣr al-ʿIyāḍī. He was also a student of Abū Bakr al-Warrāq. He is known mostly for his work entitled *al-Sawād al-aʿẓam* (The Greater Mass, i.e., Orthodox doctrine), written in 62 briefly explained articles

79 All URLs as of 15 October 2017 unless otherwise specified.

of belief (*khiṣāl al-īmān*) which he considered to be the basis of including anyone in 'the greater throng' i.e. *Ahl al-Sunna wal-Jamā'a*. The work received an expanded commentary by Ibrāhīm al-Wafi (fl. 1313/1895) (*q.v.*), Persian and Turkish translations as well as an unpublished full English translation. Its sections are:

1. He must not doubt in respect of his faith.
2. He must not run counter to the Congregation (*jamā'a*) of the Muslims.
3. He must perform the prayers behind every ruler, just and unjust; and consider it valid.
4. He must not call anyone among the people of this qibla an unbeliever through his sinning.
5. He must pray at the funeral of everyone young and old of the people of this qibla and consider it valid.
6. He must consider that the decree (*taqdīr*) of both good and evil is from Allah.
7. He must not take up sword against any of the Muslims without a just cause.
8. He must perform the prayers of the two feasts (*'Id*) and the *jum'a* prayer behind every ruler and consider it valid.
9. He must consider the wiping of the shoes valid (as a substitute for ablution) both at home and when travelling.
10. He must regard faith as the gift of Allah.
11. He must know that the deeds of people are created by Allah.
12. He must confess that the Qur'ān, the Speech of Allah, is uncreated.
13. He must believe that the punishment of the grave is a reality.
14. He must believe that the questioning by Munkar and Nakir in the grave is a reality.
15. He must believe that the prayer and alms of the living benefit the dead.
16. He must believe that the intercession of the Prophet (upon him blessings and peace) for the sinners of his Community is a reality.
17. He must believe that the Night of the Prophet's Ascent (*mi'rāj*) is a reality.
18. He must confess to the exhibition of each person's record on the Day of Resurrection and hold it to be a reality.

19. He must believe in the reckoning and hold it to be a reality.
20. He must believe that the balance of deeds is a reality.
21. He must believe in the *ṣirāṭ* (bridge over hellfire) and hold it to be a reality.
22. He must know that Paradise and hellfire are already created, will not cease to exist nor vanish and must hold this as a reality.
23. He must know that Allah reckons with His servants on the Day of Resurrection with no interpreter between Him and them.
24. He must testify that the Ten Companions of the Prophet (upon him blessings and peace) are in Paradise, and believe that is a reality.
25. He must know that none of his Companions or his Community after the Prophet was more excellent than Abū Bakr al-Ṣiddīq, and he must believe that he is caliph after the Prophet in reality.
26. He must know that after Abū Bakr al-Ṣiddīq there is no one in the whole Community more excellent than ʿUmar b. al-Khaṭṭāb, followed by ʿUthmān b. ʿAffān, followed by ʿAlī b. Abī Ṭālib, and must hold them to be rightfully caliphs.
27. He must not talk abusively of any of the Companions of the Messenger of Allah nor slander them.
28. He must know that Allah may be angry and may be pleased with anyone in creation.
29. He must believe in the reality of the vision of Allah in Paradise without asking how.
30. He must know that the status of the Prophets is higher and better than those of the walis.
31. He must not deny the miraculous power (*karāma*) of the walis, but consider it true.
32. He must know that Allah, by His justice, can change the felicitous to the wretched, and, by His generosity, the wretched to the felicitous.
33. He must know that the unbelievers' minds are not equal to the minds of the Prophets and the believers.
34. He must believe that Allah is still creating without any change of His state.
35. He must believe that Allah has knowledge and power and thus is omniscient and omnipotent.

36. He must believe that the sinners among the believers will really be punished in hell in the measure of their sins.
37. He must believe that Allah has done what He willed and will do what He wills, whether created beings understand (this act) as good or evil or not.
38. He must know that what is written on the volumes (*maṣāḥif*) is Qur'ān really, not figuratively.
39. He must know that faith is held really and not figuratively.
40. He must know that if a man has an adversary at law, and leaves this world without satisfying him, Allah will give to his adversary in the next world part of his good deeds equivalent to his claim against his (the adversary's) claim against him, and he must consider that as just on Allah's part.
41. He must know that man's obedience to Allah coincides with His grant of success (*tawfiq*) and man's disobedience to Allah coincides with His abandonment (*khidhlān*).
42. He must know that faith involves two members, the heart and the tongue.
43. He must know that whoever knows Allah in his heart and does not confess to it with his tongue is an unbeliever in reality; and he who confesses with his tongue but does not know in his heart is a hypocrite in reality.
44. He must not assert a resemblance between Allah and anything else.
45. He must not ascribe to Allah any location nor speak of His presence or absence.
46. He must know that earning is sometimes obligatory.
47. He must believe that action is different from faith.
48. He must believe that the faith of the upright person and of the sinner is equal.
49. He must believe in the resurrection.
50. He must believe in the Hour as a reality.
51. He must believe that the *witr* is three cycles with one greeting (*taslīma*).
52. He must regard the uncleanness of the Imam as uncleanness in respect of those who stand behind him (in prayer).

53. He must believe that the washing of the feet after removing the leather socks is without doubt necessary.
54. He must not consider it valid to perform ablution (*wuḍū'*) with a small quantity of stagnant water.
55. He must believe that the wiping [of the leather socks] is to be repeated if the ablution becomes invalid; and if blood flows from any part of the body or matter or pus or the like, that invalidates the ablution.
56. He must believe that faith does not increase nor decrease.
57. He must know that Iblīs was a believer in the view of Allah and the angels as long as he remained Allah's worshipper (*'abd*) whereas Abū Bakr and 'Umar were, in the view of Allah and the angels, unbelievers, as long as they worshipped images.[80]
58. He must believe that the command of Allah does not cease to be an obligation upon the man who loves Him.
59. He must fear Allah for the sake of the end (*khātima*).
60. He must not consider that despair of Allah and of His mercy is valid.

al-Samarqandī, Abū al-Layth Naṣr b. Muḥammad b. Aḥmad. *Bāb alfāẓ al-kufr* in *Khizānat al-fiqh wa-'uyūn al-masā'il.* Ed. Ṣalāḥ al-Dīn al-Nāhī. Baghdad: Sharikat al-Ṭab' al-Ahliyya, 1385/1965. Pp. 434–441.

———. *Masā'il Abī al-Layth.* In Muḥammad b. 'Umar Nawawī Banten, *Qaṭr al-ghayth fī sharḥ Masā'il Abī al-Layth.* Cairo: al-Maṭba'at al-Maymaniyya, 1307/1890. https://arh789.blogspot.com/2015/04/matan-kitab-qothrul-ghoits.html

———. *Ibid.* In A.W.T. Juynboll, 'Samarkandi's Catechismus Opnieuw Besproken,' *Bijdragen tot de Taal-, Land- en Volkenkunde van Nederlandsch-Indië*, 29ste Deel,3de Afl., [4e Volgreeks, 5e Deel] (1881), pp. 267–284.

———. *Sharḥ al-Fiqh al-absaṭ li-Abī Ḥanīfa.* In Hans Daiber, *The Islamic Concept of Belief in the 4th/10th Century: Abū al-Layth al-Samarqandī's*

80 The statement that 'Iblīs was a believer in the view of Allah and the angels' is problematic in light of the gloss of Allah's statement to them, *verily I know what you know not* (al-Baqara 2:30), as a reference—among other things—to His knowledge of Iblīs's unbelief when the angels considered him a believer as mentioned in the *Tafsīrs*. It is intended as a rebuttal of Ash'arīs, cf. Ibn al-Subkī, *Sayf* (p. 45)—and Allah knows best.

Commentary on Abū Ḥanīfah's al-Fiqh al-Absaṭ. Tokyo: Institute for the Study of Languages and Cultures of Asia and Africa, Tokyo University of Foreign Studies, 1995.

Abū al-Layth al-Samarqandī

Abū al-Layth Naṣr b. Muḥammad b. Aḥmad b. Ibrāhīm al-Samarqandī (d. 373/983) is one of the major early Ḥanafī jurists who authored works of *fiqh*, the famous admonitory books *Bustān al-ʿārifīn* and *Tanbīh al-ghāfilīn*, and a major Quranic commentary, *Baḥr al-ʿulūm*. The very brief catechism entitled *Masāʾil Abī al-Layth fil-īmān* attributed to him is compatible with both Māturīdī and Ashʿarī doctrine, but does not seem known in Ḥanafī lands or Māturīdī sources. It did achieve widespread use in Southeast Asia thanks to its brevity and doctrinal compatibility but probably mostly because a prominent Javanese scholar, Muḥammad b. ʿUmar Nawawī Banten (1813–1898), wrote a commentary on it. Abū al-Layth is also the probable author of the *Sharḥ al-fiqh al-akbar* (= *Sharḥ al-fiqh al-absaṭ*) originally published under the name of Abū Manṣūr al-Māturīdī (see Salient Themes, 'Spurious attributions/ascriptions in Māturīdī scholarship').

Daiber's edition of the *Sharḥ al-Fiqh al-absaṭ* is commendable but he all but endorses the text's anti-Ashʿarī bias and makes up additional mischaracterizations of his own. When discussing (p. 14) the Ashʿarīs' view that the same ability cannot apply to both something and its opposite he imprudently concludes that they believe that *istiṭāʿa* applies only to evil, seemingly unaware of the Māturīdī understanding that Ashʿarī *istiṭāʿa* applies to all acts (as summarized, for example, by Shaykh Zādah in the *Farāʾid*, no. 36). He falsely attributes (pp. 15, 239) to Ashʿarīs (which the *Sharḥ* reviles as 'people who doubt in their religion' at the very end) the view that the *kalām* of Allah is created. Lastly he states (p. 13): 'In contrast to the Ashʿarites and Muʿtazilites, the commentator advises (ll.188–224; 831ff.) to keep to tradition (*taqlīd*) as a way to religious knowledge.' Apart from the vague translation of *taqlīd* as 'tradition' rather than 'imitation,' Daiber here (i) misconstrues Abū al-Layth's *concession* that *taqlīd* in belief is valid as a *recommendation* to stick to *taqlīd* in belief; (ii) does not acknowledge the fact that Māturīdīs invalidate imitation as a sound basis for *knowledge* in religion (e.g. opening of Māturīdī's *Tawḥīd*; Maymūn Nasafī's *Tabṣira*, ch. 4: 'Falsifying the claim that... imitation is among the avenues of obtaining knowledge of the validity of religion'); (iii) does not acknowledge the *Sharḥ*'s mischaracterization of Ashʿarīs as invalidating the imitator's faith (whereas Pazdawī, *Uṣūl al-dīn*, ch. 39, states, 'the imitative believer is a believer by consensus: refutation of the Muʿtazila');[81] and (iv) shows unawareness that the schools that consider *ʿaql* as the basis for the obligatoriness of belief are the Māturīdīs and Muʿtazilīs, not the Ashʿarīs, who consider *naql/samʿ* as the exclusive basis for it.

81 See also Taqī al-Dīn al-Subkī, *Fatāwā al-Subkī*, 2 vols. (Cairo: Maktabat al-Qudsī, 1355–1356/1936–1938; rept. Beirut: Dār al-Maʿrifa, 1975 and Beirut: Dār al-Jīl, 1992), 2:365–368 and the very first section under Salient Themes of Māturīdism.

FIFTH/ELEVENTH CENTURY

al-Ustuwāʾī

al-Ustuwāʾī al-Naysābūrī, Ṣāʿid b. Muḥammad. *al-Iʿtiqād: ʿAqīdatun marwiyya ʿan Abī Ḥanīfa*. Ed. Sayyid Bāghajwān. Beirut: Dār al-Kutub al-ʿIlmiyya, 1426/2005.

The qadi Abū al-ʿAlāʾ Ṣāʿid b. Muḥammad b. Aḥmad b. ʿUbayd Allah al-Ustuwāʾī al-Naysābūrī (343–432/954–1040), nicknamed ʿImād al-Islām, first studied under his maternal grandfather Abū Naṣr Muḥammad b. Muḥammad b. Sahl b. Ibrāhīm al-Naysābūrī (318–388/930–998) then about a dozen others, and counts twice as many students on record. His book chainlessly anthologizes the doctrinal views of Abū Ḥanīfa and his students on:

(i) *īmān*,
(ii) *qaḍāʾ* and *qadar*,
(iii) *istiṭāʿa*,
(iv) uncreatedness of the Qurʾān,
(v) the vision of Allah,
(vi) the Balance of deeds,
(vii) the punishment of the grave,
(viii) intercession,
(ix) the Verse of *istiwāʾ*,
(x) the Companions,
(xi) obedience to rulers,
(xii) prayer behind innovators as forbidden but valid,
(xiii) narrating the Divine Attributes *bilā kayf*, and
(xiv) confining oneself, in all doctrinal matters, to what is textually established in the Qurʾān and Sunna as well as the consensus,

without recourse to personal opinion, all as directly related from him by Abū Muṭī' al-Balkhī, Ḥammād b. Abī Ḥanīfa, al-Jārūd b. Yazīd al-'Āmirī, Muḥammad b. al-Ḥasan al-Shaybānī and Abū Yūsuf, Nūḥ b. Abī Maryam, Abū Muqātil Ḥafṣ b. Salm al-Samarqandī, Wakī' b. al-Jarrāḥ, Ḥammād b. Zayd b. Dirham al-Azdī, al-Ḥasan b. Ziyād al-Lu'lu'ī, Ismā'īl b. Ziyād (or Ibn Abī Ziyād) al-Sakūnī, 'Abd al-Karīm b. Muḥammad al-Jurjānī, then from the next generation-layer such as Mūsā b. Sulaymān al-Jūzjānī, Muḥammad b. 'Ubayd b. Abī Umayya, Muḥammad b. Muqātil al-Rāzī, 'Umar b. Ḥammād, Muḥammad b. Shujā' al-Thaljī and others. The work served as one of the sources for the later *Manāqib* works of Muwaffaq al-Dīn al-Makkī and Kardarī.

Abu Shakur al-Sālimī

al-Sālimī, Abū Shakūr, *al-Tamhīd fī bayān al-tawḥīd*. Ed. Ömür Türkmen. Ankara: Türkiye Diyanet Vakfı Yayıları, 2017.

Hājjī Khalīfa in his *Kashf al-ẓunūn* described Abū Shakūr Muḥammad b. 'Abd al-Sayyid b. Shu'ayb al-Kashshī al-Sālimī's (d. after 460/1068) *Tamhīd fī bayān al-tawḥīd* as 'an abridgment on the principles of theological knowledge and pure monotheism in which he mentioned various definitions on reason, the spirit etc. and in which he cited what is permissible to discuss of the science of dialectic theology.'

Abū al-Yusr al-Pazdawī

al-Pazdawī, Abū al-Yusr Muḥammad b. Muḥammad. *Kitāb Uṣūl al-dīn*. Ed. Hans-Peter Linss. Cairo: Dār Iḥyā' al-Kutub al-'Arabiyya, 1963. Rept. Cairo: al-Maktabat al-Azhariyya lil-Turāth, 1424/2003.

———. *Zallat al-qārī'*. In Necattin Hanay, '*Kitāb Zallat al-qārī' lil-Imām Abī al-Yusr al-Bazdawī: dirāsa wa-taḥqīq*,' *Ankara Üniversitesi İlahiyat Fakültesi Dergisi*, vol. 57 no. 1 (2016) pp. 1–56.

Abū al-Yusr Muḥammad b. Muḥammad b. al-Ḥusayn b. ʿAbd al-Karīm al-Pazdawī (421–493/1030–1100) the qadi of Samarqand, nicknamed *Imām al-a'imma* in *al-Qand*, was teacher to Abū Ḥafṣ al-Nasafī among others. He "filled creation with his works on principles and the branch sciences" (*al-Qand*), including *Zallat al-qārī*, a treatise on the recitational mistakes of Quranic readers[82] and *Uṣūl al-dīn*. He prefaced the latter brief creed with the definition of who *Ahl al-Sunna wal-Jamāʿa* are and who they are not, which he goes on to detail with a survey of non-Sunni sects and positions in the heresiographical tradition of his predecessors and epigones. He forwards the majority position that human languages are divinely-ordained at their origin then man-made (*iṣṭilāḥiyya*) at a later stage.[83] Among his important refutations of the Muʿtazila, Qadariyya, Jabriyya and Jahmiyya (in which he echoes al-Ashʿarī's position and is followed in turn by ʿAlā' al-Dīn al-Usmandī, Nūr al-Dīn al-Ṣābūnī, and Rukn al-Dīn al-Samarqandī) are those of (i) *tawlīd* or *tawallud*—the position that agents generate or engender (*wallada*) acts in other than themselves, whereas in Sunnism such agents do so only superficially, according to established divine custom (*ʿāda/sunnat Allāh*), and only Allah is the effective doer—neither *generation* nor *nature*;[84] and (ii) the position that non-existents are actual entities, which is tantamount to asserting the eternity of the world.[85] Linss's edition has a reduplicative discussion of *īmān* being indissociably the same as *islām* (on p. 157 and p. 228) with Pazdawī's attribution of the dissociative position to the Muʿtazila and Rawāfiḍ exclusively; in reality the dissociative position is also that of Ashʿarīs and, arguably, that of the majority of *Ahl al-Sunna*.[86] *Uṣūl al-dīn* covers the following topics:

82 See also the same-titled work by ʿUmar al-Nasafī below.

83 On this issue see al-Rāzī, *al-Maḥṣūl fī ʿIlm Uṣūl al-Fiqh*, ed. Ṭaha Jābir al-ʿAlwānī, 2nd ed., 6 vols. (Beirut: Mu'assasat al-Risāla, 1992), 1:181–183; al-Ghazālī, *al-Mustaṣfā min ʿIlm al-Uṣūl*, ed. Ḥamza Zuhayr al-Ḥāfiẓ, 4 vols. (Medina: al-Jāmiʿa al-Islāmiyya, 1413/1993), 3:7–11; Shawkānī, *Irshād al-fuḥūl ilā taḥqīq al-ḥaqq min ʿilm al-uṣūl*, ed. Shaʿbān Muḥammad Ismāʿīl, 2 vols. (Cairo: Dār al-Kutbī, 1992), 1:69–70.

84 Cf. Daniel Gimaret, *La doctrine d'al-Ashʿarī* (Paris: Cerf, 1990), pp. 401–409.

85 Cf. Gimaret, *Doctrine*, pp. 29–32.

86 See Ibn Ḥajar's extensive commentary on the hadith of Jibrīl translated in full in Gibril Fouad Haddad, *Sunna Notes III: The Binding Proof of the Sunna* (Birmingham: al-Qur'an wal-Sunna Association, 2010), pp. 149–202.

1. On the science of *kalām*, the necessity of teaching it, and the works produced in it
2. Concrete objects (*aʿyān*) exist in reality and so do abstract meanings (*maʿānī*)
3. Avenues of knowledge for things
4. A thing is indicative of its form (*shakl)* as well as of other things and of its opposite
5. The senses and their number
6. Reports and their types
7. What is knowledge?
8. The sciences are of different types
9. The definition of the world
10. About accidents
11. The world is originated
12. Allah is one without partner
13. Allah neither resembles anything nor does anything resemble Him
14. Allah possesses no direction
15. Allah is all-hearing and all-seeing
16. Some of the divine attributes
17. Allah is willing with a will subsistent in His essence
18. All originated things (*ḥawādith*), whether concrete objects or acts, are through divine will
19. Allah is without beginning (*qadīm*) in His speech as in all His attributes
20. Bringing into being (*al-ījād*) and existentiation (*al-takwīn*)
21. Seeing Allah
22. The name, the naming and the named
23. The sending forth of messengers—upon them peace
24. The messengership of Adam—upon him peace
25. Refutation of those who denied the messengership of certain messengers
26. Allah creates the acts of creatures and the rebuttal of naysayers
27. The acts of created objects are either necessary or voluntary
28. Acts do not possess secondarily-generational or engendering force (*tawallud*)
29. Power to act does not precede acts

30. The power of every act is also generically suitable for any other act
31. On tasking beyond capacity
32. Ability comes together with the act; its subsequent elements
33. Nothing whatsoever is compulsory for Allah
34. Why Allah created the world
35. Grave sinners among the Muslims do not linger forever in hellfire
36. Does avoidance of grave sins expiate lesser sins?
37. The definition of *īmān*
38. Is *īmān* in general terms or in the particulars?
39. The imitative believer is a believer by consensus: refutation of the Muʿtazila
40. On the increase and decrease of belief
41. On *īmān* and *islām*
42. Is *īmān* created or not?[87]
43. Resurrection is real
44. The balance of deeds is real
45. The bridge over hellfire is real
46. The final reckoning is real
47. The basin of Kawthar and intercession are real
48. The reckoning in the grave and to whom it applies
49. The interrogation by Munkar and Nakīr in the grave
50. Paradise and hellfire are already created contrary to naysayers
51. Paradise and hellfire are inextinguishible contrary to Jahm and Hishām b. al-Ḥakam
52. The one murdered dies by virtue of his lifespan
53. On the infallibility of prophets and messengers
54. Can the wretched end up blissful and vice versa?
55. The caliphs after the Prophet—upon him blessings and peace
56. It is obligatory to appoint someone for political leadership (*imām sā'is*)
57. Attributes of the *imām*
58. What to do when the less qualified is made caliph
59. A caliph's appointment of a successor before death
60. Scenario of two vying caliphs
61. Can the *imām* be removed for depravity and the like?

87 See note 109 on this issue.

62. Let supplication be made for the repentance of the depraved *imām*
63. The powerful usurper is a caliph *de facto* and *de jure*
64. Did the Prophet hand over political leadership to anyone after him?
65. The best of people after the Prophet—upon him blessings and peace
66. Muʿāwiya was never a rightful *imām* or caliph in ʿAlī's lifetime but only afterwards
67. The disagreement over the status of Yazīd b. Muʿāwiya[88]
68. Who is superior, the angels or the Muslims?
69. The human messengers and the angelic messengers
70. The jinn: their rewards and punishments
71. Reason is a tool for learning about things
72. Reason makes knowledge of Allah compulsory for al-Māturīdī and the Samarqandīs, not for al-Ashʿarī and the Māturīdīs of Bukhāra
73. The taking of the covenant from Adam's progeny[89]
74. On non-existents (*al-maʿdūm*)
75. The resolve to do evil
76. On languages being divinely-ordained at their origin then man-made
77. The staggering miracle of the Qur'ān
78. All of the Qur'ān is superexcellent[90]
79. On *islām* and *īmān* [repeating previous identical section]
80. The difference between prophet and messenger
81. Things that belong to Allah without His needing them whatsoever
82. Is discussing the spirit permissible?

88 al-Qārī wrote *Qayd al-sharīd min akhbāri Yazīd*, in which he documents—as he also mentions in *Minaḥ al-rawḍ al-azhar, Sharḥ al-Shifā* and *Salālat al-risāla*—the impermissibility of cursing Yazīd in accordance with the position of most of the scholars including Imam Aḥmad according to one of two positions, al-Ghazālī, Ibn al-Ṣalāḥ, al-Nawawī and al-Haytamī in their *Fatāwā*, Ibn al-Subkī in *al-Sayf al-mashhūr*, al-Damīrī, the *Quṭb* ʿAbd Allāh al-Ḥaddād in his *ʿAqīda*, Ibn al-Qayyim in *Ijtimāʿ al-juyūsh*, al-Ardabīlī in *al-Bughāt*, al-Aṣbahānī in *al-Ḥujja*, Ibn ʿĀbidīn, and many others. An enlightened treatment of this issue is found in Shihāb al-Dīn Aḥmad al-Ramlī's (d. 958/1551) *Fatāwā fī furūʿ al-fiqh al-Shāfiʿī* (p. 704–705).

89 'If one asks how the verse of the divine convenant (al-Aʿrāf 7:172) can be binding when we cannot remember that event no matter how hard we try, the answer is that Allah caused us to forget it as a test for us because the world is the abode of trial, and we are tasked to believe in the unseen from the start.' al-Qārī, *Sharḥ al-Fiqh al-akbar*, Nafā'is ed., p. 112.

90 See al-Kumushkhānawī, heading 18.

83. Life and spirit
84. What is emptiness (*al-hawā'*)?
85. Jinn, devils and their activities
86. Repentance and when it is accepted
87. On the miraculous gifts of the friends of Allah
88. The place of children in the hereafter
89. On the union of two substances
90. Sacred law (*al-sharī'a*) and spiritual reality (*al-ḥaqīqa*)
91. Knownness (*ma'lūmiyya*) of something and its unknownness from differing angles
92. Application of the term *Ahl al-Sunna wal-Jamā'a*
93. Differing of the sub-sects of the unbelievers just as the sub-sects of the Muslims differed
94. Exposition of the schools and sub-sects of the Muslims
95. Points in which al-Ash'arī differed with the generality of *Ahl al-Sunna wal-Jamā'a*
96. Points in which Ibn Kullāb differed with the generality of *Ahl al-Sunna wal-Jamā'a*
97. Points in which the hadith scholars differed with the generality of *Ahl al-Sunna wal-Jamā'a*
98. Exposition of the school of the Rawāfiḍ
99. Exposition of the school of the Khawārij
100. Exposition of the school of the Qadariyya and Mu'tazila
101. Exposition of the school of the Jabriyya
102. Exposition of the school of the Murji'a
103. Exposition of the school of the Mujassima [anthropomorphists]

Abū al-Mu'īn Maymūn al-Nasafī

al-Nasafī, Abū al-Mu'īn Maymūn b. Muḥammad. *Baḥr al-kalām*. Ed. Walī al-Dīn Muḥammad Ṣāliḥ al-Farfūr. 2nd ed. Damascus: Maktabat Dār al-Farfūr, 1421 / 2000.

———. *Ibid.* Ed. Muḥammad al-Sayyid al-Barsījī. Amman: Dār al-Fatḥ lil-Dirāsāt wal-Nashr, 1435/2014.

———. *Sharḥ al-Ta'wīlāt*. Undated and unsourced ms. uploaded in PDF at https://archive.org/details/ala-din-samarqandi-sharh-on-tawilat-of-maturidi.

———. *Tabṣirat al-adilla fī uṣūl al-dīn*. Ed. Claude Salamé. 2 vols. Damascus: Institut Français d'Études Arabes de Damas (IFEAD), 1990.

———. *Tabṣirat al-adilla fī uṣūl al-dīn*. Ed. Hüseyin Atay. Ankara: Diyanet İsleri Başkanlığı Yayıları, 1993. Vol. 1 only.

———. *Tabṣirat al-adilla fī uṣūl al-dīn*. Ed. Muḥammad al-Anwar Ḥāmid ʿĪsā. 2 vols. Cairo: al-Maktabat al-Athariyya lil-Turāth & al-Jazīra lil-Nashr wal-Tawzīʿ, 2011.

———. *al-Tamhīd fī uṣūl al-dīn aw al-Tamhīd li-qawāʿid al-tawḥīd*. Ed. Muḥ. ʿAbd al-Raḥmān al-Shāghūl. Cairo: al-Maktabat al-Azhariyya lil-Turāth, 2006.

Born in Nasaf (also known as Nakhshab) to a distinguished family of Hanafi scholars, Sayf al-Ḥaqq Abū al-Muʿīn Maymūn b. Muḥ. b. Muḥammad b. Muʿtamad al-Nasafī al-Makḥūlī (438–508/1047–1115)[91] is the greatest single representative of the Maturidi school of dialectic theology after its founder, having single-handedly 'served his school in the same way as al-Bāqillānī, al-Juwaynī, al-Ghazālī and al-Āmidī had done in the Ashʿarī school' (ʿĪsā, 1:4). He studied under his father Muḥammad b. Muḥ. b. Muʿtamad b. Muḥammad, from whom he narrated Abū Ḥanīfa's *al-ʿĀlim wal-mutaʿallim* and he took hadith from the qadi and hadith master Abū Muḥammad ʿAbd al-ʿAzīz b. Muḥammad al-Nakhshabī and Abū Bakr Muḥammad b. Aḥmad al-Baladī among others. He authored *Manāhij al-a'imma* and *Sharḥ al-Jāmiʿ al-kabīr* in law; *Tabṣirat al-adilla*, *Baḥr al-kalām*,[92] *al-ʿUmda fī uṣūl al-dīn*, *Īḍāḥ*

91 al-Dhahabī, *Tārīkh al-Islām wa-wafayāt al-mashāhīr wal-aʿlām*, ed. ʿUmar ʿAbd al-Salām Tadmurī, 52 vols. (Beirut: Dār al-Kitāb al-ʿArabī, 1407–1421/1987–2000), [Vol. 35] Years 501–510, p. 213–214 no. 245; Ibn Quṭlūbaghā, *Tāj al-tarājim*, ed. Muḥammad Khayr Ramaḍān Yūsuf (Damascus: Dār al-Qalam, 1413/1992), p. 308 no. 303; al-Laknawī, *al-Fawā'id al-bahiyya*, p. 355; Ibn Abī al-Wafā', *al-Jawāhir al-muḍiyya*, 3:527- no. 1725; ʿĪsā, 1:13–16, 22–28.

92 This work has received at least five editions so far (Baghdad 1304/1886, Cairo 1329/1911, Cairo 1340/1922, Damascus 1421/2000, Amman 1435/2014) and a commentary by Badr al-Dīn Ḥasan b. Abī Bakr b. Aḥmad al-Maqdisī (d. 836/1433) entitled *Ghāyat al-marām fī sharḥ Baḥr al-kalām*. See its description in al-Barsījī's edition, p. 38. Al-Rūdānī attributed

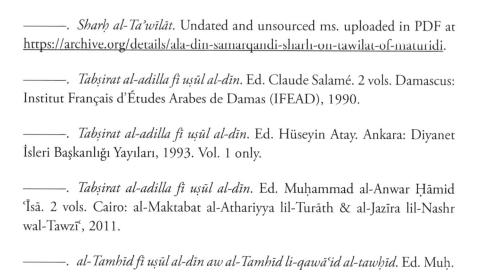

al-maḥajja li-kawn al-ʿaql ḥujja, *al-Tamhīd li-qawāʿid al-tawḥīd* in dogmatics, the latter of which received a commentary by Ḥusām al-Dīn al-Ḥusayn b. ʿAlī al-Sighnāqī (d. 710/1310) entitled *al-Tasdīd* (*q.v.*); and many other works including a heretofore unpublished commentary on Māturīdī's *Tafsīr* entitled *Sharḥ al-Taʾwīlāt* as recorded and compiled by his student ʿAlāʾ al-Dīn Abū Bakr b. Muḥ. b. Aḥmad al-Samarqandī.'[93] The latter was the author of *Mīzān al-uṣūl fī natāʾij al-ʿuqūl* and is sometimes misidentified as 'Abū Bakr Muḥammad'. Also among Maymūn al-Nasafī's students were Abū Ḥafṣ ʿUmar b. Muḥammad al-Nasafī who mentioned him in his partially extant *al-Qand fī ʿulamāʾ Samarqand*; Abū al-Maḥāmid Maḥmūd b. Aḥmad al-Shāghurjī al-Faghnawī; ʿAbd al-Rashīd b. Abī Ḥanīfa al-Waʾwālijī; Abū al-Fatḥ Aḥmad b. Muḥammad b. Aḥmad al-Khulmī; al-Qāḍī al-Ṣadr Abū al-Maʿālī Aḥmad b. Muḥammad Ibn Abī al-Yusr al-Pazdawī; Abū Bakr Masʿūd b. Aḥmad al-Kāshānī; Abū al-Muẓaffar Ismāʿīl b. ʿAdī al-Azharī al-Ṭālqānī; and others.

Muʿīn al-Nasafī's great-great-grandfather the arch-Ḥanafī Abū Muṭīʿ Makḥūl b. al-Faḍl al-Nasafī (d. 308/920 or 318/930) is the author of the first complete catalogue of the non-Sunni sects in the Māturīdī school to our knowledge, *al-Radd ʿalā ahl al-bidaʿ wal-ahwāʾ al-ḍāllat al-muḍilla wa-hum ithnāt wa-sabʿūna firqa*.[94] He is also the one who narrated that Abū Ḥanīfa had said that raising the hands before and after *rukūʿ* 'invalidates one's prayer because it constitutes too much extraneous movement,' a position which Amīr Kātib al-ʿAmīd b. Amīr Ghāzī al-Atqānī (685–758/1286–1357), among other later scholars, adduced to forbid Hanafis from praying behind Shafiʿīs.[95]

---

the *Baḥr* to Burhān al-Dīn al-Nasafī: see Salient Themes, 'Spurious attributions/ascriptions in Māturīdī scholarship.'

93 Per folio 2r of the 1186H 879-folio ms. uploaded in PDF at https://archive.org/details/ala-din-samarqandi-sharh-on-tawilat-of-maturidi. See also the entry on Abū Bakr b. Muḥ. b. Aḥmad in Ibn Abī al-Wafāʾs *al-Jawāhir al-Muḍiyya*.

94 In Marie Bernand, 'Le *Kitāb al-radd ʿalāl bidaʿ* d'Abū Muṭīʿ Makḥūl al-Nasafī,' *Annales Islamologiques* 16 (1980), pp. 39–126. On Abū Muṭīʿ Makḥūl al-Nasafī see al-Dhahabī's notices in *Tārīkh al-Islām* and the *Siyar*; and Seyit Bahçivan, 'Abū Muṭī Makḥūl b. al-Faḍl al-Nasafī wa-shakhṣiyyatuhu al-ʿilmiyya,' *e-makâlât Mezhep Araştırmaları*, V/2 (Güz 2012), ss. 31-59. (http://www.emakalat.com/tr/download/article-file/63746 as of 8 December 2020)

95 This narration was declared aberrant by the Hanafi authorities and the position was rejected by al-Sighnāqī in *al-Nihāya*, Ibn Amīr al-Ḥājj in *Ḥilyat al-muṣallī*, Ibn al-Humām in

The *Tabṣira* recommended itself for the clarity and simplicity of its style despite its length, authoritativeness and methodological depth. The latter attribute shows in the sustained comparative coverage of the multifarious doctrinal positions of the non-Māturīdī schools on any and all issues in the fashion of the *Maqālāt al-Islāmiyyīn* and other heresiographies, and the distinction of technical registers as, for example in the mention of the respective terminologies of linguists and logicians in the section on quiddity (*mā'iyya*). It is arguably the most consistently-cited Māturīdī reference in all subsequent comparative doctrinal literature.

The subject-headings of *Baḥr al-kalām* are:

1. The permissibility of debate
2. The definition of knowledge
3. The definition of *īmān* and its precondition
4. The free choice of belief and unbelief
5. Power and ability
6. Bliss and wretchedness
7. The status of those who did not receive the call [to religion]
8. The status of those who do not know the preconditions of belief
9. The originated nature of the world
10. The divine attributes have no beginning
11. The beginningless and the originated in time
12. Oneness (*al-waḥdāniyya*)
13. Applying the term 'thing' (*shay'*) to Allah
14. Applying the term 'self' (*nafs*) to Allah
15. Applying the term 'light' (*nūr*) to Allah
16. The 'hand' (*yad*) and the 'foot' (*qadam*)
17. The 'coming' (*majī'*), 'going' (*dhahāb*), and 'descent' (*nuzūl)*
18. The meaning of 'establishment' (*istiwā'*)
19. Place and withness (*ma'iyya*)
20. Seeing Allah Most High
21. The Qur'ān is the beginningless speech of Allah
22. The name and the named

Fatḥ al-Qadīr and others. Taqī al-Dīn al-Subkī firmly refuted it. See al-Laknawī, *al-Fawā'id al-bahiyya*, pp. 87–89, 355–357 and Ibn Abī al-Wafā, *Jawāhir* 2:180.

23. Sustenance
24. Coercion and free choice
25. The acts of servants
26. Belief
27. The increase of belief and its decrease
28. The one who commits a grave sin
29. Repentance from sins
30. Being taken to task for the heart's intent
31. Spiritual knowledge and belief
32. The wisdom of creating creation
33. The punishment of the damned
34. Tasking beyond capacity
35. The children of the polytheists
36. Those who are summoned to belief
37. The progeny of devils
38. Wealth and poverty
39. Acquisition (*iktisāb*)
40. Those who are neither questioned nor punished in the grave
41. Allah is creating as we speak
42. The miraculous gifts of the friends of Allah
43. Devils have some power (*wilāya*) over human beings inwardly and outwardly
44. The affirmation of Messengership
45. Our Prophet Muḥammad—upon him blessings and peace—is a Messenger as we speak
46. The night journey and heavenly ascent
47. The throne and the foot-stool
48. The recording angels
49. Those who will not perish upon the blowing of the horn
50. The perdurance (*baqā'*) of paradise and its bliss and the perdurance of hellfire and its torment
51. Good pleasure and fury
52. Allah Most High knows the exact count of the souls of the blissful and the damned
53. The five principles of the Muʿtazila

54. Intercession
55. The balance of deeds, the bridge, the basin and the reckoning
56. Paradise and hell are already created
57. The interrogation of the grave and its punishment
58. The location of spirits in the interworld (*barzakh*)
59. The inviolability (*'iṣma*) of the lives of Muslims
60. Overall leadership (*imāma*)
61. Exposition of the most preferential rank of the Companions
62. Revelation was directed to our liegelord Muḥammad
63. The seal of prophethood
64. The imam who gathered up the Qur'ān after the demise of the Prophet
65. The heavenly scriptures and folios revealed to the prophets—upon them blessings and peace
66. The number of the prophets and messengers
67. Whoever dies does not return to this world
68. The categorical prohibition of sins and indecencies
69. The wisdom behind the abrogation of [prior] heavenly laws
70. Temporary marriage
71. The rebuttal of permissivists (*ibāḥiyya*)
72. Stars are subjected, not disposers (*al-nujūm musakhkharāt ghayr mudabbirāt*)
73. The position of the spheres in relation to the seven heavens
74. Conclusion

The subject-headings of *Tabṣirat al-adilla* are:

1. The defining parameters of *'ilm*
2. The affirmation of truths and sciences
3. The avenues to the types of knowledge
4. Falsifying the claim that the heart's appreciation of something, or inspiration, or imitation are among the avenues of obtaining knowledge of the validity of religions
5. The faith of the imitator
6. The originated nature (*ḥudūth*) of the world
7. The affirmation of the originated nature of the world in all its parts and of that of accidents

8. The originated nature of substances
9. Falsifying the claim that any part of the world whatsoever has no beginning
10. The world has an originator
11. Declaring the Maker as One
12. Falsifying the doctrine of the Zoroastrians
13. Falsifying the doctrine of the dualists
14. That the First Maker is without beginning
15. The negation of the claim that the First Maker is an accident
16. Falsifying the statement of those who say that the First Maker is a substance
17. Falsifying the doctrine of the anthropomorphists
18. Falsifying the doctrine of the anthropomorphists who contravene us in name and substance
19. Falsifying the doctrine of the anthropomorphists who contravene us in name only
20. Exposition of the impossibility of describing Allah as possessing form, color, taste, smell etc.
21. Falsifying [the claim of] resemblance
22. Falsifying the doctrine of Jahm b. Ṣafwān
23. The non-likeness between Allah and other than Him
24. On quiddity
25. The impossibility that the Maker be in a spatial location
26. The affirmation of the attributes of Allah Most High
27. The attribute of knowledge (*ʿilm*)
28. Attributes and the Essence
29. The negation of createdness being part of the speech of Allah Most High
30. That the attribute of speech is uncreated
31. Falsifying the doctrine of those who neither confirm nor deny regarding the Qur'ān [being uncreated]
32. On [the term] 'the rendering (*ḥikāya*) of the speech of Allah'
33. On the difference between 'speech' and 'that which is heard' (*al-kalām wal-masmūʿ*)

34. Existentiating (*takwīn*) is other than the existentiated and is without beginning
35. Will is an attribute of Allah and is without beginning
36. The Maker of the world is all-wise
37. Affirming the possibility of the vision of Allah by reason and its necessity by revealed evidence
38. Affirming prophethood and messengership
39. Messengership is within the purview of possibilities
40. Is messengership part of the possibilities or part of the necessities?
41. The staggering miracles that establish the prophetship of the claimant to prophethood
42. Matters that establish messengership
43. The staggering miracles (*muʿjizāt*) that establish divine Messengership
44. Affirming the messengership of Muḥammad, upon him peace
45. Affirming the miraculous gifts (*karāmāt*) of the friends of Allah

The subject-headings of *al-Tamhīd li-qawāʿid al-tawḥīd* are:

1. Affirming the realities of things and the various kinds of knowledge
2. Affirming the originated nature of the world
3. That the world has an originator
4. Affirming the unicity of the Maker
5. Affirming the beginninglessness of the Maker
6. That the maker of the world is not an accident
7. That the Maker of the world is not a substance
8. That the Maker of the world is not a body
9. The impossibility of describing Allah as an image or something possessing color or taste or smell
10. Falsifying the claim of resemblance
11. Falsifying the ascription of place
12. The affirmation of attributes
13. The affirmation of the pre-existence of the speech of Allah
14. Existentiation is other than the existentiated
15. Existentiation is pre-existent and Allah is ever creating through it
16. The affirmation of will
17. That the maker of the world is all-wise

18. The affirmation of the vision of Allah
19. The affirmation of messengership
20. The affirmation of the miraculous gifts of the friends [of Allah]
21. On ability together with action
22. The affirmation of the creation of the acts of servants
23. That secondarily-generated acts (*mutawallidāt*) are created by Allah Most High
24. The murdered dies by virtue of his lifespan
25. On provisions
26. Sins are by virtue of the will of Allah (*bi-irādat Allāh wa-mashī'atih*)
27. On *qaḍā'* and *qadar* and the conclusiveness of the acts of creatures being created by Allah
28. On guidance and misguiding and the conclusiveness of acts beings created
29. Falsifying the doctrine of the fittest (*aṣlaḥ*) [as being compulsory for Allah]
30. Unbelief and sins are created by Allah even if unbelievers and sinners are harmed thereby
31. Affirmation of the punishment of the grave for the unbelievers and some sinful Muslims
32. Affirmation of the bliss of the grave for obedient servants
33. On the threat of punishment made against the depraved among Muslims
34. The affirmation of intercession
35. The quiddity of *īmān*
36. On overall political leadership

Sixth/Twelfth Century

al-Ṣaffār

al-Ṣaffār, Ibrāhīm b. Ismāʿīl. *Talkhīṣ al-adilla li-qawāʿid al-tawḥīd*. Ed. Hishām Ibrāhīm Maḥmūd. Cairo: Dār al-Salām lil-Ṭibāʿa wal-Nashr wal-Tawzīʿ wal-Tarjama, 2010.

———. *Ibid.* Ed. Angelika Brodersen. Beirut: Orient-Institut; Berlin: Klaus Schwarz in Kommission, 2011.

Little is known about the ascetic Rukn al-Islām and Rukn al-Dīn Abū Isḥāq Ibrāhīm b. Ismāʿīl b. Abī Naṣr Aḥmad b. Isḥāq al-Ṣaffār or Ṣaffārī (in Dhahabī's *Siyar*) al-Bukhārī (d. 534/1139) other than that he hailed from a distinguished scholarly family. He mentions his father in *Talkhīṣ al-adilla* as 'the imam and shahid, my father,' his grandfather Abū Naṣr, and his books *al-Ibāna ʿan ithbāt al-risālāt* and *al-Fuṣūl*, besides the *Talkhīṣ*. The headings of the latter are:

1. The science of the knowledge of Allah
    - 1.1 The reality of truth and falsehood
    - 1.2 Truth
    - 1.3 The evidence that leads to certainty
    - 1.4 Qur'ān-based evidence
    - 1.5 Sunna-based evidence
    - 1.6 Consensus-based evidence
2. Theology (*kalām*)
    - 2.1 The basis for the word *kalām*

4.8 On the Qur'ān
4.9 Belief in the Messengers and Prophets
4.10 Difference between the two
4.11 Deservedness of caliphate and imamate
4.12 Belief in the Last Day
4.13 The questioning after death
4.14 Paradise and Hell
4.15 Belief in the Decree
4.16 The apportionment of the act
4.17 Evidences for the generality of faith
4.18 Reality if the evidence
4.19 Knowledge of Allah

5. The universe (*al-ʿālam*)

5.1 The reality of the universe; the macrocosm and the microcosm
5.2 Reality of existents and reality of things
5.3 Reality of the pre-existent and of the created; time and natures
5.4 The three categories of created entities and those who deny them
5.5 The congruence of substances and bodies; accidents; abiding
5.6 Life, bodies, power, the spirit, and death
5.7 The spirit of life, the life of the spirit and the Life of Allah
5.8 Sleep and loss of consciousness; dreams; dreaming of Allah
5.9 Doubt and conjecture; inadvertence and ignorance
5.10 Secondarily-generated acts (*mutawallidāt*)
5.11 That which is correctly visible by the eye
5.12 Typology of accidents
5.13 Impossibility of the perdurance of accidents
5.14 Perdurance and existence
5.15 That for which it is valid to perdure and that for which it is not
5.16 The supposed pre-existence of prime matter (*hayūlā*)[96]
5.17 The passing away of the universe and its parts
5.18 The need for an Originator

96 See al-Bayḍāwī's commentary on al-Aʿrāf 7:54 with our annotations on the invalidation of the notion of pre-existent prime matter in Sunnī *kalām*.

6. The Maker

   6.1 The creation of the universe; justification, wisdom, tests, welfare
   6.2 The Oneness of the Maker; difference between *Wāḥid* and *Aḥad*
   6.3 Declaring Allah as One in His Names and Attributes
   6.4 The name and the attribute
   6.5 The name and the named
   6.6 The categories of the names and of the attributes
   6.7 The Names of Allah and His Attributes
   6.8 Proofs of the Book and of the Sunna; number of the Names
   6.9 Divine ordainment (*tawqīf*)
   6.10 Origin of languages and merit of Arabic
   6.11 Derivation of the name *Allāh*

7. The Names

   7.1 Exposition of the meanings of the divine Names
   7.2 Preclusion of the description of Allah by the descriptives of origination; resemblance; incapacitation; capability of wrongdoing
   7.3 Explanation of 106 divine Names alphabetically to al-Mumīt
   7.4 Life after death
   7.5 The interval between the two blows of the horn
   7.6 The dispersal of the limbs of the deceased
   7.7 The questioning of the Prophets and Messengers
   7.8 The status of children; the stillborn
   7.9 The resurrection of angels, jinns, devils, and animals
   7.10 Explanation of 65 more divine Names to al-Hādī

8. The Attributes

   8.1 What Allah may not be described with and what He may
   8.2 The ambiguous Attributes: eye, hand, side, shank, coming, etc.

9. The reality of faith

   9.1 Deeds within faith
   9.2 Faith and submission
   9.3 One does not add 'if Allah wills' (*istithnā'*) when declaring oneself a believer

9.4 Whether acts of obedience are part of faith
9.5 The declaration of the unbelief (*ikfār*) of the innovators: the Qadariyya; al-Jāḥiẓ; Maʿmar; certain Muʿtazila; al-Kaʿbī; al-Aṣamm; Shayṭān al-Ṭāq; the Kaysāniyya; the Rawāfiḍ; the Khawārij; the Yazīdiyya; the Jahmiyya; the Najjāriyya; the anthropomorphist Karrāmiyya; the Mujbira
9.6 The act of faith; the creation of faith
9.7 Dār al-Islām and Dār al-Kufr
9.8 Definitions of the names for divine will (*mashīʾa, irāda*)
9.9 The creation of all matter and acts
9.10 *Qaḍāʾ* and *qadar*
9.11 Doing what is more conducive to welfare
9.12 Affirmation of speech for Allah Most High
9.13 Definitions of speech; concerning 'Be!' (*kun*)
9.14 Divine speech and divine will
9.15 Fashioning and the fashioned
9.16 Bringing into existence
9.17 On the Qurʾān: its uncreatedness; inimitability; coherence; readings and dialects
9.18 Following the Qurʾān
9.19 Compositional arrangement of the Qurʾān
9.20 Exegesis and interpretation
9.21 Exposition of 'the three aspects of the Qurʾān'

10. Prophethood, Messengership, Friendship with Allah and Caliphate

10.1 Preference of Prophets and Messengers over the angels
10.2 Friends of Allah (*al-Awliyāʾ*) among human beings
10.3 Miraculous gifts (*karāmāt*)
10.4 Succession of the Messenger of Allah—upon him blessings and peace—per the evidences of the Book; of the Sunna; of Consensus
10.5 'Whoever says ʿAlī was a Prophet is an unbeliever, because the Messenger of Allah is the Seal of Prophets (*khātam al-Nabiyyīn*)'
10.6 The four Rightly-Guided Caliphs
10.7 Pre-condition of the arch-Imam
10.8 The splitting up into sects/faith-communities

10.9 Idol-worship; Magians/Zoroastrians; Jews and Christians; Sabians; Zendiks; Esotericists (*al-Bāṭiniyya*);
10.10 Categories of the innovators: Rāfiḍīs, Qadarīs, and the central Asian anthropomorphists

11. The hereafter

11.1 The states of the hereafter
11.2 Intercession on the Day of Resurrection
11.3 The Bridge
11.4 Reading one's record of deeds
11.5 The Balance of deeds
11.6 Paradise and Hell; their creation; the fact they are everlasting
11.7 The vision of Allah Most High; its evidence; its timing

[Pseudo-]Nasafī

[Pseudo-]Nasafī, ʿUmar b. Muḥammad. *Matn al-ʿAqāʾid*. In *Kutub al-ʿaqāʾid: Sharḥ al-Amālī, Sharḥ al-Fiqh al-akbar, ʿAqāʾid al-nūniyya, ʿAqāʾid al-Nasafī*. Istanbul: al-Maktabat al-Ḥanīfiyya, [1380/1962]. See Salient Themes, 'Spurious attributions/ascriptions in Māturīdī scholarship.'

———. *al-ʿAqāʾid al-nasafiyya*. Ed. Bassām ʿAbd al-Wahhāb al-Jābī. Beirut: Dār al-Bashāʾir al-Islāmiyya, 1414/1993.

Born in Nasaf, the jurist and 'Mufti of Humans and Jinns' (*muftī al-thaqalayn*, a title shared with Ibn Kamāl Bāshā) Najm al-Dīn Abū Ḥafṣ ʿUmar b. Muḥammad b. Aḥmad al-Nasafī (461–537/1069–1142) studied many sciences including *tafsīr*, *fiqh*, *shurūṭ*, hadith (which he said he narrated from 550 shaykhs), *uṣūl*, history, literature, poetry, and language, under Ṣadr al-Islām Abū al-Yusr Muḥammad b. Muḥammad b. al-Ḥusayn Pazdawī and his brother Fakhr al-Islām ʿAlī al-Pazdawī, ʿAṭāʾ b. Ḥamza al-Sughdī, Abū Muḥammad Ismāʿīl b. Muḥammad al-Nūḥī, Ismāʿīl al-Tanūkhī, Abū ʿAlī al-Ḥasan b. ʿAbd al-Malik al-Nasafī, and others. He authored many works in *fiqh*—in which he excelled—and hadith, but al-Samʿānī critiqued the latter as inaccurate, saying, 'He was of those who loved hadith and studied it without being granted its understanding.'[97] He is nowhere said to have been an authority in *kalām*. The attribution of the famous brief *'Aqā'id* to him is an oft-perpetuated mistake apparently first made by al-Taftāzānī. Among his students were his son Abū al-Layth Aḥmad; 'Umar b. Muḥammad al-'Uqaylī; Muḥammad b. Ibrāhīm al-Tūrabishtī; Abū Bakr b. Aḥmad al-Balkhī—also known as al-Ẓahīr—the author of a commentary on *al-Jāmi' al-ṣaghīr*; and al-Marghīnānī the author of the *Hidāya*, who read with him the *Musnadāt* of al-Khaṣṣāf (d. 261/875), the Ḥanafī specialist of inheritance laws and contracts. It is related that he went to visit Jār Allāh al-Zamakhsharī in Mecca; when he arrived the latter said, 'Who is that knocking at my door?' He said, "Umar.' Jār Allāh said, *Inṣarif!* He replied, *'Umar lā yanṣarifu ya sayyidī!* whereupon Jār Allāh said, *Idhā nukkira inṣarafa.*[98] Al-Dhahabī mentioned that he authored about 100 works.[99] Among them:

- *al-Akmal al-aṭwal fil-tafsīr*;
- *al-'Aqā'id*, a brief text and the most famous Māturīdī primer, actually authored by Burhān al-Dīn al-Nasafī rather than Najm al-Dīn (see Salient Themes, 'Spurious attributions/ascriptions in Māturīdī scholarship'). It was described as the most famous representative text of the Māturīdī school[100] and is in fact an epitome of *Tabṣirat al-adilla* by Abū al-Mu'īn al-Nasafī. It begins with the words: 'The people of truth have said: the realities of [existing] things are firmly established and knowledge of them is verifiable, in contradiction to the Sophists,' i.e. those who claim that nothing can be known for certain; it ends with the words, 'and the generality of human beings is superior to the generality of the angels.' Its main commentary was penned by Sa'd al-Dīn al-Taftāzānī (*q.v.*), whose *Sharḥ al-'aqā'id al-Nasafiyya*

97 al-Sam'ānī, Abū Sa'd 'Abd al-Karīm b. Muḥammad, *al-Taḥbīr fil-mu'jam al-kabīr*, ed. Munīra Nājī Sālim, 2 vols. (Baghdad: Ri'āsat Dīwān al-Awqāf, 1395/1975), 1:527–529 no. 514.

98 Ibn Abī al-Wafā, *al-Jawāhir al-muḍiyya*, 2:657-no. 1062.

99 al-Dhahabī, *Siyar a'lām al-nubalā'*, ed. Muḥibb al-Dīn al-'Amrawī, 19 vols. (Beirut: Dār al-Fikr, 1417/1997), 14:580 no. 4851.

100 By Hans-Peter Linss in his introduction to Muḥammad b. Muḥammad Bazdawī, *Kitāb usul ed-din: The Principles of Religion* (Cairo: Dār Iḥyā' al-Kutub al-'Arabiyya, 1963), p. 14; rept. (Cairo: al-Maktabat al-Azhariyya lil-Turāth, 1424/2003), p. 12.

received countless marginalia. The *'Aqā'id* received several English translations.[101]

- *al-Ijāzāt al-mutarjama bil-ḥurūf al-muʿjama*, a biographical dictionary of his teachers;
- *al-Ishʿār bil-mukhtār min al-ashʿār*, an anthology of his own poetry which al-Samʿānī and others praised;
- *al-Khilāfiyyāt fil-fiqh*, also known as *al-Manẓūmat al-nasafiyya* and as *Qayd al-awābid*, a poem on differences in jurisprudence which received a commentary by the *mufassir* Abū al-Barakāt al-Nasafī among other commentaries;[102]
- *al-Najāḥ fī sharḥ akhbār kitāb al-ṣiḥāḥ*, a commentary on al-Bukhārī's *Ṣaḥīḥ* which he began by listing fifty of his chains of transmission to the latter work;
- *Naẓm al-Jāmiʿ al-ṣaghīr*, a versified version of Muḥammad b. al-Ḥasan's *al-Jāmiʿ al-ṣaghīr* which he began with an 81-verse section on creed; this and the next work are the only two that al-Dhahabī mentions.
- *al-Qand fī dhikr 'ulamā' Samarqand*, a biographical dictionary of scholars that received two editions, containing 1,219 notices, *al-qand* meaning 'honey' according to some, while others aver the name *Samarqand* derives from the Sogdian words *samar*, 'rock,' and *kand*, 'fort, town.'[103]
- *Qayd al-awābid*, see above, *al-Khilāfiyyāt*;
- *Tārīkh Bukhārā*;

101 See the text embedded in the larger translation of al-Taftāzānī's commentary by Elder (see below under Taftāzānī); W.M. Watt's *Islamic Creeds: A Selection*; William Cureton in *Pillar of the Creed of the Sunnites*; and *'Aqā'id an-Nasafī: Introduction to the Islamic Creed*, transl. Musharraf Hussain, 2nd ed. (N.p.: Invitation Publishing House, 2005).

102 This work should not be confused with the *Muqaddima* on *khilāf* by Burhān al-Dīn al-Nasafī.

103 Adrian Room, *Placenames of the World: Origins and Meanings of the Names for 6,600 Countries, Cities, Territories, Natural Features and Historic Sites*, 2nd ed. (London: McFarland, 2006), p. 330.

- *Taʿdād al-shuyūkh li-ʿUmar mustaṭraf ʿalā al-ḥurūf mustaṭar*, which might be the same work as the *Ijāzāt*;
- *Tafsīr al-Nasafī*, a title used to refer to three of his Quranic commentaries: *al-Taysīr fīl-tafsīr*, of which a manuscript is kept at King Saʿūd University, *al-Muṭawwal*, and a commentary in Persian (of which neither al-Samʿānī in the *Muntakhab*, the *Taḥbīr* and the *Ansāb*, nor al-Dhahabī in the *Siyar* and *Tārīkh*, nor Ḥājjī Khalīfa in *Kashf al-ẓunūn* show any knowledge) published in Teheran in 1997 and described by the editor of al-Nasafī's *al-Qand*.[104]
- *Taṭwīl al-asfār li-taḥṣīl al-akhbār*;
- *Ṭilbat al-ṭalaba* on Ḥanafī juridical terminology, a book misattributed to al-Pazdawī by both al-Qurashī and al-Laknawī.
- *Zallat al-qārī'* (The reciter's slip) on the rulings pertaining to mistakes in the recitation of the Qur'ān. This work is preserved in four folios (Ẓāhiriyya 5564)[105] and bears the same title as an earlier work on the same subject by Abū al-Yusr al-Pazdawī (*q.v.*). The Hanafi Damascene hadith master and polymath Muḥammad b. ʿAlī b. Aḥmad b. Ṭūlūn (880–953/1475–1546) authored a commentary on it entitled *al-Ṭārī' ʿalā Zallat al-qārī'*.[106]

Ḥājjī Khalīfa in *Kashf al-ẓunūn* lists six commentaries on the *ʿAqā'id al-nasafiyya*: by Shams al-Dīn al-Aṣfahānī (674–749/1276–1349) the author of a commentary on al-Bayḍāwī's *Ṭawāliʿ al-anwār* in doctrine; by Jamāl al-Dīn Maḥmūd b. Aḥmad b. Masʿūd al-Qūnawī (d. 777/1375), entitled *al-Qalā'id*; by Shams al-Dīn Muḥammad b. Qāsim al-Shāfiʿī (fl. 871/1466); by Shams al-Dīn b. ʿUthmān al-Harawī known as Mullā Zādah (d. 900/1495); by ʿAlī b. ʿAlī al-Najjārī or al-Bukhārī al-Shāfiʿī (d. 967/1560); and by Saʿd al-Dīn al-Taftāzānī (712–793/1320–1390) (*q.v.*) which is the most widespread of all,

104 al-Nasafī, *al-Qand fī dhikr ʿulamā' Samarqand*, ed. Yūsuf al-Hādī (Teheran: Āyna Mīrāth, 1420/1999), p. 22. See https://www.academia.edu/31436366/Description_of_Umar_al_Nasafis_Persian_Tafsir.

105 Per Muṭīʿ al-Ḥāfiẓ, *Fahras makhṭūṭāt Dār al-kutub al-ẓāhiriyya: al-fiqh al-ḥanafī*, 2 vols. (Damascus: Dār Abī Bakr, 1401/1981), 1:347 (misspelt *dhalla*) and 1:405–406.

106 Ibn Ṭulūn, *al-Ṭārī' ʿalā* Zallat al-qāri', with Aḥmad b. Muḥammad b. Ismāʿīl al-Ṭaḥṭāwī's *Zallat al-qārī'*, ed. ʿUmar Yūsuf Ḥamdān (Beirut: Dār Ibn Ḥazm, 1439/2018).

having received the most editions and the most marginalia as detailed further down in Taftāzānī's notice. There is also a commentary by al-Qāwuqjī.

al-Lāmishī

al-Lāmishī al-Ḥanafī al-Māturīdī, Abū al-Thanā' Maḥmūd b. Zayd. *Kitāb al-tamhīd li-qawā'id al-tawḥīd*. Ed. 'Abd al-Majīd al-Turkī. Beirut: Dār al-Gharb al-Islāmī, 1995.

Not much is known about al-Lāmishī (fl. 539/1145) other than that he hailed from Lāmish in the Farghāna region south of Samarqand. His work is a theological primer revolving around the classic themes of the Māturīdī school and showing the influence of al-Nasafī's *Tabṣirat al-adilla*. Its section-headings are:

1. Certainty of the realities of things
2. The avenues whereby knowledge of realities befalls
3. Affirmation of the universe's origination, certainty of the Maker and His being without beginning
4. Affirmation of the oneness of the Maker
5. Negation of 'accident', 'substance', and 'body' from the Maker
6. Invalidation of any resemblance of the Maker with creatures
7. Invalidation of locality and direction for the Maker
8. Affirmation of the Attributes and Names
9. The pre-existence of the divine speech
10. Creation is other than the created
11. Affirmation of will for Allah—may He be exalted
12. Affirmation of the vision of Allah—may He be exalted
13. Affirmation of Prophetic Messengership
14. Miraculous gifts of the friends of Allah
15. Questions on human ability
16. Affirmation of the createdness of all human actions by Allah
17. Secondarily-generated acts (*mutawallidāt*) are all created
18. The one killed is killed by virtue of his life-term
19. On provisions
20. Disobedient sins are all by the will of Allah

21. On the foreordained Decree (*qaḍā'* and *qadar*)
22. Invalidation of the view that Allah is obligated to do what is most conducive to welfare (*al-aṣlaḥ*)
23. Affirmation of the punishment of the grave
24. The threat of punishment for the depraved Muslim sinners
25. Definition of the nature of faith
26. It neither increases nor decreases
27. Faith is created as a human act, uncreated as divine guidance
28. The faith of an imitator in belief who is sincere but ignorant of the proofs is valid, contrary to the Muʿtazila
29. Adding 'if Allah wills' (*istithnā'*) when declaring oneself a believer is impermissible
30. Imamate of the Umma

al-Usmandī

al-Usmandī, 'Alā' al-Dīn. *Lubāb al-kalām*. Ed. Mehmet Sait Özervarlı. Istanbul: Nashriyyāt Markaz al-Buḥūth al-Islāmiyya = İSAM, İslâm Araştırmaları Merkezi Yayınları, 2005.

Born in the town of Usmand in Samarqand, 'Alā' al-Dīn Muḥammad b. 'Abd al-Ḥamīd b. al-Ḥasan b. al-Ḥusayn al-Samarqandī al-Usmandī (488–552/1095–1157)[107]—known as al-'Alā' al-'Ālim—was a foremost Hanafi debater who authored in law, legal theory, the divergences of the jurists, and *tafsīr*. He took law from Ashraf b. Muḥammad al-'Alawī and hadith from Burhān al-Amīn 'Umar b. 'Abd al-'Azīz b. Muʿādh al-Bukhārī, known as al-Ṣadr al-Shahīd (d. 536/1142) and Abū al-Ḥasan 'Alī b. 'Umar al-Kharrāṭ. Among his students were Abū al-Muẓaffar al-Asʿadī b. Ḥusayn al-Karābīsī, Abū al-Muẓaffar 'Abd al-Raḥmān b. 'Abd al-Karīm al-Sāmʿānī (d. 613/1217), and Niẓām al-Dīn 'Umar b. Burhān al-Dīn 'Alī al-Marghīnānī. He died in Bukhārā. Abū al-Muẓaffar al-Sāmʿānī's son, Abū Saʿd al-Samʿānī, often met

107 al-Samʿānī, *al-Ansāb*, ed. 'Abd al-Raḥmān al-Muʿallamī et al., 12 vols. (Hyderabad Deccan: Dā'irat al-Maʿārif al-'Uthmāniyya, 1962; 2nd ed. Cairo: Maktabat Ibn Taymiyya, 1400–1405/1980–1984), 1:255–256; al-Qurashī, *Jawāhir*, 3:208–209 no. 1356; Özervarlı, pp. 28 ff.

him in Samarqand but relates in his *Ansāb* that he 'did not hear any hadith from him because he made no secret of his drinking alcohol (*khamr*).' The latter charge is most likely a misrepresentation of al-Usmandī's own Kufan-*fiqh* position that *khamr* is defined exclusively as fermented grape juice, a well-known Hanafi divergence from the *jumhūr*. Among his extant works: *Ḥaṣr al-masā'il wa-qaṣr al-dalā'il*, a commentary or emendation of 'Umar al-Nasafī's poem on the science of divergences (*'ilm al-khilāf*), of which several manuscripts are kept at the Süleymaniye Library; *Ṭarīqat al-khilāf fil-fiqh bayn al-a'immat al-aslāf*, published in Cairo in 1990; *Badhl al-naẓar fil-uṣūl*, published in Cairo in 1992. He should not be confused with his namesake 'Alā' al-Dīn Aḥmad b. Muḥammad al-Samarqandī (d. 540/1145) who authored *Tuḥfat al-fuqaha'*, *Mīzān al-uṣūl*, *Sharḥ al-Jāmi' al-ṣaḥīḥ*, and *Sharḥ Ta'wīlāt al-Qur'ān*. Also known as *Taṣḥīḥ al-i'tiqād fi uṣul al-dīn*, the *Lubāb al-kalām* contains nearly all the headings of Abū al-Mu'īn's *Tabṣira* as well as many additional fine points. Among them is the remark (p. 36) that all the types of knowledge without exception, including *siḥr*, are beautiful in themselves but may end up prohibited with respect to their practical use and the reference (p. 101) to Ash'arīs and Kullābīs as *mutakallimū ahl al-ḥadīth*. The subject-headings of *Lubāb al-kalām* are:

1. Preliminaries of indispensible knowledge in the fundamentals of doctrine
2. Knowledge and theory
3. The defining parameters of knowledge and its reality
4. The sciences are all good in themselves
5. The hierarchy of the sciences and the preferentiality of some over others[108]
6. Exposition of the divisions of the sciences
7. Exposition of the avenues of the sciences
8. Rational investigation (*naẓar al-'aql*)
9. The obligation of rational investigation concerning knowledge of Allah
10. Inspiration
11. Imitation

108 On the highest science see al-Ghazālī's first book of his *Iḥyā' 'ulūm al-dīn* entitled the Book of Knowledge.

12. The possibility that reason can apprehend the beauty or ugliness of things
13. The originated nature of the world, the affirmation of its Maker, and the fallacies of the naturalists (*ṭabāʾiʿiyyīn*)
14. The divine attributes: existence, beginninglessness, absolute oneness
15. The fact that the Maker of the world is neither an accident nor a substance nor a body
16. Falsifying the attribution of form (*ṣūra*) and compoundedness (*tarakkub*) to Allah
17. The Maker of the world is neither in a direction nor in a place
18. The Maker of the world does not resemble the world nor anything in it
19. The permissibility of saying that Allah is a thing
20. On the Names and Attributes
21. Falsifying the claims that the divine speech is originated
22. Exposition that Allah Most High is described by those attributes by meanings other than the Essence but subsisting in it
23. Exposition of the beginninglessness of the divine attributes
24. Exposition that these meanings are neither the Essence itself nor other than it nor partly it
25. Existentiation (*takwīn*) is other than that which is existentiated (*mukawwan*)
26. Exposition of the possibility of seeing Allah Most High
27. The affirmation of prophethood and messengership
    - 27.1 Exposition of the rational possibility of sending messengers
    - 27.2 That sending messengers is among the compelling dictates (*wājibāt*) of wisdom
    - 27.3 Concerning the evidentiary proofs for sending a specific messenger
    - 27.4 Affirming the messengership of our Prophet Muḥammad—upon him blessings and peace
28. The fallacies of the deniers of the inimitability of the Qur'ān and their refutation
29. The fallacy brought up by the Jews in denial of our Prophet's prophethood
30. Exposition of the meaning of the inimitability of the Qur'ān in detail
31. Exposition of the extent to which inimitability is found in the Qur'ān

32. The state of prophets and their being immune to sin
33. The preferentiality of messengers over the angels
34. The preferentiality of some prophets over others
35. The miraculous gifts of the friends of Allah
36. The acts of [Allah's] slaves—school divergences
37. On capacity
38. Falsifying the position of the determinists (Jabriyya) and affirming that the slave actuates in reality (*lil-ʿabdi fiʿl ʿalā al-taḥqīq*)
39. Falsifying the position of the absolute libertarians (Qadariyya)
40. On tasking beyond one's ability
41. Falsifying the position that actions are generated/engendered secondarily (*tawlīd*)
42. On the murdered dying by virtue of his lifespan
43. On providences
44. On the fact that sins are by virtue of the will of Allah and His decision
45. On foreordained destiny past (*qaḍāʾ*) and future (*qadar*)
46. On guidance and misguidance
47. On what is fittest (*al-aṣlaḥ*) and divine kindness (*al-luṭf*)
48. On divine favors to unbelievers
49. On the fact that causing all creatures to enter the fire is not deemed excellent in wisdom
50. On the absolute libertarians
51. The quiddity of belief (*īman*) and its corollaries
52. That belief (*īman*) and submission (*īslām*) are one and the same
53. That belief (*īman*) neither increases nor decreases
54. Negating pendency [on the divine decision] (*istithnāʾ*) in [the declaration of] belief
55. That belief is created[109]
56. On the designations and statuses [of sinners in relation to belief or damnation]
57. On eschatological reports (*samʿiyyāt*)
58. The affirmation of intercession

109 That belief is created is the position of the masters of Samarqand, while the masters of Bukhārā went so far as to claim that whoever holds that belief is created commits unbelief. See al-Badāyūnī, *al-Muʿtaqad*, pp. 234–237.

59. Miscellaneous next-worldly matters
60. Is the non-existent (*al-maʿdūm*) considered a thing?
61. Issues of overall leadership
62. The obligation to set up an overall leader
63. Setting up two overall leaders at one and the same time
64. Description of the overall leader and the preconditions of overall leadership
65. How overall leadership takes place
66. The affirmation of overall leadership for the rightly-guided caliphs and its sequence

al-Ūshī

al-Ūshī, ʿAlī b. ʿUthmān. *Badʾ al-amālī fī uṣūl al-dīn*. In ʿAlī al-Qārī, *Sharḥ al-Amālī*. Cairo: al-Maṭbaʿat al-ʿĀmira, 1293/1876. Pp. 46–48.

Sirāj al-Dīn Abū Muḥammad ʿAlī b. ʿUthmān b. Muḥammad b. Sulaymān al-Taymī al-Farghānī al-Ūshī al-Shahīdī (d. 575?/1180? of the plague) was a Maturidi scholar from Ūsh, a village near Farghāna in Transoxiana. He studied under Nāṣir al-Dīn Muḥammad b. Yūsuf al-Samarqandī and taught the qadi Abū Naṣr Aḥmad b. Muḥammad al-Zāhidī al-Bukhārī.[110] Among his works are (i) *Ghurar al-akhbār wa-durar al-ashʿār*; (ii) *al-Lāmiyya fī uṣūl al-dīn*, a 68-verse *lām*-rhymed poem on Sunni doctrine known as *Badʾ al-amālī* which received several commentaries, among them Muḥammad b. Abī Bakr al-Rāzī's *Hidāya min al-iʿtiqād*, dated 751/1350 by Ḥajī Khalīfa; ʿIzz al-Dīn Ibn Jamāʿa's (d. 819/1416) comparative work *Darj al-maʿālī*, which received an authoritative critical edition;[111] Mullā ʿAlī al-Qārī's (*q.v.*) *Ḍawʾ al-maʿālī*; ʿAbd al-Raḥīm b. Abī Bakr b. Sulaymān al-Marʿashī (d. 1068/1658);[112] *ʿUqūd al-durar al-ghawālī* by a certain Qāsim al-Ḥasanī al-Ḥanafī;[113] Muḥammad

110 Bāmakhrama al-Ḥimyarī, *al-Nisba ilā al-mawāḍiʿ wal-buldān* (Abu Dhabi: Markaz al-Wathāʾiq wal-Buḥūth, 2004), *s.v.* ʿŪsh.'

111 ʿIzz al-Dīn Muḥammad b. Abī Bakr b. Jamāʿa, *Darj al-maʿālī sharḥ Badʾ al-amālī*, ed. Majdī Ghassān Maʿrūf (Beirut: Muʾassasat al-Kutub al-Thaqāfiyya, 2011/1432).

112 al-Marʿashī, *Sharḥ Badʾ al-Amālī*, ed. Aḥmad Darwīsh Muʾadhdhin (Qahrumān Maʿash: n.p., 2014).

113 https://archive.org/details/20200726_20200726_1544 as of 7 December 2020.

b. ʿAbd Allāh al-Naysābūrī's (fl. 1096/1685) *ʿUqūd al-laʾālī fī sharḥ Badʾ al-amālī*;[114] an anonymous Osmanli commentary entitled *Sharḥ al-Lāmiyya fī uṣūl al-dīn* (undated MS Arab 283, Houghton Library, Harvard University, 8 leaves, seq. 317–330); an anonymous supercommentary (on Qārī's commentary) authored in 1164/1751 entitled *Tuḥfat al-aʿālī ʿalā sharḥ al-Qārī*, first published in Cairo in 1296/1879 then 1891 then in Istanbul in 1308/1890 at Maṭbaʿat Ikhtar; Muḥammad b. Sulaymān al-Ḥalabī al-Rayḥāwī al-Ḥanafī's (d. 1228/1813) *Nukhbat al-laʾālī*;[115] al-Qāwuqjī's (*q.v.*) *al-Durr al-ghālī*, and *Jāmiʿ al-laʾālī*; Sulaymān b. Samḥān b. Muṣliḥ's (1268–1349/1851–1930) *ʿUqūd al-jawāhir al-laʾālī fī muʿāraḍat Badʾ al-amālī*; a thorough but non-Māturīdī comparative commentary by the late head qadi of Lebanon Muḥammad Aḥmad Kanʿān (1944–2011) already mentioned; and the beneficial two-volume *Badr al-layālī sharḥ Badʾ al-amālī* by the contemporary Mufti Riḍāʾ ul-Ḥaqq of Darul Uloom Zakariyya in South Africa; (iii) *Mashāriq al-anwār fī sharḥ niṣāb al-akhbār li-tadhkirat al-akhyār*; (iv) *Mukhtalaf al-riwāya*, a commentary on ʿUmar al-Nasafī's poem on juridical differences; and (v) *Thawāqib al-akhbār*. The topical headings of *Badʾ al-amālī* are:

1. Monotheism
2. The divine attributes
3. The name and the named
4. Transcendence (*al-tanzīh*)
5. The vision of Allah
6. The divine speech
7. The finalization of all divine messages with the Muḥammadan law
8. The night journey and heavenly ascension
9. Intercession
10. Infallibility
11. The descent of ʿĪsā b. Maryam
12. Miraculous gifts
13. The Arch-liar
14. Preferential ranks among the Companions

114 Partially damaged and defective Ms. 4921, King Saud University in 27 folios.

115 *Nukhbat al-laʾālī li-sharḥ Badʾ al-amālī*, ed. Aḥmad Ḥilmī al-Qūghī (Istanbul: Hakîkat Kitâbevi, 1994).

15. Imitation in belief
16. What constitutes unbelief
17. Apostasy
18. The punishment of the grave
19. The non-existent
20. Reward is a bounty and punishment is justice
21. The reckoning
22. The weighing of deeds
23. The bridge over hellfire
24. The intercession of the righteous
25. Supplication
26. The originated nature of the world and nullity of 'primal matter' (*hayūlā*)

al-Ṣābūnī

al-Ṣābūnī, Nūr al-Dīn. *Kitāb al-bidāya min al-kifāya fil-hidāya fī uṣūl al-dīn.* Ed. Fatḥ Allāh Khalīf. Alexandria: Dār al-Ma'ārif, 1969. 155 pp.

———. *al-Kifāya fil-hidāya.* Ed. Muhammed Aruçi. Istanbul: İSAM; Beirut: Dār Ibn Ḥazm, 1435/2014. 432 pp.

Es-Sâbûnî, Nûreddin. *Mâtürîdiyye Akaidi.* [*al-Bidāya fī uṣūl al-dīn.*] Ed. and transl. Bekir Topaloğlu. Ankara: Diyanet İsleri Başkanlığı Yayıları, 2005.

Born in Bukhara to a wealthy family of soap (*ṣābūn*) traders, Nūr al-Dīn Abū Muḥammad Aḥmad b. Maḥmūd b. Abī Bakr al-Ṣābūnī al-Bukhārī (d. 580/1184)[116] taught 'Abd Allāh b. 'Alī b. Ṣāyin al-Farghānī (551–616/1156–1219) and Shams al-A'imma Muḥammad al-Kardarī (d. 642/1244) and debated Rashīd al-Dīn over the impossibility of seeing the nonexistent (cited in Nasafī's *I'timād*), Fakhr al-Dīn al-Rāzī and others. Nothing of his teachers is known other than that he narrated hadith from Sadīd al-Dīn Abū al-Riḍā Muḥammad b. Maḥmūd b. Mas'ūd al-Asadī al-Ṭirāzī, from Muḥyī al-Sunna

116 al-Laknawī, *al-Fawā'id al-bahiyya*, p. 74 no. 63; Khayr al-Dīn Ziriklī, *al-A'lām*, 1:253–254; and the Turkish and Arabic introductions to the Topaloğlu ed. of the *Kifāya*.

al-Baghawī. He was buried in the cemetery of the seven qadis in Bukhara. He is mostly known as the author of the oft-copied and oft-quoted *al-Bidāya min al-kifāya* on dogma, also known as *ʿAqīdat al-Ṣabūnī*, which received a thorough bilingual edition and Turkish translation under the title *Mâtürîdiyye Akaidi*. He abridged the latter from his larger *al-Kifāya min al-hidāya*. The *Bidāya* received a recent commentary entitled *al-Hidāya*.[117] He also authored *al-Mughnī fi uṣūl al-dīn* and *al-Muntaqā min ʿIṣmat al-anbiyā* (preserved in full in the Süleymaniye Library, ms. 2426), an abridgment of Abū al-Ḥusayn Muḥammad b. Yaḥyā al-Bashāgharī's *al-Mawsūm bi-kashf al-ghawāmiḍ min aḥwāl al-anbiyā'*, known simply as *ʿIṣmat al-anbiyā'*. (The latter is also the title of an extant work in print by al-Razī.) The *Bidāya* sums up all the tenets of the Māturīdī creed in a medium-sized textbook authoritatively written with an eye to comparative religion. This heresiographical method defines the Sunni middle ground in positive assertions as well as through the sustained negation of what it is not, as shown in the very first chapter (*al-qawl fi madārik al-ʿulūm*) which throws the gauntlet to Sophists, the Summaniyya and Brahmans of India, atheists, the Rāfiḍa, anthropomorphists and the Muʿtazila just as al-Nasafī had done in the first chapter of his *Tabṣira* with the various sects of the Muʿtazila, the Ashʿarīs and others. The subject-headings of *al-Bidāya min al-kifāya* are:

1. The senses by which the types of knowledge are grasped
2. The created nature of the world and the necessity of the Maker
3. Declaring the Maker as One
4. Declaring the Maker as transcendent beyond the characteristics of createdness
5. The attributes of Allah
6. The name and the named
7. The negation of sameness and likeness
8. The beginninglessness of the speech of Allah
9. Existentiation (*al-takwīn*) and that which is existentiated *(al-mukawwan)*
10. The possibility of seeing Allah Most High

117 Niḍāl b. Ibrāhīm Āl Rashī, *al-Hidāya sharh al-Bidāya fi uṣūl al-dīn lil-ʿallāma Nūr al-Dīn al-Ṣābūnī* (Diyār Bakr: Maktabat Diyār Bakr, 2017). There is also an English translation of the *Bidāya* as of 2020.

11. Section: on seeing Allah in dream[118]
12. Will
13. Affirming the Messengers
14. The evidence for the truthfulness of our Prophet, upon him blessings and peace
15. The characteristics of Prophethood
16. The wondrous miracles of the friends of Allah
17. Imamship and its collaterals
18. The imamship of the rightly-guided caliphs, may Allah be well-pleased with them
19. The questions of declaring one just and declaring one unjust
20. Ability
21. The creation of the actions of creatures by Allah
22. Nullifying secondary engenderment (*tawlīd*)
23. Tasking beyond capacity
24. Declaring all things willed as included in the divine will
25. Section: the non-existent pertains neither to the divine will nor to the divine sight. [Al-Ṣābūnī debated Rashīd al-Dīn at length in Persian on the latter issue as chronicled by Ḥāfiẓ al-Dīn al-Nasafī in *al-Iʿtimād*.]
26. The negation of the incumbency of doing what is fittest [on Allah]
27. Provisions
28. Life-terms
29. Past and future foreordained destiny
30. Guidance and misguidance
31. Those who commit enormous sins
32. Section: Four questions
    - 32.1 Intercession
    - 32.2 Is forgiveness for unbelief and polytheism rationally possible?
    - 32.3 Can Allah be described as able to be unjust, or foolish, or to lie?[119]
    - 32.4 Enormous sins and lesser sins
33. *Īmān* and *Islām*
34. The reality of faith
35. The faith of the imitator

118 See al-Badayūnī's summation on this in his *Muʿtaqad*.
119 See 'Salient Themes'.

36. Section: The increase and decrease of faith
37. What makes faith incumbent by virtue of revealed evidence

al-Ghaznawī

al-Ghaznawī, Jamāl al-Dīn Aḥmad b. Muḥammad. *Kitāb Uṣūl al-dīn*. Ed. ʿAmr Fārūq al-Dāʿūq. Beirut: Dār al-Bashā'ir al-Islāmiyya, 1419/1998. 366 p.

Jamāl al-Dīn Aḥmad b. Muḥammad b. Maḥmūd b. Saʿīd al-Ghaznawī (d. 593/1197) was a student of the famous Masʿūd al-Kāsānī the author of *Badā'iʿ al-Ṣanā'iʿ*, one of the main reference-works of the Ḥanafī School. Ghaznawī authored books on legal theory, jurisprudence, juristic differences, and Māturīdī doctrine. It is possible, but not certain, that *Uṣūl al-dīn* is the same as his *Rawḍat al-mutakallimīn* or its abridgment, *al-Muntaqā min rawḍat al-mutakallimīn*. The main chapter-headings of *Uṣūl al-dīn* are:

1. The divine Attributes

   1.1 The pre-eternal existence and oneness of the Maker
   1.2 The attributes precluded from Him such as direction and place
   1.3 The gist (*mafhūm*) of *istiwā'*, *nuzūl*, *yad* and *wajh*
   1.4 Non-resemblance of the Creator to anything created
   1.5 The foremost divine Attributes and the detailing of speech
   1.6 His knowledge is not acquired

2. The divine Names

   2.1 The divine Names are His Attributes
   2.2 They are by divine ordainment (*tawqīfiyya*)
   2.3 *Takwīn* and *takhlīq*
   2.4 All the divine Attributes are pre-existent

3. The vision of Allah

4. Prophethood, angels and friends of Allah

   4.1 The possibility of Messengers
   4.2 The wisdom of sending Messengers
   4.3 The sending of a specific person

4.4 The sending of Prophets as Messengers
4.5 The heavenly ascent is a reality
4.6 The immunity of Prophets from sin
4.7 The preference of certain angels over others
4.8 The preference of certain human beings over angels
4.9 The angels are immune from sin
4.10 The covenant taken from human beings
4.11 The miraculous gifts of the friends of Allah
4.12 A *walī* is never better than a Prophet

5. The acts of servants

5.1 The servant never creates his own acts
5.2 Reward and punishment hinge on acts
5.3 One act may be subject to divine creation and human earning
5.4 Secondarily-generated acts are from the act of servants
5.5 There is no tasking beyond capacity
5.6 Allah is not obligated to do what is most conducive to welfare

6. Reward and punishment

6.1 Acts of obedience are marks of divine reward
6.2 The one killed dies by virtue of his life-term
6.3 Provision is what reaches one, and each takes his in full
6.4 The divine will conforms to the divine knowledge
6.5 Command and prohibition apply to unbelievers also
6.6 Divine foreknowledge does not predetermine a servant's acts

7. Foreordained destiny and those who commit enormities

7.1 Predeterminism
7.2 Good and evil, guidance, uprightness, and misguidance
7.3 Market prices
7.4 The reality of blessings
7.5 The wisdom of divine acts
7.6 The depraved believer does not perdure in Hellfire
7.7 His status upon leaving this life unrepentant

8. The signs of the Hour and false prophets

    8.1 Descent of ʿĪsā—upon him peace
    8.2 It is obligatory not to believe in seers, fortune-tellers etc.
    8.3 The status of pseudo-prophets
    8.4 Differences concerning the children of polytheists
    8.5 Concerning the recording angels
    8.6 The unbelievers' recording angels
    8.7 The resurrection of animals
    8.8 The Maker of the universe has power to resurrect all existents
    8.9 The reality of death and its agonies

9. Matters of the unseen

    9.1 The angel of death
    9.2 The punishment of the grave is a reality
    9.3 The dead benefit from donated rewards
    9.4 The trumpet-blow is a reality and resurrection is a reality
    9.5 The gathering of all creatures
    9.6 Divine wrath and divine contentment
    9.7 The reading of records, the balance of deeds, and the Basin
    9.8 Intercession, Paradise, and the termination of the Reckoning
    9.9 The Bridge and the entrance of the believers into Paradise
    9.10 Those who have the station of intercession

10. Paradise and Hell

    10.1 Levels of the believers in Paradise
    10.2 The sinful believers
    10.3 The perduring of the unbelievers in Hellfire
    10.4 Paradise and Hellfire are already created
    10.5 The people of Paradise and the people of Hellfire

11. Faith

    11.1 Meaning of faith
    11.2 Acts of worship are part of the rulings on faith
    11.3 Faith does not increase or diminish
    11.4 When can a human being be said to be a believer

SEVENTH/THIRTEENTH CENTURY

al-Tūrabashtī

al-Tūrabashtī, Shihāb al-Dīn Abū ʿAbd Allāh Faḍl Allāh b. Ḥasan. *al-Muʿtamad fil-muʿtaqad.* Madras: Maṭbaʿ Maẓhar al-ʿAjāʾib, 1286/1869. Rept. Istanbul: Hakîkat Kitabevi, n.d.

al-Tūrabashtī (d. 661/1263) was a Hanafi jurist whom al-Qārī cites in his works, among them *Sharḥ al-Fiqh al-akbar* where he says, ʻal-Tūrabashtī said in his *Muʿtaqad* that *al-Mawjūd* and *al-Qadīm* are among the [divine] names of the essence.ʼ[120]

Burhān al-Dīn al-Nasafī

al-Nasafī, Burhān al-Dīn. *al-ʿAqāʾid.* See [Pseudo-]Nasafī, ʿUmar b. Muḥammad.

Burhān al-Dīn Abū al-Faḍl Muḥammad b. Muḥammad b. Muḥammad (600–687/1203–1288) is probably the actual author the *ʿAqāʾid* attributed to Najm al-Dīn ʿUmar al-Nasafī according to the Moroccan transmissologist Muḥammad b. Sulaymān al-Rūdānī (1037–1094/1628–1683). He is less probably also that of *Baḥr al-kalām* rather than Abū al-Muʿīn Maymūn al-Nasafī. See Salient Themes, ʻSpurious attributions/ascriptions in Māturīdī scholarship.ʼ

120 al-Qārī, *Sharḥ al-Fiqhl a-akbar*, Dār al-Nafāʾis ed., p. 43.

al-Khabbāzī

al-Khabbāzī, ʿUmar b. Muḥammad b. ʿUmar. *Kitāb al-Hādī fī uṣūl al-dīn*. Ed. Adil Bebek. Istanbul: Marmara İlâhiyat Vakfı Yayınları (İFAV), 2006.

This is a detailed compendium of Maturidi creed written by one of the major authorities of its school, Jalāl al-Dīn ʿUmar b. Muḥammad b. ʿUmar al-Khabbāzī al-Khujandī (d. 691/1292).[121] Its chapter-headings are:

1. Exordium
   - 1.1 Defining knowledge (*ʿilm*) and its means of acquisition
   - 1.2 On the senses (*madārik*) by which the types of knowledge are grasped
   - 1.3 That inspiration is not among the avenues of knowledge of creeds
2. TOPICS RELATED TO GODHEAD (*masāʾil al-ilāhiyyāt*)
   - 2.1 On the originated nature of the world and the existence of the pre-eternal Maker
   - 2.2 That the world is not without beginning nor self-made *ex nihilo*
   - 2.3 That the Particularizer (*mukhaṣṣiṣ*) of the world is necessarily Existent (*wājib al-wujūd*)
   - 2.4 On the name and the named
   - 2.5 On the impossibility of the Creator being an accident or a substance or a body or anything that characterizes origination in time
   - 2.6 That Allah is not an image
   - 2.7 That Allah is not in any direction
   - 2.8 That Allah is not a locus for originated matters
   - 2.9 Falsifying resemblance (*tashbīh*)
   - 2.10 On the affirmation of affirmatory attributes[122]
   - 2.11 That Allah is all-knowing
   - 2.12 The non-existence of anything which Allah knows to exist is precluded

121 Published by Ayedh S. Aldosari as *Hanafi Maturidism: Trajectories of a Theological Legacy. With a Study and Critical Edition of al-Khabbazi's* Kitab al-Hadi (Sheffield, UK and Bristol, CT Equinox Publishing, 2017).

122 Cf. al-Qārī, *Sharḥ al-Fiqhl a-akbar*, Dār al-Nafāʾis ed., p. 62: *al-ṣifāt al-dhātiyya al-thubūtiyya.*

2.13 That Allah is all-powerful
2.14 That Allah is all-living
2.15 That Allah is all-hearing and all-seeing
2.16 On the negation of originated nature from the divine speech
2.17 On will
2.18 On existentiation and the existentiated
2.19 On the rational possibility of seeing Allah and its necessity by virtue of transmission
2.20 The non-existent cannot be seen
2.21 Allah is not an 'efficient cause' (*ʿilla*) for the existence of the world
2.22 On ability (*istiṭāʿa*)
2.23 The creation of the acts of servants
2.24 On acquisition (*kasb*)
2.25 Secondarily-generational or engendering force (*al-tawlīd wal-tawallud*)
2.26 That to which will pertains (*mutaʿallaq al-irāda*)
2.27 Nothing is incumbent on Allah
2.28 Lifespans
2.29 Sustenance
2.30 Guidance and misguiding
2.31 On tasking beyond capacity
2.32 Divine bounty

3. TOPICS RELATED TO PROPHETHOOD (*masāʾil al-nubuwwāt*)

3.1 On the affirmation of messengership
3.2 The messengership of our Messenger—upon him blessings and peace
3.3 On infallibility (*ʿiṣma*)
3.4 That prophets are preferable to angels
3.5 On miraculous gifts (*karāmāt*)

4. TOPICS RELATED TO ESCHATOLOGY (*masāʾil al-samʿiyyāt*)

4.1 On resurrection
4.2 On the questioning of the grave
4.3 On the punishment of the grave

4.4 On the balance of deeds
4.5 On the bridge [over hellfire]
4.6 On the divine threat of punishment (*al-waʿīd*)
4.7 On intercession
4.8 On forgiveness for unbelief
4.9 It is not permissible to describe Allah as able to wrong or to lie
4.10 Faith is confirmation in the heart according to Abū Ḥanīfa, al-Māturīdī and al-Ashʿarī
4.11 Faith is not mere affirmation as the Karrāmiyya claim
4.12 That faith neither increases nor decreases
4.13 On the obtainment of one's foreordained sustenance in full (*muwāfāt*)
4.14 On the imitator's faith
4.15 On overall leadership
4.16 On the respective caliphates of Abū Bakr, ʿUmar, ʿUthmān and ʿAlī
4.17 On preferentiality among the Companions

Muḥammad b. al-Samarqandī

al-Samarqandī, Muḥammad b. Ashraf. *al-Maʿārif fī sharḥ al-Ṣaḥāʾif*. Ed. ʿAbd Allāh Muḥammad ʿAbd Allāh. 2 vols. Cairo: al-Maktabat al-Azhariyya lil-Turāth, 2015.

———. *al-Ṣaḥāʾif al-Ilāhiyya*. Ed. Aḥmad ʿAbd al-Raḥmān al-Sharīf. Kuwait: Maktabat al-Falāḥ, 1985. Pp. 517.

Little is known of the arch-expert (*muḥaqqiq*) Muḥammad b. Ashraf al-Ḥakīm al-Ḥasanī or al-Ḥusaynī al-Samarqandī (d. after 690/1291) besides his being the author of books in *kalām*, logic, *adab al-baḥth* (ethics of scientific research and debate), astronomy and Euclidian geometry as cited in *Sullam al-wuṣūl ilā ṭabaqāt al-fuḥūl*, *Kashf al-ẓunūn* and other bio-bibliographical works. The *Ṣaḥāʾif* or 'Folios' is a hefty work divided into two *Maqṣid*s ('Propositions'), the first entitled *Fīl-mabādiʾ* ('On First Principles') and the second *Fīl-masāʾil* ('On the Questions'), divided into nineteen sections entitled 'folios.' The work is imbued with philosophical terminology, showing familiarity with the positions of the Muʿtazilīs, Shīʿīs and other non-Sunnī sects, as well as those of the Māturīdīs and Ashʿarīs on a vast range of questions, in which the author defends and illustrates the Māturīdi position. He also wrote a large commentary on the same work, the *Maʿārif.* The latter was in turn glossed by the chief mufti of the Mughal army, ʿAbd al-Salām al-Kirmānī al-Dīwī (d. 1039/1630), the teacher of the logician ʿAbd al-Ḥakīm al-Sayālkūtī (d. 1067/1657)[123] among others.

Rukn al-Dīn al-Samarqandī

al-Samarqandī, Rukn al-Dīn ʿUbayd Allāh b. Muḥammad. *al-ʿAqīdat al-rukniyya fī sharḥ Lā ilāha illā Allāh Muḥammadun rasūl Allāh.* Ed. Mustafa Sinanoğlu. Istanbul: Manshūrāt Markaz al-Buḥūth al-Islāmiyya = İSAM, İslâm Araştırmaları Merkezi Yayınları, 1429/ 2008.

The Hanafi Sufi imam Rukn al-Dīn Abū Muḥammad ʿUbayd Allāh b. Muḥammad b. ʿAbd al-ʿAzīz al-Samarqandī (d. 12 Ṣafar 701/17 October 1301)—also called Walī al-Dīn and Bārsāh or Bārshāh—studied at the Mustanṣiriyya in Baghdad under Muẓaffar al-Dīn Aḥmad b. ʿAlī b. al-Sāʿātī (d. 694/1295) who licensed him to teach his book *Majmaʿ al-baḥrayn wa-multaqā al-nayyirayn* in 690/1291. Among his students in *fiqh* was Yaḥyā b. Sulaymān b. ʿAlī al-Rūmī al-Ādharbayjānī. He lived the last ten years of his life in Damascus teaching at the Ẓāhiriyya and praying 100 daily voluntary *rakʿa*s. After he was found strangled and drowned, the caretaker of Dār al-Ḥadīth, ʿAlī al-Ḥawrānī, was arrested and jailed, confessed to his murder two months later and was hanged at the gate of the school. Among Rukn al-Dīn's works preserved at the Sulaymāniyya are:

(i) *ʿAqāʾid al-Shaykh Rukn al-Dīn al-Samarqandī*, a larger work than the *Rukniyya* bearing on *kalām*, philosophy and *taṣawwuf*, preserved in a unique manuscript that is partially washed out;

(ii) the *Rukniyya*, in which he blends text-based (e.g., section on *samʿiyyāt*) and reason-based proofs ('Accidents are not in any dimension,' 'The quiddity of

123 Asad Q. Ahmed and Reza Pourjavady, "Theology in the Indian Subcontinent," in *The Oxford Handbook of Islamic Theology*, ed. Sabine Schmidtke (Oxford: Oxford University Press, 2016) p. 613.

belief neither increases nor decreases,' '*īmān* and *islām* are inseparable') with a cross-*madhhab* contrastive approach—especially with the Ashʿarī school ('al-Ashʿarī said... al-Rāzī said...,' 'tasking beyond capacity,' '[the injunction to] worship is not addressed to the unbelievers')—and a cross-sect heresiological approach including the rebuttal of Shiʿis ('of the preconditions of caliphate is that the caliph be visible not hidden'), philosophers ('the entirety of the universe is finite,' 'prophethood is of a purely gifted nature,' 'the universe is not inside something, and void exists between its parts'), Muʿtazilis ('Allah knows all universals and all particulars'), Kharijis ('the divine rebukes of the Prophet are a mark of his truthfulness'), or both ('sin neither annuls good deeds nor negates belief'), like the creeds of previous and later Maturidi masters, but with briefer treatment and many more topics including anthropomorphism ('Allah is not in any dimension'), 'Sufi' issues ('it is possible for the walī to know that he is a walī,' 'is it possible for the walī to be expelled from his *wilāya*?' 'a slave's obedience to Allah is more honorable than paradise'), eschatology, *alfāẓ al-kufr* ('the unbeliever's resolve [to believe] does not bring him out of unbelief as long as he does not actually believe, while the believer's resolve to disbelieve even years later brings him out of belief on the spot'), and oddities ('invoking the mercy of Allah upon the Prophet is praiseworthy,' 'A blind person's repentance from prohibited gazing and an impotent person's repentance from fornication of the genitals');

(iii) *Sharḥ al-asmā' al-ḥusnā*;

(iv) epistle on belief and unbelief;

(v) epistle on repentance;

(vi) *Jāmiʿ al-uṣūl*, a work on Hanafi-Shafiʿi divergences in legal theory;

(vii) *Talkhīṣ Jāmiʿ al-usūl*, an abridgment of the preceding;

(viii) *al-Qawāʿid al-fiqhiyya*;

(ix) *Iʿjāz al-Qur'ān*, bearing on the linguistic and stylistic inimitability of the Qur'ān;

(x) *Tafsīr al-Samarqandī*, a 50-folio manuscript on selected verses in their sequential ordering;

(xi) *Mulakhkhaṣ Sharḥ ma'ānī al-āthār*, an abridgment of al-Ṭaḥāwī's book by that title;

(xii) an epistle on *al-Rūḥ*;

(xiii) *Risāla fī 'ālam al-malakūt* on the divisions of the world;

(xiv) *al-Risālat al-insāniyya* on the position of human beings in the hierarchies of existent things, the *rūḥ* and the *nafs*;

(xv) *Risālat al-'ubūdiyya* on the nature of spiritual slavehood and the preconditions of worship and obedience;

(xvi) *Risāla fī ḥaqīqat al-'ālam* on the wisdom of creation, the divisions of the world, and the Muḥammadan light.

The subject-headings of *al-'Aqīdat al-rukniyya* are:

1. Belief is the witnessing to the existence of Allah and His perfections, and to the prophethood of Muḥammad the Messenger of Allah
2. The imitator is a believer
3. Detailing this unqualified belief in Allah and His Messenger
4. The entirety of the universe is finite
5. The paths of acquirable knowledge are three
6. The types of intuitive knowledge do not depend on acquisition
7. The inspiration (*ilhām*) of the Prophet is a proof binding upon him and other than him
8. What Allah created is a manifestation of His existence
9. Allah is clear of any indwelling
10. Allah is not an accident
11. Allah differs from all created things
12. Allah is single in His essence and one in His attributes
13. Perfect monotheism
14. Allah is not in any dimension
15. Spirits are not in any dimension
16. Accidents are not in any dimension
17. Truths cannot be subverted
18. Allah precedes all things
19. Belief in ambiguous verses

20. The existence of Allah is His very essence
21. What is non-existent (*ma'dūm*) is not a thing nor its quiddity
22. It is incumbent to believe that Allah did not create the world in vain
23. The divine attributes
24. The 'immaterial spirit endowed with speech' (*al-rūḥ al-nāṭiqa al-rūḥaniyya*) has primordial knowledge of Allah
25. Allah has countless Attributes and Names from pre-existence to eternity
26. The Attributes of Allah are not His very Essence
27. The Name *Allāh* is underived
28. Allah is Creator from pre-existence to eternity
29. Indwelling is impossible in relation to Allah
30. The Qur'ān is the speech of Allah
31. The hearing of the speech of Allah
32. Existentiating (*takwīn*) is the attribute of Allah
33. The existence of the world is through its bringing into existence (*ījād*) by Allah
34. Allah is willer
35. Allah Most High is perduring
36. Hearing and sight are two meanings besides the knowledge of Allah
37. The Maker of the world is All-Wise
38. Allah knows all universals and all particulars
39. The knowledge-contents (*ma'lūmāt*) of Allah and the apportionments of His power (*maqdūrāt*) are infinite (*UṣGh*)
40. It is impermissible that Allah be described as having power to commit injustice or to lie
41. Tasking beyond capacity
42. Causing pain to the innocent
43. Allah is Creator of all the world
44. The effects of the acts of animals are by the creating of Allah without their choice nor acquisition
45. The murdered dies by virtue of his lifespan
46. Sins are brought into existence through the foreordained Decree of Allah
47. The fittest (*al-aṣlaḥ*) is not incumbent upon Allah

48. There is neither contradiction nor reduplication among the Attributes of Allah or His Names
49. The Attributes of Allah and His Names are countless
50. There is no overlapping (*tadākhul)* among the beautiful Names and Attributes of Allah and it must not be said that one is preferable to another
51. Seeing Allah
52. Seeing Allah is among the ambiguities
53. The exact nature of the reality of the Essence of Allah cannot be known
54. Knowledge of Allah to the extent imaginable by His slaves are of three categories
55. Seeing Allah while asleep
56. Everyone for whom bliss was inscribed on the Tablet shall die blissful
57. Allah tests His slaves
58. The prohibited is also part of providence (*al-ḥarām rizq*)
59. Allah may prefer some of His creatures over others
60. The slave has no freedom from the slavehood of servanthood and legal responsibility
61. Not taking the slaves to task for error and forgetfulness
62. Gratitude for the favors of Allah
63. Prophetic matters and corollaries such as miraculous gifts and caliphate issues
64. Exposition of the preconditions of messengership
65. Supernatural events are of different categories
66. The exact number of Prophetic Messengers is not known
67. The possibility of the miraculous gift of the friend of Allah
68. The concomitants of prophethood
69. The Prophet remains a Prophet after his death
70. The Prophet may exert juridical estimation (*ijtihād*)
71. The divine rebukes of the Prophet are a mark of his truthfulness
72. Some of the Messengers and Prophets were preferred over others
73. Prophets and Messengers have transparent primordial dispositions and pure physical frames
74. Prophethood is of a purely gifted nature

75. It is impermissible to ascribe preferentiality of certain Prophets over others in particular
76. Our Prophet went on a heavenly ascent
77. The wives of our Prophet are the purified mothers of the believers
78. The friend of Allah (*walī*) never reaches the level of a prophet
79. Neither prophethood nor friendship with Allah eliminate fear
80. It is possible for the *walī* to know that he is a *walī*
81. A Messenger is not [defined as] a Messenger by virtue of staggering miracles (*muʿjizāt*)
82. Infallibility (*ʿiṣma*) is not a precondition of friendship with Allah (*wilāya*)
83. Is it possible for the *walī* to be expelled from his *wilāya*?
84. Concerning caliphate
85. Of the preconditions of caliphate is that the caliph be visible not hidden
86. The affirmation of caliphate
87. Eschatological issues (*samʿiyyāt*)
88. Preferentiality between human beings and angels
89. Belief is a categorical obligation in all the heavenly scriptures
90. Abrogation is possible in the branch issues contrary to Jewish beliefs
91. The reality of belief and its corollary rulings
92. A mature rational person who remains ignorant is not excused for being ignorant of his Maker
93. Acquired knowledge (*maʿrifa*) is not a subset (*dākhila*) of the quiddity of belief
94. Belief professed at the time one despairs [of living further] is not accepted
95. The blissful might end up wretched and the wretched might end up blissful
96. The quiddity of belief neither increases nor decreases
97. Sin neither annuls good deeds nor negates belief
98. *Īmān* and *islām* are inseparable
99. Belief between fear and hope
100. The unbeliever's mere resolve [to believe] does not bring him out of unbelief as long as he does not actually believe, while the believer's

resolve to disbelieve even years down the future brings him out of belief on the spot

101. If the believer dies as a corrupt sinner (*fāsiq*) through small or grave sins, he does not remain eternally in hellfire
102. Apostatizing those who pray to the Qibla is impermissible
103. [The injunction to] worship is not addressed to the unbelievers
104. In relation to an act of worship, its integrals and preconditions, fatwa asserts permissibility but not acceptance, because that is hidden from us
105. A slave's obedience to Allah is more honorable than paradise
106. The good deed expiates the bad one while the bad one does not annul the good deed
107. Supplications that fulfill their preconditions carry far-reaching effectiveness
108. Invoking the mercy of Allah upon the Prophet is praiseworthy
109. Visiting graves, supplicating for their dwellers and giving alms on their behalf carries innumerable benefits
110. The precondition of repentance
111. Repentance for a single sin is valid
112. The repentance of the murderer is accepted
113. Repentance from grave sins is not an automatic reason for the forgiveness of small ones
114. A blind person's repentance from prohibited gazing and an impotent person's repentance from fornication of the genitals
115. The pursuit of the religious types of knowledge is a categorical obligation
116. Even if knowledge is complete it does not suffice without practice and effort
117. Allah is the one alone who possesses knowledge of the unseen
118. The earning of licit income as defined by the sacred law
119. Solid objects perform a type of magnification
120. Affirming the existence of jinns and devils
121. Witchcraft and the evil eye are effective in certain ways
122. The universe is not inside something, and void exists between its parts
123. All bodies in the world are a single genus and quiddity for *Ahl al-Sunna*

124. Preferentiality among creatures
125. Rulings pertaining to the hereafter
126. Where souls dwell
127. Interrogation in the grave is a reality
128. The punishment of the grave is a reality
129. Resurrection is taking place inevitably
130. The reading of personal records is a reality
131. The reckoning is a reality
132. Bodies will be resurrected alongside souls
133. Children will be resurrected and also the insane
134. Whoever was amputated for a crime then apostatized and died will be punished in his entire body
135. On the great gathering
136. On the balance of deeds
137. On contentions
138. On the bridge over hellfire
139. The Prophet's basin is a reality
140. Perduring in paradise is a reality and perduring in the fire is a reality
141. Worship and other excellent deeds do not compel bliss and entrance into paradise
142. Sins do not compel wretchedness and entrance into hellfire

Eighth/Fourteenth Century

ʿAbd Allāh al-Nasafī

al-Nasafī, ʿAbd Allāh b. Aḥmad. *al-Iʿtimād fil-iʿtiqād.* Ms. 3157. 77 folios. Copied 710/1310 by Bisṭām b. al-Ḥājjī Khiḍr. Riyadh: King Fayṣal Center for Islamic Studies. http://www.ahlalhdeeth.com/vb/showthread.php?t=318347 as of 4 December 2020

———. *Sharḥ al-ʿUmda fī ʿaqīdat Ahl al-Sunna wal-Jamāʿa al-musammā bil-Iʿtimād fil-iʿtiqād.* Ed. ʿAbd Allāh Muḥammad Ismāʿīl. Cairo: al-Maktabat al-Azhariyya lil-Turāth, 2012.

———. [*ʿUmdat al-ʿaqāʾid.*] *ʿUmdat ʿaqīdat Ahl al-Sunna wal-Jamāʿa. Pillar of the creed of Sunnites: being a brief exposition of their principal tenets by Háfidh-uldín Abú'lbarakát Abdullah Alnasafi. To which is subjoined a shorter treatise of a similar nature by Najmuldín Abú Hafs Umar Alnasafi.* Ed. William Cureton. London: Society for the Publication of Oriental Texts, 1843.

Abū al-Barakāt Ḥāfiẓ al-Dīn ʿAbd Allāh b. Aḥmad b. Maḥmūd al-Nasafī (d. 710/1310) was a Hanafi jurist, exegete, legal theorist and Māturīdī *mutakallim* that is primarily known for his oft-studied *Tafsīr*, entitled *Madārik al-tanzīl wa-ḥaqāʾiq al-taʾwīl*, a title patterned after his exact contemporary al-Bayḍāwī's *Anwār al-tanzīl wa-asrār al-taʾwīl*, from which he frequently quotes, both of their works being reworkings of al-Zamakhsharī's *Kashshāf*. He studied under Wajīh al-Dīn al-Rāzī, Shams al-A'imma al-Kardarī, al-Sirāj al-Thaqafī, al-Zayn al-Badawānī and others. Among his students was Ḥusām al-Dīn al-Sighnāqī. He was an ardent defender of Ibn al-ʿArabī and Ibn al-Fāriḍ. Also among his works are *Kanz al-daqāʾiq* in Hanafi and comparative jurisprudence, which received many subsequent commentaries, most famously those of Zaylaʿī and

Ibn Nujaym respectively entitled *Tabyīn al-ḥaqā'iq* and *al-Baḥr al-rā'iq*; *al-Manār*, a short text on juridical principles which Kāfī Ḥasan Afandī al-Aqḥiṣārī (*q.v.*) emendated; a commentary on the *Manār* entitled *Kashf al-asrār*; another text entitled *al-Manār* on credal doctrine which received a commentary by Sa'd al-Dīn Abū al-Faḍā'il al-Dihlawī entitled *Ifāḍat al-anwār fī iḍā'at uṣūl al-Manār*; *'Umdat al-'aqā'id* (edited by William Cureton), in which he was said to have confused the Māturīdī position with the Mu'tazilī stance in many places;[124] its commentary entitled *al-I'timād fil-i'tiqād*, also in print;[125] and other works. The headings of *al-I'timad* are as follows:

1. The affirmation of truths
2. On the originated nature of the world
3. On the affirmation of the Maker
4. On the attribute of unicity (*waḥdāniyya*)
5. On the attribute of pre-existence (*qidam*)
6. That He—Most High—is not an accident
7. That He—Most High—is not a substance
8. That He—Most High—is not a body
9. That He—Most High—is not in a direction
10. That He—Most High—is not located in a place
11. On the attributes of perfection
12. On the attribute of speech
13. On the attribute of existentiation
14. On the attribute of will
15. On the attribute of wisdom
16. Affirmation of seeing Allah
17. Affirmation of seeing Allah in dream
18. Affirmation that the non-existent cannot be seen
19. Affirmation of messengership
20. Affirmation of the messengership of Muḥammad—upon him blessings and peace
21. The special qualities (*khawāṣṣ* = *khaṣā'iṣ*) of Prophethood

124 According to al-Badāyūnī in his *Mu'taqad* (2.4.19)—per Ibn al-Humām (note 190 below).

125 Published as *Sharḥ al-'Umda fī 'aqīdat Ahl al-Sunna wal-Jamā'a al-musammā bil-I'timād fil-i'tiqād*, ed. 'Abd Allāh Muḥammad Ismā'īl (al-Maktabat al-Azhariyya lil-Turāth, 2012).

22. The miraculous gifts of the friends of Allah
23. On ability
24. On the acts of creatures
25. On secondarily-generated acts (*mutawallidāt*)
26. That the one murdered dies by virtue of his lifespan
27. That He—Most High—wills both obedience and sins
28. Affirmation of the issue of guidance and misguiding
29. On what is fit and fittest (*al-ṣalāḥ wal-aṣlaḥ*)
30. On foreordained destiny past and to come
31. On the status of tasking beyond one's capacity
32. On sustenance
33. One the obligatoriness of belief
34. On the quiddity of belief
35. That belief neither increases nor decreases
36. On in whom confirmation subsists is a true believer
37. The status of the imitator's faith
38. That *īmān* and *islām* are one and the same
39. The status of one who commits a grave sin
40. On intercession
41. The Ashʿarī ruling of the [rational] possibility of the forgiveness of unbelief (IKB 7)
42. Allah is not describable as able to commit injustice, foolishness and lying
43. That good deeds eliminate bad ones
44. Eschatology
45. The great gathering of bodies
46. The reading of the records is real
47. The balance [of deeds] is real
48. The bridge [over hellfire] is real
49. On paradise and hell
50. The jinn unbeliever will be punished in hellfire
51. The *walī* does not reach the level of a *nabī*
52. The ranks of preferentiation between human beings and angels
53. The covenant Allah took from Adam and his progeny is real
54. On overall political leadership
55. Preferential ranking among the Companions

Ḥusām al-Dīn al-Sighnāqī

al-Sighnāqī, Ḥusām al-Dīn Ibn ʿAlī. *al-Tasdīd fī sharḥ al-Tamhīd.* Ed. ʿAlī Ṭāriq Ziyād Yalmāz. Unpubl. diss. https://archive.org/details/20200119_20200119_1351 as of 4 December 2020.

Ḥusām al-Dīn al-Ḥusayn b. ʿAlī b. al-Ḥajjāj al-Sighnāqī or Sughnāqī (d. 710/1310)—after the town of Sughnāq near Bukhārā—was a Ḥanafī jurist, legal theorist, linguist and debater, the foremost student of Ḥāfiẓ al-Dīn Abū al-Faḍl Muḥammad b. Muḥammad b. Naṣr al-Nasafī among others. Sighnāqī authored several works,[126] among them *al-Nihāya*, a major commentary on Marghīnānī's *Hidāya* in *fiqh*. His voluminous commentary on Maymūn al-Nasafī's *al-Tamhīd li-qawāʿid al-tawḥīd* (*q.v.*), entitled *al-Tasdīd fī sharḥ al-Tamhīd,*[127] should not be confused with the same-titled commentary on Ibn al-Bāqillānī's *Tamhīd* by the Moroccan Qadi Abū al-Qāsim ʿAbd al-Jalīl b. Abī Bakr al-Rabaʿī al-Qarawī al-Dībājī—known as Ibn al-Ṣābūnī—authored in 478/1085.

Najm al-Dīn al-Ṭarasūsī

al-Ṭarasūsī, Najm al-Dīn Ibrāhīm b. ʿAlī. *Urjūza fī maʿrifat mā bayna al-Ashāʿira wal-Ḥanafiyya min al-khilāf fī uṣūl al-dīn.* In Ṣalāḥ al-Dīn Khalīl b. Aybak al-Ṣafadī, *Aʿyān al-ʿaṣr wa-aʿwān al-naṣr.* Ed. ʿAlī Abū Zayd et al. 6 vols. Beirut: Dār al-Fikr al-Muʿāṣir; Damascus: Dār al-Fikr, 1418/1998. 1:102–103.

Najm al-Dīn Ibrāhīm b. ʿAlī b. Aḥmad b. ʿAbd al-Wāḥid al-Ṭarasūsī (721–758/1321–1357) was born in Damascus where he succeeded his father as head judge, a post which he held irreproachably until his death. Despite his brief life and busy profession he also taught in several madrasas and authored works in Ḥanafī *fiqh* and legal theory, pilgrimology, fatwas, juridical terminology used by judges and witnesses, advice to Turkish rulers on the superiority of the Ḥanafī school to the heretofore preponderant Shāfiʿī school in statecraft, political theory and administration, the classification of the sciences, scholarly biographies, and the above two-page poem on twelve of 'the differences in the

126 See https://islamansiklopedisi.org.tr/signaki as of December 2020.
127 His chain of transmission to Maymūn al-Nasafī is cited in *al-Jawāhir al-muḍiyya.*

foundations of the faith between the Ashʿarīs and the Ḥanafīs' which Ṣafadī said he and his son heard from him. Ibn Ḥajar also mentions it in the entry devoted to him in *al-Durar al-kāmina*.

Tāj al-Dīn [Ibn] al-Subkī

[Ibn] al-Subkī, Tāj al-Dīn ʿAbd al-Wahhāb. *al-Qaṣīdat al-nūniyya fil-khilāf bayna al-Ashāʿira wal-Māturīdiyya*. In *Ṭabaqāt al-Shāfiʿiyya al-Kubrā*. Ed. Maḥmūd al-Ṭannāḥī and ʿAbd al-Fattāḥ al-Ḥilw. 2nd. ed. 10 vols. Jīza: Dār Hijr, 1992. 3:377–389.

———. *Ibid*. In al-Jābī, Bassām ʿAbd al-Wahhāb, *al-Masāʾil al-khilāfiyya* (*q.v.*).

———. *Ibid*. In Badeen, Edward, *Sunnitische Theologie in osmanischer Zeit*, pp. 1–18 (Arabic).

———. *al-Sayf al-mashhūr fī ʿaqīdat Abī Manṣūr*. Ed. Muṣṭafā Ṣāʾim Yabram. Istanbul: n.p., 2000. 95 p. 2nd ed. Ankara: Sharikat Aydam, 1432/2011. 118 p.

Shaykh al-Islām Qāḍī al-quḍāt Tāj al-Dīn Abū al-Naṣr ʿAbd al-Wahhāb b. Abī al-Ḥasan ʿAlī b. ʿAbd al-Kāfī al-Subkī al-Shāfiʿī al-Qāhirī al-Dimashqī (727–771/1327–1370) is famous as a foremost chronicler of the Ashʿarī school with his masterpiece *Ṭabaqāt al-Shāfiʿiyya al-kubrā* among many other extant works. In North African schools his seminal text on legal theory entitled *Jamʿ al-jawāmiʿ* is known simply as *Ibn al-Subkī*. In his 144-line *nūn*-rhymed poem entitled *al-Nūniyya* he asserts six meaningful differences and seven terminological differences between Ashʿarīs and Māturīdīs, while considering the rest inauthentic. The *Nūniyya* is also identified as *al-Sayf al-mashhūr fī ʿaqīdat Abī Manṣūr* and received a commentary by the Shāfiʿī grammarian and logician ʿAlī b. Ibrāhīm b. Muḥammad al-Ḥusaynī al-Juwaymī known as Nūr al-Dīn al-Shīrāzī (785–860/1383–1456), on which Abū ʿAdhaba built his own compendium entitled *al-Rawḍat al-bahiyya* (*q.v.*).

Both Ibn al-Subkī and his father, the Shāfiʿī Shaykh al-Islām, legal theorist and hadith master Taqī al-Dīn al-Subkī, take up the Māturīdī position in dissent of the Ashʿarī position on several key points. For example, although both Imām al-Ḥaramayn in *al-Irshād* and al-Ghazālī in *al-Mankhūl* allow the possibility of small sins for Prophets,[128] Ibn al-Subkī says in *al-Nūniyya*:

> They [Māturīdīs] said Allah precludes small sins from Prophets; and in our [Ashʿarī] school there are two positions. / Preclusion is narrated from the Master [=Abū Manṣūr ʿAbd al-Qāhir al-Baghdādī] and al-Qāḍī ʿIyāḍ, and it is the strongest position. / It is the position I take and was that of my father,[129] exempting their rank from any defect. / Al-Ashʿarī is our Imam but in this we differ with him one and all. / And we say that we are on his path but his companions are split in two parties over the matter. / Some Ashʿarīs even said Prophets are completely free of forgetfulness. / Yet all are considered al-Ashʿarī's followers. This dissent does not expel them from that status.[130]

The fact that the above appears to be the strongest position among Ashʿarīs—contrary to how they are generally characterized in the comparative Māturīdī-Ashʿarī literature on this particular issue (e.g. al-Ṭarasūsī's *Urjūza*)—shows in the fact that it was also held by Abū Isḥāq al-Isfarāyīnī (d. 418/1027) and others.[131]

128 'As for sins considered small... minds do not deny them [as possible for Prophets]. I did not come upon a categorically explicit transmitted proof either negating them or asserting them [as possible]. For explicitly categorical proofs come either from explicit texts (*nuṣūṣ*) or from consensus (*ijmāʿ*) and there is no consensus [either], since the ulema differ over the possibility of small sins for Prophets. The explicit, unambiguous or uninterpretable texts that would categorically establish the principles pertaining to this issue are simply not found. So if it is said that since the matter is conjectural, what is the strongest conjecture in the matter in your opinion? We say: Our strongest conjecture is that they are possible. The stories of the Prophets in many a verse of the Book of Allah Most High bear witness to that [conjecture]. But Allah knows best what is right.' Ibn al-Juwaynī, *al-Irshād ilā qawāṭiʿ al-adilla fī uṣūl al-iʿtiqād*, ed. Asʿad Tamīm (Beirut: Mu'assasat al-Kutub al-Thaqāfiyya, 1996), pp. 298–299; cf. al-Ghazālī, *al-Mankhūl min taʿlīqāt al-uṣūl*, ed. Muḥammad Ḥasan Hītū (Beirut: Dār al-Fikr, 1970), p. 223.

129 See Shaykh al-Islām ʿAlī b. ʿAbd al-Kāfī al-Subkī, *al-Ibhāj fī sharḥ al-Minhāj*, ed. Shaʿbān Muḥammad Ismāʿīl, 2 vols. (Maktabat al-Kulliyyāt al-Azhariyya, 1401/1981), 2:263.

130 Ibn al-Subkī, *Ṭabaqāt al-Shāfiʿiyya al-kubrā*, 3:387–388.

131 See http://www.livingislam.org/fiqhi/sp2-gfh_e.html#1.

Ibn Abī al-ʿIzz

Ibn Abī al-ʿIzz, ʿAlī b. ʿAlī. *Sharḥ al-ʿAqīdat al-Ṭaḥāwiyya*. Ed. ʿAbd Allāh b. ʿAbd al-Muḥsin al-Turkī and Shuʿayb al-Arnaʾūṭ. 8th ed. 2 vols. Beirut: Muʾassasat al-Risāla, 1416/1995.

———. *Ibid.* Ed. Muḥammad Nāṣir al-Albānī et al. 9th ed. Beirut: al-Maktab al-Islāmī, 1408/1988.

Ṣadr al-Dīn Abū al-Ḥasan ʿAlī b. ʿAlāʾ al-Dīn ʿAlī b. Shams al-Dīn Muḥammad b. Abī al-ʿIzz al-Dimashqī al-Ṣāliḥī (731–792/1331–1390) is not a Māturīdī scholar and was included in this study only because his commentary on the *Ṭaḥāwiyya* is the most well-known in our time, although firmly heretical by Māturīdī and Ashʿarī standards. He is unknown in the Hanafi biographical sources but is mentioned in other sources due to the affair that led to his eleven-month imprisonment from 784 to 785. Ibn ʿImād (d. 1089/1678) devoted five lines to him in *Shadharāt al-dhahab* (Year 792) in which he mentioned that Ibn Abī al-ʿIzz was the Hanafi judge for Damascus then for Cairo for one month, after which he excused himself and came back to Damascus. There, he was imprisoned for a certain blunder and remained incarcerated until a new governor came and gave him amnesty. The story is told by Ibn Ḥajar in his *Inbāʾ al-ghumr* that when the poet ʿAlī b. Aybak al-Ṣafadī wrote a poem in praise of the Prophet and circulated it among the scholars for perusal, Ibn Abī al-ʿIzz wrote negative remarks in the margins, among them: Next to the line *ḥasbī Rasūl Allāh* (sufficient for me is the Messenger of Allāh) he wrote, 'This cannot be said except for Allāh.' Next to the line *ishfaʿ lī* (intercede for me!) he wrote, 'Intercession is not asked of him.' Next to the line, *tawassaltu bika* (I have you as my means) he wrote, 'One does not use him as one's means' *(la yutawassalu bihi)*. Next to the line, *al-maʿṣūm min al-zalal* (made immune against lapses) he wrote, 'Except the lapse earning [divine] rebuke' *(illā min zallat al-ʿitāb)*. Next to the line, 'O best of all creatures!' he wrote, 'The preponderant position is that angels are better' *(al-rājiḥ tafḍīl al-malāʾika)*. Interrogated before a judge about the above, Ibn Abī al-ʿIzz admitted saying them then said: 'I take back those statements and now believe other than what I first said.' He was let go but when the case was later reviewed before the collected judges they decided that he should be flogged, the Ḥanbalī

Ibn Mufliḥ abstaining. The Shāfiʿī head qadi then commuted the sentence into imprisonment which was carried out, and ordered that *tawassul* poetry be recited by all the muezzins of Damascus after the dawn prayer.[132]

The first printing of Ibn Abī al-ʿIzz's commentary on the *Ṭaḥāwiyya* was in 1930 in Mecca at the hands of ʿAbd Allāh b. Ḥasan b. Ḥusayn, a descendant of the Najdī Muḥammad b. ʿAbd al-Wahhāb. Aḥmad Shākir (d. 1958) brought out another edition in 1954 and, more recently, al-Albānī and his friends. The Ashʿarī Murtaḍā al-Zabīdī in his monumental *Itḥāf al-sādat al-muttaqīn* quotes some lines from the *Sharḥ* then comments: 'After examining these words [of Ibn Abī al-ʿIzz] carefully, I have found them to be in contravention of the principles of the school of his Imam. In fact, he seems to be rejecting the imams of the Sunna as if he were the advocate of their opponents, speaking rashly and trespassing bounds until he compares the position of *Ahl al-Sunna* with the sayings of Christians. Let the reader beware!'[133] Mullā ʿAlī al-Qārī said: 'One must not pay any attention to what the innovators imagine on rational bases, and the commentator of al-Ṭaḥāwī's *ʿAqīda* [*i.e.* Ibn Abī al-ʿIzz] blundered in this regard when he said: "Can any vision be rationally conceived without face to face encounter? And in it there is a proof for His elevation *(ʿulūw)* over His creatures." It seems that he applies the upward direction to his Lord, whereas the doctrine of *Ahl al-Sunna wal-Jamāʿa* is that He—exalted is He—is not seen in any direction! The saying of the Prophet—upon him blessings and peace, *You shall see your Lord just as you see the moon on the night it is full* [narrated from Abū Hurayra by al-Tirmidhī (*ḥasan gharīb*) and, with a slightly different wording, from Jarīr b. ʿAbd Allāh al-Bajalī by al-Bukhārī and Muslim] is a simile (*tashbīh*) between two types of sightings generally speaking, not a simile between two objects of vision from every perspective.'[134] Al-Kawtharī referred to Ibn Abī al-ʿIzz when he said: "A commentary was published [on the *Ṭaḥāwiyya*], authored by an unknown spuriously affiliated with the Hanafi school, but whose handiwork proclaims his ignorance of this discipline and

---

132 Ibn Ḥajar, *Inbāʾ al-ghumr bi-aʿmār al-ʿumr*, ed. Ḥasan Ḥabash, 4 vols. (Cairo: Lajnat Iḥyāʾ al-Turāth al-Islāmī, Wizārat al-Awqāf, 1994), 1:258–260 (year 784).

133 al-Zabīdī, *Itḥāf al-sādat al-muttaqīn*, 10 vols. (Cairo: al-Maṭbaʿat al-Maymaniyya, 1311/1893), 2:146.

134 al-Qārī, *Sharḥ al-Fiqh al-akbar*, Nafāʾis ed., p. 180.

the fact that he is an anthropomorphist who has lost his compass.'[135] Shaykh Muḥammad Abū al-Hudā al-Yaʿqūbī said that his father the late Sayyid Ibrāhīm al-Yaʿqūbī raised the possibility that the commentary attributed to Ibn Abī al-ʿIzz was in fact by Ibn Qayyim al-Jawziyya (d. 751/1350) on the basis of the author's systematic abandonment of Sunnī positions on several key points in favor of Ibn Taymiyya's,[136] as shown below. This seems precluded by Ibn Abī al-ʿIzz's mention of Ibn Kathīr (d. 774/1373) as his teacher in two places of the *Sharḥ*, unless such a mention is a later interpolation. What is likeliest is that Ibn Abī al-ʿIzz was completely absorbed into the orbit of Ibn Taymiyya's influence and abandoned whatever Māturīdī principles he may have held at one time in doctrine, adopting new views on *tawassul* and even the curt manners and disdain for scholars for which that strain achieved notoriety from its inception to our time.

Among the revealing comments Ibn Abī al-ʿIzz made in his *Sharḥ* (1:195): 'Whoever claims that Allah is seen without direction, let him check his reason,' although al-Ṭaḥāwī had explicitly said, 'The seeing of Allah by the people of paradise is real without their vision being all-encompassing and *without the manner of their vision being known*' ... 'He is beyond having limits placed on Him, or being restricted, or having parts or limbs. Nor is He contained by the six directions as all created things are,' while Abū Ḥanīfa's position in the *Waṣiyya* is, 'The meeting *(liqā')* of Allah Most High with the dwellers of Paradise is by visual sight *without modality, nor simile, nor direction' (liqā' Allāh taʿālā li-ahl al-janna bil-ru'yat al-baṣariyya bi-lā kayf wa-lā tashbīh wa-lā jiha)*, as cited by al-Qārī in *Sharḥ al-Fiqh al-akbar* (Nafā'is ed., pp. 176–177). Ibn Abī al-ʿIzz's view in this respect combines pure Muʿtazilism—which negates all vision of Allah on the grounds that nothing can be seen except in a direction—and anthropomorphism, which subsumes Allah under created entities such as spatiality and dimensionality.[137] Another heresy is Ibn Abī al-ʿIzz's endorse-

135 al-Kawtharī, *al-Ḥāwī fī sīrat al-imām al-Ṭaḥāwī* (Cairo : Maṭbaʿat al-Anwār, 1948; rept. Cairo: al-Maktabat al-Azhariyya lil-Turāth, 1995), pp. 38–39.

136 Class communication.

137 Ibn al-Juwaynī, *al-Irshād*, p. 167: 'Among their [the Muʿtazila's] insinuations are claims that stem, in fact, from pure conjecture, such as their saying that one who sees must be facing opposite what he sees, or virtually facing *(al-rā'ī yajib an yakūna muqābilan lil-mar'ī aw fī ḥukm al-muqābil)*. We say to them: Do you know for certain what you are claiming, or do you know it on speculative bases? If they claim that they know it for certain and accuse

ment of Ibn Taymiyya's doctrine (strenuously defended by Ibn al-Qayyim in *Hādī al-arwāḥ ilā bilād al-afrāḥ*) that hellfire is of finite duration and shall come to an end, in flat contradiction of al-Ṭaḥāwī's statement: 'The Garden and the Fire are created and shall never be extinguished nor come to an end.'[138] Ibn Abī al-ʿIzz also adopted Ibn Taymiyya's triadic monotheism as expressed in his famous devising of three *tawḥīds*: one for Godhead *(tawḥīd al-ulūhiyya)*, one for Lordship *(tawḥīd al-rubūbiyya)*, and one for the Divine Names and Attributes *(tawḥīd al-asmā' wal-ṣifāt)*.[139] This is found, to our knowledge, in no other commentary of the *Ṭaḥāwiyya*, not even the 'Salafī' commentary by Ḥasan al-Busnawī, although the latter does follow Ibn Abī al-ʿIzz in other matters. Finally, Ibn Abī al-ʿIzz also subscribes, like Ibn Taymiyya, to the philosophy that contingencies subsist *(qiyām al-ḥawādith)* in the Godhead; that the world is 'generically pre-existent' *(qadīm bil-nawʿ)*; that Allah speaks with letters and sounds; and that He has 'limits which He alone knows' although he also admitted that 'The *Salaf* all agree that human beings have no knowledge of any limit for Allah and that they do not give any of His Attributes any limits. Abū Dāwūd al-Ṭayālisī said [as narrated by al-Bayhaqī in *al-Asmā' wal-ṣifāt* (Kawtharī ed., p. 426; Ḥāshidī ed., 2:334)], "Sufyān, Shuʿba, Ḥammād b. Zayd, Ḥammād b. Salama, Sharīk and Abū ʿAwāna did not attribute any limits [to Allah], nor any likeness, nor any simile."'[140]

---

whoever disagrees with them of denial, their credibility collapses and their untruth becomes manifest. The same reasoning applies to the anthropomorphists.... And the Creator sees His creation without direction, therefore it is possible that He be seen without direction.' In their tiny supercommentaries on Ibn Abī al-ʿIzz, ʿAbd al-ʿAzīz b. Bāz and Nāṣir al-Albānī reject al-Ṭaḥāwī's preclusion of the concept of limbs and limits with relation to the Deity by claiming, '*Allāh is beyond limits that we know, buthas limits which He knows*.' The latter also denies the authenticity of the manuscripts of the *Ṭaḥāwiyya* that carry the wording 'He [Allah] encompasses everything and all that is above it [the Throne],' affirming only the wording, 'He encompasses everything and is above it' on the grounds that 'there is nothing created above the Throne,' in imitation of Ibn Ḥazm's identical claim. See al-Albānī, *al-ʿAqīda al-Ṭaḥāwiyya sharḥ wa-taʿlīq* (Beirut: al-Maktab al-Islāmī, 1978), pp. 46, 56.

138 *Sharḥ* (2:427–430). Ibn Taymiyya was refuted by al-Taqī al-Subkī in his *al-Durra al-muḍiyya fil-radd ʿalā Ibn Taymiyya* and by Muḥammad b. Ismāʿīl al-Ṣanʿānī in his *Rafʿ al-astār li-ibṭāl adillat al-qā'ilīn bi-fanā' al-nār* (Nullification of the proofs of the claimants that hellfire shall come to an end).

139 In his *Fatāwā* (1:219, 2:275); *Minhāj al-Sunna* (2: 62); *Risālat Ahl al-Suffa* (p.34) and elsewhere.

140 Ibn Abī al-ʿIzz, *Sharḥ al-ʿaqīda al-Ṭaḥāwiyya* (1:262–263).

Sa'd al-Dīn al-Taftāzānī

al-Taftāzānī, Sa'd al-Dīn Mas'ūd b. 'Umar et al. *Sharḥ... al-Taftāzānī... 'alā matn al-'Aqā'id lil-Shaykh Najm al-Dīn Abī Ḥafṣ 'Umar b. Muḥammad al-Nasafī... wa-bi-hāmishih Ḥāshiyat al-Mawlā Mūṣliḥ al-Dīn Muṣṭafā al-Kassatlī... wa-talīhimā Ḥāshiyat al-Mawlā Aḥmad b. Mūsā al-Khayyālī... wa-bi-hāmishihā Ḥāshiyat al-Shaykh Ramaḍān al-Bahshatī.* 2 vols. Istanbul: Dār Sa'ādat, 1326/1908. 200 p. + 111 p. Rept. Baghdad: Maktabat al-Muthannā, [1970 or 1980].

———. *Majmū'at al-ḥawāshī al-bahiyya 'alā Sharḥ al-'Aqā'id al-nasafiyya al-mushtamil 'alā Sharḥ al-'Aqā'id al-nasafiyya lil-Taftāzānī wa-'alā Ḥāshiyat Mullā Aḥmad al-Janadī 'alayh wa-'alā Ḥāshiyat al-Khayyālī 'alayh wa-'alā Ḥāshiyat 'Abd al-Ḥakīm al-Sayālkūtī 'alā al-Khayyālī wa-'alā Jāmi' al-taqārīr 'alā 'Abd al-Ḥakīm li-ba'ḍ afāḍil al-muḥaqqiqīn.* With the *Ḥāshiya* of 'Iṣām al-Dīn al-Isfarāyīnī on Taftāzānī and the supercommentaries of Walī al-Dīn and al-Kafawī on it and with the *Ḥāshiya* of Shujā' al-Dīn and al-Sharīf al-Jurjānī on al-Khayyālī. Ed. *Jam' min afāḍil al-'ulamā'.* 2 vols. Cairo: Maṭba'at Kurdistān al-'Ilmiyya, 1329/1911.

al-Taftāzānī, Sa'd al-Dīn Mas'ūd b. 'Umar. *Sharḥ al-'Aqā'id al-Nasafiyya.* Ed. Muḥammad 'Adnān Darwīsh. [Damascus: n.p., 1411/1990.]

———. *Ibid.* Ed. Aḥmad Ḥijāzī al-Saqqā. Cairo: Maktabat al-Kulliyyāt al-Azhariyya, 1408/1988.

———. *Sharḥ al-'Aqā'id al-Nasafiyya al-muḥashshā bi-'Iqd al-farā'id 'alā Sharḥ al-'Aqā'id.* Mawlāna Muḥammad 'Alī. Karachi: Maktabat al-Bushrā, 1430/2009.

———. *Sharḥ al-'Aqā'id al-Nasafiyya ma'a ḥāshiyatih Jam' al-farā'id bi-inārat sharḥ al-'Aqā'id wa-yalīhimā Sharḥ Mīzān al-'Aqā'id.* Ṣadr al-Warā al-Miṣbāḥī and Shāh 'Abd al-'Azīz al-Dihlawī. 2nd ed. Karachi: Maktabat al-Madīna, 1433/2012.

———. *A Commentary on the Creed of Islam: Sa'd al-Dīn al-Taftāzānī on the Creed of Najm al-Dīn al-Nasafī.* Transl. Earl Edgar Elder. New York: Columbia University Press, 1950.

Al-Taftāzānī (712–793/1320–1390) was a Māturīdī Ḥanafī scholar[141] that hailed from an Afghan family that settled in a village near Nasā in Khurasan. He studied in Sarakhs under ʿAḍud al-Dīn al-Ījī then in Damascus under Quṭb al-Dīn al-Rāzī al-Taḥtānī who lived on the ground floor of the Ẓāhiriyya. He then moved to Khwārizm where he took up writing until Timur-Lang summoned him first to Sarakhs then to Samarqand. Among his students were Ḥusām al-Dīn al-Ḥasan b. ʿAlī al-Abīwardī the author of *Rāʿī al-jinān fil-maʿānī wal-bayān*, Burhān al-Dīn Ḥaydar al-Harawī the teacher of Mullā Khusrū al-Shīrāzī; and Jalāl al-Dīn Yūsuf al-Awbahī to whom he gave a full *ijāza* to all his works and transmissions. Among his works: a *tafsīr* in Persian entitled *Kashf al-asrār wa-ʿuddat al-abrār*; a famed commentary on al-Zamakhsharī's *Kashshāf*; several books in Ḥanafī *fiqh* including a collection of fatwas; several works on legal theory, the most important being *al-Talwīḥ ilā kashf ḥaqā'iq al-Tanqīḥ*; a commentary on al-Nawawī's Forty Hadiths, in print; several books on *kalām*, among which *al-Maqāṣid*, its *Sharḥ*, and the *Sharḥ al-ʿaqā'id al-nasafiyya*; several books on grammar such as *al-Irshād*, *al-Iṣbāḥ*, and *Ḥall al-maqāʿid fī sharḥ al-qawāʿid*; two books on morphology: *Sharḥ al-taṣrīf al-ʿizzī* and *Qawānīn al-ṣarf*; two books on logic: *Sharḥ al-risālat al-shamsiyya* and *Sharḥ al-manṭiq wal-kalām*; *Sharḥ al-Sarrājiyya* on inheritance law; and *al-Niʿam al-sawābigh fī sharḥ al-kalim al-nawābigh* on the philosophy of language.

Taftāzānī's inspired *Sharḥ al-ʿaqā'id* received no less than 28 super-commentaries or marginalia (*ḥawāshī*) including by Shāfiʿī authorities such as ʿIzz al-Dīn Ibn Jamāʿa, Aḥmad al-Bardaʿī, Shaykh al-Islām Zakariyyā al-Anṣārī (recently published), Shams al-Dīn al-Ghazzī, Shihāb al-Dīn al-Ḥaskafī, Manṣūr al-Ṭabalāwī, Burhān al-Dīn al-Biqāʿī and Ibrāhīm al-Laqānī. Among the famous Māturīdī marginalia on Taftāzānī are those of ʿIṣām al-Dīn al-Isfarāyīnī (pub. 1913) who also authored a commentary on Bayḍāwī's *Tafsīr*; Abū al-Fayḍ al-Kafawī; ʿAbd al-ʿAzīz al-Dihlawī (a one-page epitome entitled *Mīzān al-ʿAqā'id* 'authored in half a minute' and its commentary); Ramaḍān b. Muḥammad Efendi (pub. 1320/1902, 1326/1908); Muṣliḥ al-Dīn Muṣṭafā

141 See ʿAbd al-Fattāḥ Abū Ghudda's notes on al-Laknawī's *Iqāmat al-ḥujja*, pp. 16–18.

al-Kassatlī (d. 901/1496) (pub. 1326/1908); Muḥammad ʿAbd al-ʿAzīz al-Farhārī's *al-Nibrās*; and al-Qārī's hadith documentation entitled *Farāʾid al-qalāʾid*. One of the most important is that by Shams al-Dīn Aḥmad b. Mūsā al-Khayyālī (829–862/1425–1458) which he based on the *ḥāshiya* of Ibn Abī Sharīf al-Maqdisī the student of Ibn Humām and which received, in turn, no less than 10 super-supercommentaries. Among them are those by Sājuqlī Zādah and by the Indian logician ʿAbd al-Ḥakīm al-Sayālkūtī (who also commented al-Bayḍāwī's *Tafsīr*) (1297/1880), on which the erudite Ismāʿīl al-Kalanbawī (see Table 5) in turn wrote a supersupercommentary.[142] The chapter-headers of Taftāzānī's *Sharḥ al-ʿaqāʾid* are as follows:

1. Knowledge of firm truths
2. The avenues of knowledge and its acquisition
3. The senses
4. True reports
5. Reason/mind
6. Inspiration
7. The world
8. Dividing the world into objects and accidents
9. Accidents and the locus of its occurrence
10. The Originator of the world is Allah
11. Some divine Attributes and their definitions
12. Speech
13. The Qurʾān is the speech of Allah and uncreated[143]
14. Existentiating (*takwīn*)
15. Will
16. The vision of Allah
17. The acts of creatures
18. Their voluntary acts
19. Capacity
20. Slaves are tasked with what lies within their capacities

142 Kalanbawī also wrote a treatise on 'necessary' versus 'merely possible' existence entitled *Risālat al-imkān* (Istanbul: Dār Saʿāda, 1309/1892). On 'compulsoriness' in the sense of necessity see note 156.

143 'What is recited is without beginning, while the recitation itself is originated.' al-Qārī, *Sharḥ al-Fiqh al-akbar*, Nafāʾis ed., p. 70, cf. pp. 16, 71.

21. The murdered dies by virtue of his lifespan
22. Illicit sustenance [also] counts as *rizq* and each gets one's *rizq* in full
23. The one who guides or misguides is Allah
24. What is fit or fittest is not obligatory for Allah
25. The interrogation of Munkar and Nakīr
26. The Balance of deeds
27. The Bridge
28. Paradise and Hellfire
29. Enormous sins and the narrations as to their number
30. Intercession
31. Belief neither increases nor decreases
32. *Īmān* and *islām* are one and the same
33. A believer should not say 'I am a believer *in shā Allāh*'
34. The blissful and the wretched
35. The dispatching of Messengers
36. The staggering miracles of Prophets
37. Exposition of the number of the Prophets
38. The angels
39. The Books of Allah
40. The heavenly Ascent
41. The miraculous gifts of the Prophets
42. The best of people after Prophets
43. Caliphate and the caliphs
44. Time span of the rightly-guided caliphate
45. The obligation of instituting the overall leader (*naṣb al-imām*)
46. The overall leader is not impeached because of depravity
47. Prayer is enjoined behind every righteous and unrighteous [leader]
48. We refrain from mentioning the Companions other than in good terms
49. The Ten promised Paradise
50. Wiping on top of leather socks
51. The status of date mash (*nabīdh*)
52. A *walī* does not reach the rank of prophets
53. Qur'ān and Sunna texts are primarily literal
54. Holding sin to be licit or making light of it is *kufr*

55. Despairing of or feeling safe from Allah is *kufr*
56. Supplication
57. The major preconditions of the Hour
58. The *mujtahid* can err
59. Ranks and levels between human beings and angels

Ninth/Fifteenth Century

ʿIzz al-Dīn Ibn Jamāʿa

Ibn Jamāʿa, ʿIzz al-Dīn Muḥammad b. Abī Bakr *Darj al-maʿālī sharḥ Badʾ al-amālī.* Ed. Majdī Ghassān Maʿrūf. Beirut: Muʾassasat al-Kutub al-Thaqāfiyya, 2011/1432.

The celibate Cairene Shāfiʿī Shaykh al-Islām and polymath ʿIzz al-Dīn Abū ʿAbd Allāh Muḥammad b. Abī Bakr b. ʿIzz al-Dīn ʿAbd al-ʿAzīz b. Muḥammad b. Ibrāhīm b. Saʿd Allāhb. Jamāʿa al-Ḥamawī (759–819/1358–1416) hailed from a prestigious family of qadis and scholars in all fields of the Islamic sciences. He memorized the Qurʾān in one month and went on to excel in every science, studying under Ibn al-Subkī, al-Sirāj al-Bulqīnī and Ibn Khaldūn among others. He was the teacher of al-Fayrūzābādī and of Zayn al-Dīn al-ʿIrāqī whom he instructed to devote himself to hadith, and the latter's student Ibn Ḥajar al-ʿAsqalānī also took from him—among countless other students—and would call him *Imām al-aʾimma.* He died of the plague in Cairo, having authored over a thousand works, among them the above commentary on al-Ūshī's *Badʾ al-amālī* which he wrote not as a Māturīdī but as a comparatist.

Badr al-Dīn al-Maqdisī

al-Maqdisī, Badr al-Dīn Ḥasan b. Abī Bakr. *Ghāyat al-marām fī sharḥ Baḥr al-kalām.* Ed. ʿAbd Allāh Muḥammad Ismāʿīl and Muḥammad al-Sayyid Aḥmad Shaḥḥāta. Cairo: al-Maktaba al-Azhariyya lil-Turāth, 1432/2011. 869 p.

Badr al-Dīn Ḥasan b. Abī Bakr b. Aḥmad al-Maqdisī, known as Ibn Buqayra (760–836/1359–1433) was a Cairene Ḥanafī qadi and grammarian whose career had started in his native Quds then Damascus and finally Cairo where he taught at the Shaykhuniyya among other madrasas and at the Mardānī mosque, and was the head preacher at the Barqūqiyya. He relatedly authored two works, a commentary on Maymūn al-Nasafī's *Baḥr al-kalām* entitled *Ghāyat al-marām*,[144] and another on Ibn Hishām's *al-Shudhūr* on grammar, entitled *al-Surūr*.

ʿAlāʾ al-Dīn al-Bukhārī

al-Bukhārī, ʿAlāʾ al-Dīn Muḥammad b. Muḥammad. *Risāla fil-Iʿtiqād*. Ed. Saʿīd ʿAbd al-Laṭīf Fawda. Kuwait: Dār al-Ḍiyāʾ, 1433/2012.

The Ashʿarī Ḥanafī jurist ʿAlāʾ al-Dīn Muḥammad b. Muḥammad b. Muḥammad b. al-ʿAlāʾ al-Bukhārī al-Mizzī (779–841/1377/1438) is generally famous for his declaration of apostasy against Aḥmad b. Taymiyya and Ibn ʿArabī, but is actually a distinguished student of al-Taftāzānī (on whose commentary on Zamakhsharī's *Kashshāf* he wrote a supercommentary) from a scholarly family, his father being his other main teacher and his maternal uncle al-ʿAlāʾ ʿAbd al-Raḥmān al-Tishlāqī being a student of ʿAḍud al-Dīn al-Ījī. He shone in Shāfiʿī *fiqh* as well, together with legal theory, doctrine, logic, debate, rhetoric and prosody as well as *taṣawwuf* and Arabic literature until he became 'the Imam of his time' (Ibn Ḥajar). He lived parts of his life in Gulbarga in India, as well as Mecca, Cairo, and finally Damascus, achieving quick fame everywhere he went. He taught no less than 45 distinguished students documented in the above edition (pp. 56–80), whose benefit to the present bibliography is that it provides a comparative approach to some of the doctrinal positions over which Ashʿarīs and Māturīdīs famously differ.

Ibn al-Humām

Ibn al-Humām, Kamāl al-Dīn. *al-Musāyara fī ʿilm al-kalām wal-ʿaqāʾid al-tawḥīdiyya al-munjiya fil-ākhira*. Ed. Muḥammad Muḥyī al-Dīn ʿAbd

144 See its description in al-Barsījī's edition of *Baḥr al-kalām* (p. 38).

al-Ḥamīd. Cairo: al-Maṭbaʿat al-Maḥmūdiyya al-Tijāriyya fī Miṣr, 1348/1929. Rept. Jubayl, Lebanon: Dār wa-Maktabat Bīblyūn, 2015.

Born in Alexandria, the Hanafi jurist and theologian Kamāl al-Dīn Muḥammad b. ʿAbd al-Wāḥid b. ʿAbd al-Ḥamīd Ibn al-Humām (790–861/1388–1457) of superlative eloquence and incisiveness, 'the arch-scholar of people on earth' (al-Sakhāwī), is famed for three works: *Sharḥ fatḥ al-Qadīr*, an authoritative commentary on the *Hidāya* in *fiqh* (which he read with al-Sarrāj); the *Musāyara* on a synthesis of Ashʿarī and Maturīdi positions based on the topical headings of al-Ghazālī's *Qawāʿid al-ʿaqāʾid*; and *al-Taḥrīr fī uṣūl al-fiqh* on legal principles. He also excelled in Quranic commentary, debate, language, inheritance law, arithmetic, *taṣawwuf*, rhetoric, music and logic. He flourished in Cairo where he studied under prestigious Shāfiʿī masters such as Ibn ʿAbd al-Salām, al-Bisāṭī, al-Shumunnī, al-Walī al-ʿIraqī, Ibn Ḥajar and al-ʿIzz Ibn Jamāʿa. After living in Aleppo and the Hijaz for a while he once again settled in Cairo, first as a teacher in the Mamluk sultan al-Ashraf Barsbay's school, then as head shaykh of the Khānaqa Shaykhūniyya, each time quitting his position after a short while, preferring a life of seclusion, writing, and private teaching.

Al-Shawkānī relates in his biographical notice on Ibn al-Humām in *al-Badr al-ṭāliʿ* that the latter surpassed many of his teachers in his insight and the precision of his thought. His ability to synthesize shows in his work on legal theory, *al-Taḥrīr fī uṣūl al-fiqh al-jāmiʿ bayn iṣṭilāḥ al-Ḥanafiyya wal-Shāfiʿīyya*. This aspect of Ibn al-Humām's mind is certainly confirmed by his elucidations in the *Musāyara*, where he offers advanced insights on points of commonality or resolutions (*taqrīrāt*) that escaped the notice of both Ashʿarīs and Māturīdīs in their rebuttals of the Muʿtazila and other non-Sunnī sects. An example of this approach is his considering as two offshoots of Ghazālī's fifth foundation (i.e. that excellence and ugliness are not compelling determinants of divine commands, prohibitions and acts, contrary to the Muʿtazila's claim) the assertion of the possibilities (i) that Allah may task a soul beyond its capacity and (ii) that He may punish creatures without prior transgression on their part nor future recompense for them. He follows up with a defense of the Maturidi position that the 'capacity to lie' is precluded from the divine attributes as an absurd impossibility.[145] The book received several commentaries, notably those of his two students the Hanafi master al-Qāsim b. Quṭlūbaghā (802–879/1399–1474) and the Shāfiʿī al-Kamāl b. Abī Sharīf (Muḥ. b. Muḥ. b. Abī Bakr b. ʿAlī al-Maqdisī 822–906/1419–1501), entitled *al-Musāmara.*[146] The headings of the *Musāyara* are as follows:

1. Introduction on the definition of *kalām*
2. FIRST INTEGRAL: KNOWLEDGE OF ALLAH
   - 2.1 First principle: knowledge of His existence
   - 2.2 Second principle: that He is pre-eternal, without beginning
   - 2.3 Third principle: that He is everlasting
   - 2.4 Fourth principle: that He is not a substance subject to dimensionality
   - 2.5 Fifth principle: that He is not a body
   - 2.6 Sixth principle: that He is not an accident
   - 2.7 Seventh principle: that He has no specific direction
   - 2.8 Eighth principle: that He has established Himself on the Throne
   - 2.9 Ninth principle: that He is seen with eyesights
   - 2.10 Tenth principle: that He is One without partner
3. SECOND INTEGRAL: KNOWLEDGE OF HIS ATTRIBUTES
   - 3.1 First to sixth principle: that He is able, knowing, living, willing, hearing-seeing, and speaking
4. THIRD INTEGRAL: KNOWLEDGE OF THE ACTS OF ALLAH
   - 4.1 The attributes of acts
   - 4.2 First principle: that there is no creator other than Him
   - 4.3 Second principle: the movement that typifies servants is called 'acquisition' (*kasb*)
   - 4.4 On resolve (*ʿazm*)

145 Ibn al-Humām, *al-Musāmara fī ʿilm al-kalām wal-ʿaqāʾid al-tawḥīdiyya al-munjiya fil-ākhira*, ed. Muḥammad Muḥyī al-Dīn ʿAbd al-Ḥamīd (Cairo: al-Maṭbaʿat al-Maḥmūdiyya al-Tijāriyya fī Miṣr, 1348/1929), pp. 90–118.

146 Ibn Abī Sharīf, *Kitāb al-Musāmara fī sharḥ al-Musāyara* (Bulaq: al-Maṭbaʿat al-Kubrā al-Amīriyya, 1317/1899); rept. Istanbul: Çağrı Yayınları, 1979; *ibid.* (Cairo: Maṭbaʿat al-Saʿāda, 1347/1929), rept. in 2 vols. Cairo: al-Maktabat al-Azhariyya, 2006.

4.5 On divinely-granted success (*tawfīq*)
4.6 On ability (*istiṭāʿa*)
4.7 Third principle: A servant's act is by the enabling will (*mashīʾa*) of Allah
4.8 On will and foreordained destiny
4.9 Fourth principle: Allah bestows His favor through creation and invention
4.10 Fifth principle: Ratiocinative determination of what is beautiful and what is ugly
4.11 It is possible for Allah to task his servants beyond their capacity
4.12 Allah may cause suffering to His creation
4.13 The sending of prophets is not an impossibility contrary to what Brahmans hold
4.14 The preconditions of Prophethood
4.15 Infallibility (*ʿiṣma*)
4.16 The witnessing that Muḥammad is the Messenger of Allah sent to all creatures
4.17 The Qur'ān and its evidence of the prophetship of the Messenger of Allah

5. FOURTH INTEGRAL: ESCHATOLOGY

5.1 Resurrection and the great gathering
5.2 The questioning of Munkar and Nakīr, the punishment of the grave and its bliss
5.3 The balance of deeds is real
5.4 The Kawthar
5.5 The bridge
5.6 The preconditions of overall leadership
5.7 In case knowledge and justice are not found in the aspirants to overall leadership
5.8 What is understood by *īmān*, what it refers to, and its status

Tenth/Sixteenth Century

Ibn Kamāl Bāshā

Ibn Kamāl Bāshā [Kemalpaşazâde]. *Masā'il al-ikhtilāf bayna al-Ashā'ira wal-Māturīdiyya*. Ed. Sa'īd 'Abd al-Laṭīf Fawda. Amman: Dār al-Fatḥ lil-Dirāsāt wal-Nashr, 1430/2009. 2nd ed. Amman: Dār al-Fatḥ lil-Dirāsāt wal-Nashr, 1432/2011.

———. *Ibid*. In Badeen, Edward, *Sunnitische Theologie in osmanischer Zeit*, pp. 19–23.

The Ottoman qadi, polymath and Shaykh al-Islam Shams al-Dīn Aḥmad b. Sulaymān, known by his pen name Ibn Kemal or Kemalpaşazâde (873–940/1469–1534), authored *Tevarih-i Al-i Osman* (Chronicles of the House of Osman) among numerous other works in almost every science, including *Daqā'iq al-ḥaqā'iq* on philology, a supercommentary on al-Bayḍāwī's *Tafsīr*, *Ṭabaqāt al-mujtahidīn*, a *Risāla fil-jabr wal-qadar*, *Īḍāḥ al-Iṣlāḥ* in Hanafi *fiqh*, *Taghyīr al-Tanqīḥ* in legal theory, and a Turkish translation of Tughrīburdā's *al-Nujūm al-zāhira*. In his *Masā'il al-ikhtilāf bayna al-Ashā'ira wal-Māturīdiyya* Ibn Kamāl Bāshā numbers the differences between the two schools as twelve *in toto*:[147]

1. Existentiation (*al-takwīn*)
2. The divine speech
3. The wisdom of the Maker

147 A number with which Abū 'Adhaba will concur two centuries later, although his headings differ. For an English rendering of Ibn Kamāl Bashā's text see https://muslimanswersfiles.files.wordpress.com/2013/04/the-disagreements-between-the-ashe28098aris-and-maturidis.pdf, http://marifah.info/articles/disagreementsbetweenasharisandmaturidis-ibnkamalbasha.pdf, both as of 22 November 2018.

4. Divine will[148]
5. Tasking beyond capacity
6. Reason and its relationship with the rulings of legal liability
7. Wretchedness and bliss
8. Pardon for unbelief
9. Is the believer's abiding in hellfire and the unbeliever's abiding in paradise forever possible?
10. The name and the named
11. Maleness as a precondition of Prophethood
12. The acts of servants, acquisition and creation

Nawʿī Efendi

Nawʿī Efendi. *Risāla fil-farq bayna madhhab al-Ashāʿira wal-Māturīdiyya.* In Badeen, *Sunnitische Theologie.* Pp. 25–29 (Arabic).

The Istanbul *mutakallim* and poet Yaḥyā b. ʿAlī b. Naṣūḥ al-Rūmī, known as Nawʿī Efendī (940–1007/1533–1599), was tutor to the children of Sultan Murād before devoting himself to authorship. Among his works is a commentary on al-Fanārī's *al-Risāla al-qudsiyya*; another on *Taʿlīm al-mutaʿallim*; *Muḥaṣṣal al-masāʾil al-kalāmiyya*; marginalia on *Hayākil al-nūr*; a very brief epistle on the differences between Ashʿarīs and Māturīdīs where he lists seven or eight differences; several works of poetry in Turkish; a Turkish translation of *Fuṣūṣ al-ḥikam*; and other works.[149]

148 This difference is a historical inaccuracy in the Māturīdī books on differences, as the Ashʿarī position is the same as the Māturīdī on this point, namely, that "disobedience takes place by His will without His contentment" (Ibn Khafīf, *ʿAqīda*, §38), in Ibrāhīm al-Dusūqī Shattā, *Sīrat al-Shaykh al-kabīr Abī ʿAbd Allāh Muḥammad ibn Khafīf al-Shīrāzī* (Cairo: al-Maṭābiʿ al-Amīriyya, 1397/1977), pp. 340–365. See also Ibn al-Subkī, *Ṭabaqāt*, 4:286–287 and 10:295.

149 al-Ziriklī, *al-Aʿlām*, 8:159.

ELEVENTH/SEVENTEENTH CENTURY

Mullā ʿAlī al-Qārī

al-Qārī, ʿAlī b. Sulṭān Muḥammad. *Ḍawʾ al-maʿālī ʿalā manẓūmat Badʾ al-amālī*. Ed. ʿAbd al-Salām Shannār. Damascus: Dār al-Bayrūtī, 1427/2006.

———. *Ḍawʾ al-maʿālī ʿalā manẓūmat Badʾ al-amālī*. Ed. Muḥammad ʿAdnān Darwīsh. Damascus: Dār Iqraʾ, 2002.

———. *Minaḥ al-Rawḍ al-azhar sharḥ al-Fiqh al-akbar*. With *al-Taʿlīq al-muyassar ʿalā Sharḥ al-Fiqh al-akbar* by the editor. Ed. Wahbī Sulaymān Ghāwjī. Beirut: Dār al-Bashāʾir al-Islāmiyya, 1419/1998.

———. *Sharḥ al-Amālī*. Cairo: al-Maṭbaʿat al-ʿĀmira, 1293/1876.

———. *Sharḥ al-Amālī*. Istanbul: Maṭbaʿat al-ʿĀlam, 1319/1901.

———. *Sharḥ Ḍawʾ al-maʿālī ʿalā manẓūmat Badʾ al-amālī*. Ed. ʿAbd al-Laṭīf Ṣāliḥ Farfūr. [Damascus:] Maktabat al-Maʿārif, [1970].

———. *Sharḥ al-Fiqh al-akbar*. Ed. Marwān Muḥammad al-Shaʿār. Beirut: Dār al-Nafāʾis, 1417/1997.

———. *Sharḥ al-Fiqh al-akbar*. Beirut: Dār al-Kutub al-ʿIlmiyya, 1404/1984.

Mullā Nūr al-Dīn Abū al-Ḥasan ʿAlī b. Sulṭān Muḥammad al-Qarī al-Harawī *thumma* al-Makkī (d. 1014/1605) the polymath Imam, jurisprudent, canonist, exegete, heresiographer, calligrapher, *Ḥajj* specialist, philologist, logician, 'magnificent *muḥaddith* and noble verifier, one of the renewers' (al-Laknawī and Ibn ʿĀbidīn), ʻone of the great Hanafi hadith masters' (al-Kawtharī), ʻone of the forerunners of knowledge and the peerless scholar of his time, most remarkable in his analyses and the elucidation of language' (al-Muḥibbī), ʻthe encyclopedist of the sciences of transmission and reason, imbued with the Prophetic Sunna, one of the foremost erudite scholars and great perspicuous memorizers' (Shawkānī), was born in the major Khurasanian city of Herat in present-day Afghanistan. He shone in memorization, the science of canonical readings and the leadership of prayer in *tarāwīḥ*, hence his nickname of *qārī* (reciter) before he became famous as *mullā*, a Persian scholarly title of distinction derived from *mawlā*, in use mostly in the non-Arabic regions of Central and South Asia. He sustained himself and his dependants through his calligraphy of volumes of Qur'ān and its commentary in a handwriting which one of his contemporaries described as ʻone of the wonders of the world.' The sale of one such volume sufficed him the sustenance of an entire year. Al-Qārī probably moved to Mecca shortly after 952/1545 where he remained until his death and was buried in al-Maʿlāt cemetery—Allah have mercy on him. Al-Muḥibbī in *Khulāṣat al-athar* said that when news of his death reached the ulema of Egypt, they held the funeral prayer in absentia at al-Azhar in a throng of over 4,000. His teachers included Ibn Ḥajar al-Haytamī; ʿAlī al-Muttaqī al-Hindī the author of *Kanz al-ʿummāl*; the *musnid*, jurist, grammarian and qadi, Mullā ʿAbd Allāh b. Saʿd al-Dīn al-ʿUmarī al-Sindī; the mufti, historian and commentator of the Qur'ān Abū ʿĪsā Quṭb al-Dīn Muḥammad b. Aḥmad b. Muḥammad al-Gujarātī al-Nahrawālī whom al-Qārī called ʻthe reliance of latter-day scholars and the cream of the oceans of erudition, our teacher, the mufti of the Muslims in the safe Sanctuary of Allah;' and the jurist and admonisher Sinān al-Dīn Yūsuf b. ʿAbd Allāh al-Amāsī al-Rūmī. Al-Qārī could have received his knowledge of the Maturidi school from any and all of the above as well as others. Among his works on doctrine are:

(i) *Ḍaw' al-maʿālī li-Bad' al-amālī*, a commentary on al-Ūshī's (d. 569/1174) poem on Māturīdī doctrine which al-Qārī said he finished in 1010/1602. It has received several editions and supercommentaries, among them the anonymous 104-page *Ḥāshiya li-baʿḍ al-muḥaqqiqīn tusammā Tuḥfat al-aʿālī ʿalā sharḥ al-ʿallāma ʿAlī... al-Qārī al-musammā Ḍaw' al-maʿālī* which received two early editions.[150] In *Ḍaw' al-ma'ālī* al-Qārī compared the way of the *Khalaf* to worship *('ibāda)* and deeds *('amal)* which both end in the hereafter and that of the *Salaf* to servanthood *('ubūdiyya)* and total assent *(riḍā)* which both continue in the hereafter, hence the latter's superiority;

(ii) *al-Qawl al-sadīd fī khulf al-wa'īd* (in print), a treatise in which al-Qārī presents the proofs to his argument that the possibility that Allah Most High might relent from what He threatens is not the Consensus but is disputed by a sizeable number of doctrinal specialists who held that it was precluded; and

(iii) an extensive and oft-studied commentary on *al-Fiqh al-akbar* which received several editions. The only complete one to our knowledge is that of our teacher Wahbī Sulaymān Ghāwjī, which comprises al-Qārī's continuation, past the last line of his actual commentary, into an encyclopedic series of additional discussions on major points of doctrine. Below are the section-headings of the Ghāwjī edition of *Minaḥ al-rawḍ al-azhar*:

1. The superexcellence of the science of pure monotheism over others
2. The principle of *tawḥīd*; correct belief in accordance with it
3. What the legally-liable person must profess belief in
4. Belief in resurrection after death
5. Belief in divine foreordainment
6. Allah is One not in the sense of number but in the sense of being without partner
7. Nothing of creation resembles Allah
8. Explanation of the attributes of essence and exposition of their referents
9. The attribute of speech and the scholars' difference of opinion concerning it
10. Attributes of act and the differences between Māturīdis and Ash'arīs concerning them
11. The almighty Creator is described through the attributes of essence and acts
12. The Qur'ān is the speech of Allah and is neither created nor brought into being
13. The almighty Creator's attributes do not resemble those of creatures

150 Cairo: Maṭba'at Akhtar, 1308/1890 and Cairo: al-Maṭba'at al-Maymaniyya, 1309/1891.

14. The almighty Creator possesses *yad*, *wajh* and *nafs* 'without how'
15. Allah Most High brought created things into existence from nothing
16. Foreordainment foregone (*qaḍā'*) and yet-to-come (*qadar*) are pre-existing divine attributes
17. Allah created creatures free of unbelief and belief
18. Allah does not coerce anyone He created to disbelieve
19. All the acts of creatures are their acquisition (*kasb*) and it is Allah Who creates them
20. All the acts of creatures are part of His knowledge and out of His *qaḍā'* and *qadar*
21. Prophets are kept clear of both enormous sins and minor sins
22. Affirming the prophethood of Muḥammad—upon him blessings and peace
23. The best of people after him are the four rightly-guided caliphs in the order of their rules
24. The enormous sin does not expel a believer from the pale of belief
25. Sins harm those who commit them contrary to what some sects hold
26. Acts of true obedience are accepted while sins other than polytheism may be forgiven by Allah
27. Prophets' staggering miracles and the miraculous gifts of the friends of Allah are real
28. Concerning supernatural feats at the hands of unbelievers and corrupt people
29. Allah will be seen in the hereafter 'without how'
30. Belief is affirmation with the tongue and confirmation in the heart
31. Belief neither increases nor decreases
32. All believers are on the same level in belief but of differing ranks in deeds
33. The meaning of *islām* and its relation to *īmān*
34. The denominate of *dīn* and its being a conglomerate name for all divine laws
35. Intercession from Prophets and the righteous is real
36. The weighing of deeds on the Day of Resurrection is real
37. Paradise and hell are already created contrary to what the Mu'tazila hold

38. The returning of the soul to the dead in the grave is real
39. The pressure of the grave and its punishment are real
40. The meaning of the Creator's nearness and remoteness from creatures
41. The children of the Prophet—upon him and them blessings and peace
42. What one must believe in case anything of monotheism is unclear to one
43. The ascension to heaven is real
44. The coming out of the Arch-liar and all the endtimes details the Sunna mentions are real

SUPPLEMENTS: NECESSARY ISSUES ON POINTS OF DOCTRINE

- S1. The preferential ranks of some prophets over others
- S2. The preferential ranks of angels and the difference of opinion thereabout
- S3. The preferential ranks of the Companions after the rightly-guided caliphs
- S4. The preferential ranks of the Successors
- S5. The preferential ranks of women
- S6. The preferential ranks of the Companions' children
- S7. The friend of Allah never reaches the rank of a prophet
- S8. The pubescent is never excused from legal liability as long as he is rational
- S9. Are the texts of the Qur'ān and Sunna taken in their manifest locutions or interpreted?
- S10. The possibility of seeing the Almighty Creator in this world
- S11. Concerning the sighting of Allah in dream
- S12. The one murdered dies by virtue of his lifespan
- S13. Exposition: the unbeliever enjoys divine favors in this world
- S14. Allah is in no way compelled to observe what is fit and fittest (*al-ṣalāḥ wal-aṣlaḥ*)
- S15. Exposition: the illicit is also considered provision (*rizq*)
- S16. Allah misguides whomever He wills and guides whomever He wills
- S17. What is fittest for the servant is not incumbent on Allah
- S18. Leaving a threat unfulfilled (*khulf al-wa'īd*) is an act of generosity and is thus possible on His part

S19. The possibility of punishment for small sins even if one avoids enormous ones
S20. Supplication for the dead benefits, contrary to what the Muʿtazila hold
S21. The supplication of the unbeliever does not benefit
S22. The unbelievers among the jinn are punished in hellfire
S23. Devils can influence human beings
S24. Everything narrated about the description of paradise and hell is real
S25. The striving scholar (*mujtahid*) in ratiocinations can err and can be correct
S26. Belief neither increases nor decreases
S27. *Īmān* and *islām* are one and the same thing
S28. Reason is but a tool for acquiring knowledge, and the real compeller is Allah
S29. Allah is never described as 'having power to commit injustice'
S30. When confirmation and affirmation are there it is valid for one to say 'I am a true believer'
S31. The statement 'I am a believer *in shā' Allāh*'
S32. Being tasked beyond capacity is not permissible
S33. Is faith created or not?
S34. Faith remains with sleep, inattention, unconsciousness and death
S35. The faith of the imitator is permissible
S36. Witchcraft and the evil eye are real
S37. The non-existent is not a thing fimly established to exist outwardly
S38. Setting up an overall leader is obligatory
S39. Despairing of the mercy of Allah is unbelief
S40. The status of giving credence to a soothsayer
S41. The word *qur'ān* is a name for both the compositional structure (*naẓm*) and the meaning (*maʿnā*)
S42. To consider a (definitively established) sin licit—even a minor one—is unbelief
S43. Repentance and its preconditions

SECTION: BADR AL-RASHĪD ON STATEMENTS THAT CONSTITUTE UNBELIEF[151]

1. Statements related to the Qur'ān and prayer
2. Statements related to knowledge and scholars
3. Explicit and allusive *kufr*
4. Saying 'I am a believer, *in shā' Allāh*'
5. Denial and ignorance of the definition of *islām* and *īmān*
6. Contentment with unbelief for oneself or for another
7. Deeming the illicit licit and vice versa or wishing it were
8. Statements that contain unbelief and statements that do not
9. Statements and acts that constitute unbelief
10. Imitating non-Muslims
11. Whoever equates the licit and the illicit or denies the existence of those who practice the licit
12. Whoever wishes or loves for the illicit to be licit
13. Whoever deems obedience to Allah a heavy burden or considers it punishment
14. Whoever refuses repentance or deems fine his depravity and sins

Ḥasan Kāfī al-Aqḥiṣārī

al-Aqḥiṣārī, Kāfī Ḥasan Afandī. *Rawḍāt al-jannāt fī uṣūl al-i'tiqādāt*. In Badeen, *Sunnitische Theologie*. Pp. 31–60 (Arabic).

The pious and erudite *mujāhid* Ḥasan Kāfī Afandī al-Aqḥiṣārī (951–1024/1544–1615) was a qadi of Bosnian origin who excelled in Arabic, Turkish and Persian. He authored *Samt al-wuṣūl ilā 'ilm al-uṣūl*; *Tamḥīṣ al-Talkhīṣ*; the famous *Uṣūl al-ḥikam fī niẓām al-'ālam*; a commentary on al-Qudūrī's primer in Ḥanafī *fiqh*; another one on Ibn al-Ḥājib's *Kāfiya* in grammar; *Niẓām al-'ulamā' ilā Khātam al-anbiyā'* in which he lists his teachers; a creed entitled *Rawḍāt al-jannāt fī uṣūl al-i'tiqādāt* (The groves of paradises on the foundations of beliefs),[152] and another, a commentary on the *Ṭaḥāwiyya* entitled

151 See above, introduction, section entitled 'Māturīdī literature in the sub-genre of blasphemous expressions.'

152 al-Ziriklī, *A'lām*, 2:194.

Nūr al-yaqīn fī uṣūl al-dīn which received a thorough study in Bosnian.[153] The *Rawḍāt* is in eight sections called 'groves' covering the reality of belief, belief in Allah, belief in the angels, belief in the Books of Allah, belief in the Messengers of Allah, belief in the last day, belief in resurrection after death, and belief in the foreordained decree. It ends with a supplement reporting al-Māturīdī's description of the relation of *islām* and *īmān* to the chest (*ṣadr*), heart (*qalb*), core (*fu'ād*), secret (*sirr*), and hiddenmost (*khafī*) of a human being with respect to three particular verses: *Is he whose chest Allah expanded for surrender, so that he beholds a light from his Lord* (al-Zumar 39:22), *But Allah made faith beloved to you and embellished it in your hearts* (al-Ḥujurāt 49:7), and the Verse of Light (al-Nūr 24:35) in which he concludes, '*Tawḥīd, ma'rifa, īmān* and *islām* are neither a single thing nor different from one another.'[154]

[Pseudo-]Shaykh Zadah

[Pseudo-]Shaykh Zadah, 'Abd al-Raḥīm b. 'Alī. *Kitāb Naẓm al-farā'id wa-jam' al-fawā'id fī bayān al-masā'il al-latī waqa'a fīhā al-ikhtilāf bayna al-Māturīdiyya wal-Ashā'ira fil-'aqā'id.* Cairo: al-Maṭba'at al-Adabiyya, 1317/1899.

———. *Ibid.* In al-Jābī, Bassām 'Abd al-Wahhāb, *al-Masā'il al-khilāfiyya* (*q.v.*).

This is one of the synthesizing works on the differences between the two schools of the Māturīdīs and the Ash'arīs from the perspective of the former, listing them as forty 'singularities' (*farā'id*). Many editions attribute this work to Shaykh Zādah 'Abd al-Raḥīm b. 'Alī b. al-Mu'ayyad al-Amāsī (d. 944/1537), an impossibility since the work refers to such as al-Qārī (d. 1014/1605) and Ibrāhīm al-Laqānī (d. 1041/1632). It has been claimed that in reality it is the work of a later Ottoman scholar from Gallipoli, 'Abd al-Raḥmān b. Muḥammad b. Sulaymān al-Dāmād, known as Shaykhī Zādah (d. 1078/1667) but this is also open to question since he cites (cf. *Farīdas* 23 and 27) *Ishārāt al-marām* by al-Bayāḍī (1044–1098/1634–1687) (*q.v.*). It is noteworthy that the

153 Zuhdija Adilović, *Hasan Kafija Pruščak i njegovo djelo: svjetlost istinske spoznaje o temeljima vjere: komentar Tahavijeve poslanice iz akaida* (Zenica: Islamska pedagoška akademija, 2004).

154 al-Māturīdī as quoted by al-Aqḥiṣārī in Badeen, *Sunnitische Theologie*, pp. 59–60 (Arabic).

Farā'id include all of the twelve *masā'il* listed by Ibn Kamāl Bāshā (*q.v.*) (IKB) in his list of the differences between the two schools a century earlier and some of those listed by Abū 'Adhaba (AA) a century later. An abridged edition of the *Farā'id* with a brief critical commentary was published recently under the name of 'Īsā al-Ḥimyarī, the former head of *Awqāf* in Dubai.[155] The *Farā'id* covers the following headings:

1. Explanation of 'compulsoriness' (*wujūb*)[156] (AA 2.1.1)
2. Is compulsoriness non-existential or not?
3. Is existence additional to the essence or is it essence itself?
4. Is perdurance the same as existence?
5. Explanation of the attribute of power (*qudra*)
6. The attribute of will does not comprise love and good pleasure (*riḍā*) (IKB 4, AA 1.5)
7. The attribute[s] of hearing and sight
8. The attribute of speech (IKB 2, AA 2.4.1)
9. Exposition of internal speech (*al-kalām al-nafsī*) (IKB 2, AA 2.4)
10. Exposition of the attribute of existentiation (*takwīn*) (IKB 1)
11. The existentiated nature of things (IKB 1)
12. Is the name the very same as the thing named? (IKB 10, AA 3))
13. Exposition of foreordainment foregone (*qaḍā'*) and yet-to-come (*qadar*)
14. Concerning ambiguities (*mutashābihāt*)
15. Exposition of divinely-granted success (*tawfīq*) (IKB 7)
16. Exposition of the tasking beyong capacity (IKB 5, AA 2.5)
17. The concomitance of wisdom in all the divine acts (IKB 3)
18. Is wisdom a beginningless attribute? (IKB 3)
19. Is it permissible to attribute to Allah the retracting of a threat (*khulf al-wa'īd*)? (IKB 8)
20. Allah never does something ugly (IKB 6)

155 'Īsā al-Ḥimyarī, *al-Qalā'id fī taḥrīr al-Farā'id* (Beirut: Dār al-Aḥbāb lil-Ṭibā'a wal-Nashr wal-Tawzī', 1420/2009).

156 'The compulsory (*wājib*) is that whose absence is rationally inconceivable; the impossible is that whose certainty (*thubūt*) is rationally inconceivable, and the possible (*jā'iz*) is that whose certainty or absence is rationally possible.' 'Abd Allāh 'Arwānī, *Uṣūl al-'aqā'id* ([Damascus:] Maktabat al-Ghazālī, [1975?]), p. 20 n.

21. Is the pardon of unbelief possible? (IKB 8)
22. Ratiocinative beauty and ugliness (IKB 6)
23. Is belief in Allah made compulsory by reason?
24. The reality/literal meaning of belief (*īmān*)
25. Does belief increase and decrease or not?
26. Is the imitator's belief valid or not? (AA 1.6)
27. Does transmissive evidence constitute definitive knowledge?
28. Is belief created or not?[157] (AA 4)
29. Are *īmān* and *islām* one and the same or not?
30. Are the last words and acts what is decisive in *īmān* or not?
31. Can [foreordained] bliss and wretchedness be interchanged or not? (IKB 7, 9, AA 1.2)
32. *Istithnā'* (saying *in shā Allāh*) with regard to one's *īmān* (AA 1.1)
33. All messengers and prophets are still messengers and prophets literally (AA 1.4)
34. Is maleness a precondition of prophethood? (IKB 11)
35. Is the general population of pious human beings better than angels or not?
36. Can real power apply to opposites or not?
37. Does the servant's power have any kind of effectiveness or not? (IKB 12, AA 1.7)
38. Is 'occasioning' (*īqā'*) a state, or is it purely non-existent?[158]
39. Do good deeds count again after an apostate's repentance or not?
40. Will the unbelievers be punished for neglecting categorical obligations or not?

al-Shurunbulālī

al-Shurunbulālī, Abū al-Ikhlāṣ Ḥasan b. 'Ammār. *Marāqī al-sa'ādāt fī 'ilmāy al-tawḥīd wal-'ibādāt*. Ed. Muḥ. Riyāḍ al-Māliḥ. Preface by Muḥammad Abū al-Yusr 'Ābidīn. Beirut: Dār al-Kitāb al-Lubnānī, [1973].

157 See note 109 on this issue.

158 *Īqā'* is related to the question of 'partial will' and was discussed by al-Kawtharī in his work in rebuttal of Shaykh al-Islām Muṣṭafā Ṣabrī Bāshā, *al-Istibṣār* (*q.v.*).

This brief manual is one of more than seventy that were authored by the Egyptian Ḥanafī jurist of al-Azhar Abū al-Ikhlāṣ Ḥasan b. ʿAmmār al-Shurunbulālī al-Wafāʾī (994–1069/1586–1659) on various topics.[159] Its second part bears on juristic matters while its first part bears on doctrine. The latter part's subheadings are:

1. Doctrinal conviction
2. The questioning in the grave after the soul is brought back
3. The gathering of the bodies and the description of the Bridge
4. The foundation of the foreordained Decree (*qadar*)
5. Belief in the preserved Tablet
6. The Ascent to heaven is true as is the Night Journey
7. No *walī* may be preferred over any Prophet
8. Holding fast to the congregation and obeying those in charge
9. The divine Names are ordained (*tawqīfiyya*)
10. The coming out of Dajjāl, Yaʾjūj and Maʾjūj, the Beast of the earth and the descent of ʿĪsā

al-Bayāḍī

al-Bayāḍī, Kamāl al-Dīn Aḥmad. *Ishārāt al-marām min ʿibārāt al-Imām*. Ed. Yūsuf ʿAbd al-Razzāq al-Mashhadī al-Shāfiʿī. Cairo: Muṣṭafā Bābī al-Ḥalabī, 1368/1949. Foreword by Muḥammad Zāhid al-Kawtharī. Rept. Karachi: Zam Zam Publishers, 1425/2004.

———. *Ishārāt al-marām min ʿibārāt al-imām Abī Ḥanīfata al-Nuʿmān*. Ed. Aḥmad Farīd al-Mazyadī. Beirut: Dār al-Kutub al-ʿIlmiyya, 1428/2007.

Kamāl al-Dīn Aḥmad b. al-Ḥasan b. Sinān al-Dīn Yūsuf al-Busnawī al-Rūmī al-Bayāḍī (1044–1098/1634–1687), known as Bayāḍī Zādah ('Bayāḍī's son,' as his father was qadi of Mecca), was a Hanafi jurist and doctrinal expert of Bosnian origin. Born in Istanbul, he was qadi of Aleppo in 1077 then Bursa (in Marmara province, northwestern Turkey), then Mecca in 1083 (where,

159 It was translated as *Marāqī al-saʿādāt, Ascent to Felicity: A Manual on Islamic Creed and Ḥanafī Jurisprudence*. Trans. Faraz A. Khan. London and Santa Barbara: White Thread Press, 2010.

in his youth, he had attended the gatherings of Shams al-Dīn al-Bābilī who gave him *ijāza*), then Istanbul in 1086 after a brief stay in Damascus (where al-Muḥibbī met him, thereafter describing him as 'a mountain of knowledge'), and finally Rumelia (present-day Bulgaria). All his moves to new posts were as a result of dismissal (*'azl)* from previous ones. In his last post, after a verdict of guilt was reached against a woman in a case of *zinā* in which he gave a sentence of lapidation (*rajm*) which was carried out—an unprecedented case other than in the early period of Islam—he was once again dismissed and remained in his home in Istanbul until his death. Among his teachers was the mufti of Jerusalem ʿAbd al-Raḥīm b. Abī al-Luṭf. During his qadiship of Aleppo he and its mufti, Muḥammad b. Ḥasan al-Kawākibī, held learned scholarly debates that became famous. He authored a commentary on the *Waṣāyā*, *Sawāniḥ al-ʿulūm fī sittati funūn* also known as *Sawāniḥ al-muṭāraḥāt wa-lawā'iḥ al-mudhākarāt fil-ʿulūm*, *al-Fiqh al-absaṭ*, and *Ishārāt al-marām min ʿibārāt al-Imām*, a commentary on Abū Ḥanīfa's *al-Fiqh al-akbar* containing a meticulous summary of Maturidi doctrine.[160] This work contains some of the sharpest refutations of Sunna-contrariant and Islam-contrariant positions that are just as relevant today as they were 350 years ago and that still await adequate indexing (such as by sect and heresy) and study beyond al-Kawtharī's detailed table of contents. Al-Bayāḍī also provides one of the most precise lists of fifty doctrinal and terminological differences between Māturīdīs and Ashʿarīs, 'each of which to be detailed in its proper place with its sourcing and its evidence as inferred from the discourse of the Imam in his books through one of several ways for such inference including wording, allusion, indicativeness, presupposition, and counter-implication' (يُفَصَّل إن شاء الله تعالى في محلّه كلٌّ منها بنقله ودليله المستفاد من كلام الإمام في كتبه بأحد وجوه الاستفادة من العبارة والإشارة والدلالة والاقتضاء ومن مفهوم المخالفة)[161] such as, for example, the position that '[divine] will is not necessarily concomitant with [divine] good pleasure or love,' contrary to some of the Ashʿarīs such as al-Āmidī. He shows impressive command of Ashʿarī references (including what he calls *al-Tabṣirat al-Baghdādiyya*, by which he means ʿAbd al-Qāhir al-Baghdādī's *Uṣūl*

160 See Muḥammad Amīn al-Muḥibbī, *Khulāṣat al-athar fī aʿyān al-qarn al-ḥādī ʿashar*, ed. Muḥammad Ḥasan Ismāʿī, 4 vols. (Beirut: Dār al-Kutub al-ʿIlmiyya, 1427/2006) 1:210–211 no. 140.

161 *Ishārāt*, p. 56.

al-dīn)[162] and often cites al-Subkī's *Nūniyya*, which he calls *Sharḥ al-Subkī ʿalā ʿaqīdat Abī Manṣūr*. He lists the 50 Māturīdī majority positions that differ with majority Ashʿarī positions—in his estimation—as follows:[163]

1. Existence (*wujūd*) and compulsoriness (*wujūb*) are the essence itself and this is al-Ashʿarī's choice also
2. The name is the same as the named when the referent (*madlūl*) is meant
3. The name is not sub-divided like attributes to self (*ʿayn*) or other or neither
4. The Maker is known truly and in reality
5. The attributes of act refer back to an essential attribute which is existentiation (*al-takwīn*)
6. Existentiation is not one and the same with the existentiated (*al-mukawwan*)
7. Perdurance (*al-baqāʾ*) is permanent existence and not an additional attribute
8. Hearing—without organ—is an attribute other than knowledge
9. Sight—without organ—is an attribute other than knowledge
10. The perception of smell, taste and touch are not an attribute other than knowledge with regard to Him
11. The apprehension of something with one of the senses is not knowledge of it but the medium thereof
12. Reason is not knowledge of some of the necessary propositions

13–22. Reason makes it compulsory to know the existence of Allah, His oneness, His knowledge, His power, His speech, His will, the originated nature of the world, the probative force of the staggering miracle towards the truthfulness of the messenger, confirmation thereof, and the fact that it is prohibited to disbelieve in him or belie him in his mission and the reach of his call

23. Beauty and ugliness are avenues to know the wisdom of the Maker, not rational imperatives
24. Reward by paradise and punishment by hellfire are legal rationales

162 al-Kawtharī, *ʿAqīdat al-tanzīh*, in *Maqālāt al-Kawtharī*, ed. (Cairo: al-Maktabat al-Tawfīqiyya, n.d.), pp. 312–316.
163 *Ishārāt*, pp. 53–56.

25. What is unjustifiable to annul on grounds of beauty or ugliness is unabrogable[164]
26. Beauty and ugliness are the tokens (*madlūl)* of command and prohibition
27. Beauty is reason's expectation of an act's good consequence while ugliness is the reverse
28. Everything that comes from Allah is beautiful by consensus
29. It is rationally inconceivable that Allah be described as doing injustice or what is unsuitable/not right; hence reason precludes that He punish the righteous or pardon unbelief
30. Tasking beyond capacity is impermissible, as chosen by the two Isfarāyīnīs (Abū Isḥāq and Abū Ḥāmid)
31. The acts of Allah are causated (*mu'allala*) by the welfare of servants and wisdom, without compulsion as to what is fittest
32. Ambiguities are not to be interpreted figuratively but their knowledge is resigned to Allah
33. Internal speech is not heard, but rather its indicators, as in Abū Mu'īn al-Nasafī's *Tabṣira*
34. Internal speech is what Allah mentioned in pre-existence without voice nor letter
35. Dream vision is a type of witnessing for the spirit
36. Mass-transmitted evidence to a single meaning through multiple paths conveys certitude
37. Love is in the sense of praise, not will, and pertains only to righteousness
38. Ability is suitable for contraries
39. The servant's choice (*ikhtiyār*) is described as effective but without any power of origination
40. Belief neither increases nor decreases, in the sense of categorical confirmation
41. The belief of those dwelling in the wild is deemed imitation of those who instruct them
42. Saying *in shā' Allāh* when professing belief conveys doubt about one's faith on the spot

164 Such as the necessity of belief and the prohibition of unbelief.

43. The wretched at present can be blissful in the future and vice versa, and the unbeliever enjoys divine favor in the world
44. The unbeliever is not tasked with the obligatory types of worship on the spot and the despairer's repentance is accepted
45. Prophets are immune against wilful small sins and against major sins in absolute terms[165]
46. Maleness is a precondition of prophethood
47. The *mujtahid* can err and can be right, and truth is one in the divine presence
48. The overall leadership of someone who is not the best candidate is valid
49. Death is a creational and existential matter, not merely through the termination of endurance
50. Accidents are not restored (*al-aʿrāḍ lā tuʿād*) [i.e. resurrected] [*Bar* 64][166]

Al-Bayāḍī also turns the arguments of anthropomorphists on their head, as shown by his commentary on a passage of the *Fiqh al-absaṭ* that states: 'Whoever says, "He is on the Throne and I do not know whether the Throne is in the heaven or on earth" is a disbeliever.' Al-Bayāḍī comments: 'This is because he implies that the Creator has a direction and a boundary, and anything that possesses direction and boundary is necessarily created. So this statement explicitly attributes imperfection to Allah. The believer in [divine] corporeality and direction is someone who denies the existence of anything other than objects that can be pointed to with the senses. They deny the essence of the Deity Who is transcendent beyond that. This makes them positively guilty of disbelief.' He also refutes their suggestion that '*kalām* is a newfangled innovation because the Companions did not get involved in it' by stating that in their time they mostly used political authority to quell heresies rather than arguments and that, even so, there are several examples of *kalām*-like arguments

165 '*Ahl al-Sunna wal-Jamāʿa* said that Yūsuf's brothers became prophets only after they had committed their enormities.' al-Qārī, *Sharḥ al-Fiqh al-akbar*, Nafā'is ed., p. 111.

166 Comment by Shaykh Samer al-Nass: 'This is neither the position of the Ashʿarīs nor that of the Māturīdīs, but rather the view of some of the Shaykhs, and it requires evidence. It is more appropriate for us to say that accidents are in fact returned.' (Private communication, 16 December 2020)

and debates related from them, both in the time of the Prophet and thereafter.[167] He also addresses quandaries of logic, such as the 'liar paradox' or inherently contradictory statement dubbed 'the barren stump' (*al-jadhr al-aṣamm*) that asserts, 'everything I say is false.'[168]

167 *Ishārāt*, pp. 33–34.
168 This statement, if a lie, is truthful, and if truthful, is a lie. Cf. *Ishārāt*, p. 81.

Twelfth/Eighteenth Century

al-Isbīrī Qādīzāde

Isbīrī Qādīzāde *Mumayyizāt madhhab al-Māturīdiyya ʻan al-madhāhib al-ghayriyya.* In Badeen, *Sunnitische Theologie.* Pp. 61–79 (Arabic).

———. 'Traité sur le libre arbitre: Différences entre les Doctrine des Matoridites et celles des autre sectes de l'Islam, par Qâdy Zâdeh.' In Anthonin de Vlieger. *Kitâb al-qadr: Matériaux pour servir à l'étude de la doctrine de la prédestination dans la théologie musulmane.* Leyde: E.J. Brill, 1903. Pp. 170–187 (in French).

Muḥammad al-Isbīrī Qādī Zādah (fl. 1130/1718) is known only for this small treatise in which he shows his mastery of Ḥanafī and other sources in the science of *kalām* with specific emphasis on the Māturīdī understanding of the relationship of divine foreknowledge with human free will and accountability.

Abū al-Ḥasan al-Sindī

Abu al-Hasan al-Sindī, Muḥammad b. ʻAbd al-Hādī. *al-Ifāḍat al-Madaniyya fīl-irādat al-juz'iyya.* Ed. ʻAlī b. ʻAbduh ʻAlī al-Almaʻī. Riyadh: Maktabat al-Rushd, 1428/2007.

Abū al-Ḥasan Nūr al-Dīn Muḥammad b. ʻAbd al-Hādī al-Sindī (d. 1138/1727) studied under Ibrāhīm al-Kūrānī and Muḥammad al-Barzanjī (author of *Anhār al-salsabīl,* a commentary on Bayḍāwī's *Anwār al-tanzīl)* in Tustar among others. He took up residence in Medina where he taught until his death, authoring mostly hadith commentaries such as on al-Nasā'ī, Abū Dāwūd, Aḥmad's *Musnad* and al-Nawawī's *Adhkār,* but also a commentary on Bayḍāwī's *Tafsīr* and on Ibn al-Qāsim's commentary on *Jamʿ al-jawāmiʿ* on legal theory. Among his students were Muḥammad Ḥayāt al-Sindī and others. He wrote this treatise on the issue of human free will and accountability within the larger purview of the foreordained divine decree (*qaḍāʾ* and *qadar*) and the divine creation of all the acts of servants according to the tenets of Sunni doctrine between the two extremes of determinism (*jabr*), represented by the Jabriyya and Jahmiyya, and libertarianism (*qadar*) represented by the Muʿtazila and Qadariyya. The work comprises an extensive discussion of the famous debate related between Ādam and Mūsā on free will. As Haida notes in his thesis on Ashʿarī-Māturīdī debates in Ottoman scholarship, "the overriding concern in Sindī's *Ifaḍa* is the conciliation of theological conflict, particularly between Ashʿarism and Salafī-Ḥanbalī doctrines, and to a lesser extent between Ashʿarism and Māturīdism."[169] It must be pointed out that the above Wahhābī edition actually attempts to distort al-Sindī's Māturīdī thought by misrepresenting the position of Ashʿarīs and Māturīdīs as separate from the position of *Ahl al-Sunna wal-Jamāʿa* in his text through the interpolation of headings to that effect, whereas Sindī patently considered the Ashʿarī and Māturīdī positions as forming the core subset and substance of Sunni creed, not a separate section.

al-Nābulusī

al-Nābulusī, ʿAbd al-Ghanī b. Ismāʿīl. *al-Ḥadīqat al-nadiyya sharḥ al-Ṭarīqat al-Muḥammadiyya*. 2 vols. Cairo: s.n., 1276/1860.

———. *al-Kawkab al-sārī fī ḥaqīqat al-juzʾ al-ikhtiyārī*. Ed. Muḥammad Rāghib al-Ṭabbākh. Aleppo: al-Maṭbaʿa al-ʿIlmiyya, 1349/1931. p. 25

———. *al-Qawl al-sadīd fī jawāz khulf al-waʿīd wal-radd ʿalā al-jāhil al-Rūmī al-ʿanīd*. Maktabat al-Ḥaram al-Makkī. MS 3820. In Haida, *Debates*, p. 194.

———. *Taḥqīq al-intiṣār fī ittifāq al-Ashʿarī wal-Māturīdī ʿalā khalq al-ikhtiyār*. In Badeen, *Sunnitische Theologie*. Pp. 81–132 (Arabic).

169 Haida, *Debates*, pp. 192–193.

———. *Taḥrīk silsilat al-widād fī masʾalat khalq afʿāl al-ʿibād*. In *Letters of a Sufi Scholar: The Correspondence of ʿAbd al-Ghanī al-Nābulusī (1641–1731)*. [= *Wasāʾil al-taḥqīq wa-rasāʾil al-tawfīq*.] Ed. Samer Akkach. Leiden: Brill, 2010. Pp. 55–74 (Arabic).

———. *Ibid.* In *Wasāʾil al-taḥqīq wa-rasāʾil al-tawfīq*. Ed. Bakrī ʿAlāʾ al-Dīn. Damascus: Dār Nīnawā lil-Dirāsāt wal-Nashr wal-Tawzīʿ, 2010.

———. *al-Wujūd al-ḥaqq*. Ed. Bakrī ʿAlāʾ al-Dīn. Damascus: Institut Français d'Études Arabes de Damas (IFEAD), 1995.

The major Damascene Ḥanafī jurist and Qādirī-Naqshbandī Sufi ʿAbd al-Ghanī b. Ismāʿīl b. ʿAbd al-Ghanī al-Nābulusī (1050–1143/1640–1731), author of several hundred works, is famous for his defense of the licitness of smoking, Sufi dancing and using musical instruments as well as the defense of Ibn ʿArabī with regard to the unity of being and the status of Firʿawn as a believer. He authored several texts on *kalām* which have not yet received analysis save for *al-Wujūd al-ḥaqq* which is more of a Sufi treatise and his most important defense of Ibn ʿArabī and the unity of being, entirely based on al-Ashʿarī's doctrine that 'divine existence is the divine Essence itself' (*al-wujūd ʿayn al-dhāt*). The *Wasāʾil al-taḥqīq* comprise 72 scholarly letters described by Samer Akkash in his edition (pp. 55–74), of which one is of particular interest with regard to the present bibliography, namely Letter Four on free will and the creation of acts, entitled *Taḥrīk silsilat al-widād fī masʾalat khalq afʿāl al-ʿibād* (Activating the links of love with regard to the issue of the creation of the acts of God's slaves). In this work al-Nābulusī rebuts the positions promulgated by the major Kurdish Ashʿarī-Shāfiʿī master Ibrāhīm al-Kūrānī (d. 1101/1690), author of more than a hundred works, in his treatise *Maslak al-sadād fī masʾalat khalq afʿāl al-ʿibād* (The rightful course on the issue of the createdness of the acts of man).[170] Other *kalām* works in which al-Nābulusī tends to take a more Ashʿarī position (in line with his sufism) include *al-Ḥadīqat al-nadiyya*, a commentary on a work by the Ottoman scholar al-Birkawī (Mehmet Efendi Birgivî); a shorter work entitled *al-Kawkab al-sārī fī ḥaqīqat al-juzʾ al-ikhtiyārī* (The moving star on the reality of the decisional particular), "in which he

170 On Kūrānī see Haida, *Debates*, pp. 191–192. The latter does not appear aware of al-Nābulusī's rebuttal.

defines the problem, and confines divergent opinions to three sects: the Literalists, Ashʿarīs and Māturīdīs. Nābulusī sufficiently dwells on the latter doctrine in order to explain it. In the end, he determines—in line with his Ṣūfī interpretation of Ashʿarism, and contrary to the Māturīdīs—that 'as dictated in the majority of creeds, nothing ultimately affects anything; and good deeds have no influence on [bringing about] God's contentment [with the righteous];'"[171] *al-Qawl al-sadīd fī jawāz khulf al-waʿīd wal-radd ʿalā al-jāhil al-Rūmī al-ʿanīd* (The sound argument on the possibility of breach of the threat of punishment, and the rebuttal of the stubborn and ignorant Anatolian) in which he refuted an anonymous tract declaring upholders of that view (by which Atharīs and Ashʿarīs are meant) unbelievers; and the *Taḥqīq al-intiṣār fī ittifāq al-Ashʿarī wal-Māturīdī ʿalā khalq al-ikhtiyār* (Achieving victory: on the agreement between Ashʿarī and Māturīdī that human choice is created) in which he rebuts what he calls Bayāḍī's 'reviling' (*tashnīʿ*) of al-Ashʿari's doctrine and asserts that disputation between the two schools is a needless latecomer into Sunnī theology because the Māturīdīs are one and the same with Ashʿarīs 'if one reads the classical texts of theology (*kutub al-mutaqaddimīn fī ʿilm al-kalām*).'[172]

al-Khādimī

al-Khādimī, Abū Saʿīd. *Barīqa Maḥmūdiyya fī sharḥ Ṭarīqa Muḥammadiyya wa-sharīʿa Nabawiyya fī sīrat Aḥmadiyya.* With Rajab b. Aḥmad's commentary on al-Birkawī's *Ṭarīqa Muḥammadiyya.* Ed. Aḥmad Rifʿat b. ʿUthmān Ḥilmī. 2 vols. Istanbul: Maṭbaʿat Sharikat Ṣaḥāfiyya, 1318/1900.

———. *Ibid.* 4 vols. Cairo: Muṣṭafā Bābī al-Ḥalabī 1348/1929.

Born in the village of Khādim near Konya (hence his moniker of Qūnawī as well), Abū Saʿīd Muḥammad b. Muṣṭafā b. ʿUthmān al-Khādimī (1113–1176/1701–1763) studied under Aḥmad b. Muḥammad al-Qāz Ābādī and narrates from his father, from Muḥammad b. Aḥmad al-Ṭarasūsī, from

171 al-Nābulusī, *al-Kawkab al-sārī,* in Haida, *Debates,* pp. 193–194.

172 Haida, *Debates,* p. 195; see Badeen, *Sunnitische Theologie,* pp. 110–114 and Rudolph (English), pp. 10–11.

Muḥammad b. ʿAlī al-Kāmilī, from Khayr al-Dīn al-Ramlī, from Aḥmad b. Muḥammad Amīn al-Dīn b. ʿAbd al-ʿĀl, from his father, from Shaykh al-Islām Zakariyyā al-Anṣārī.[173] Al-Khādimī taught Quranic commentary at Hagia Sophia in Istanbul and authored several works, among them *Majāmiʿ al-ḥaqā'iq wa-jawāmiʿ al-rawā'iq wal-fawā'id* on legal theory and its commentary *Manāfiʿ al-daqā'iq*, both of which received editions in 2016 and 1308/1890 respectively; marginalia on Mullā Khusraw's *Durar al-ḥukkām fī shaḥ ghurar al-aḥkām* in Hanafi law; a commentary on al-Ghazālī's *Ayyuhā al-walad*; a commentary on Sūrat al-Fātiḥā; *ʿArā'is al-nafā'is* in logic; and a commentary on Birkawī's (929–981/1523–1573) *Ṭarīqa al-muḥammadiyya* entitled *Barīqa maḥmūdiyya* which he finished in 1168/1755. In the *Barīqa maḥmūdiyya* al-Khādimī often points out the congruence of the positions of the Muʿtazilīs with those of the philosophers as already discussed in the introduction. Al-Khādimī also integrates and expands on al-Bayāḍī's (1044–1098/1634–1687) recension of the majority differences between Māturīdīs and Ashʿarīs, ending up with a total of *73 purported points of divergence* (Istanbul ed. 1:314–316) as follows:

1. Knowledge of Allah is a rational imperative, not a legal one[174]
2. Even if Allah did not send a messenger it would be compulsory for people to know him
3. The Maker is truly known with His Attributes
4. Existence and necessity are the Essence itself upon verification
5. The beauty or ugliness of certain matters is perceived rationally
6. All attributes of acts go back to the essential attribute of existentiation (*takwīn*)
7. Every essential or active Attribute is necessarily Existent, not merely possible
8. The attributes of act such as Creator, Originator and Sustainer go back to existentiation (*takwīn*)
9. Existentiation is other than the existentiated
10. Perduring (*al-baqā'*) is not an additional attribute

173 al-Kawtharī, *al-Taḥrīr al-wajīz*, p. 38, see also p. 20.
174 Al-Qārī explicitly holds the opposite view.

11. Hearing and sight are two attributes distinct from knowledge of what is heard and seen
12. The perception of what is smelled, tasted and touched is not other than knowledge for Allah
13. The divine acts have causation of wisdom and welfare
14. Divine will does not presuppose good pleasure nor love
15. Allah is 'speaker' (*mutakallim*) from pre-existence, not 'addressing' (*mukallim*) from pre-existence
16. Some parts of the Qur'an are greater (*aʿẓam*) than other parts
17. The pre-existent divine address does not pertain to non-existents
18. The existence of things takes place with existentiation (*ījād*), not with the address 'Be' (*kun*); for Pazdawī it takes place through both together
19. Belief neither increases nor decreases, as agreed upon by Imām al-Ḥaramayn
20. Saying *in shā Allāh* in the profession of faith is impermissible whether for present or future
21. The currently wretched might be blissful in the future and vice versa
22. While sight can pertain to every created thing, hearing cannot
23. Mūsā—upon him and our Prophet blessings and peace—did not hear internal speech but speech made of letters and sounds[175]
24. Tasking beyond capacity is impermissible
25. The punishing of the righteous and rewarding of the unbeliever is rationally impermissible, as are putting the believer in hellfire and the unbeliever in paradise eternally, all of which is unjust
26. Allah cannot be seen in dream even if most Hanafis assert He can
27. Dream vision is not false imagination but a type of actual witnessing by the spirit
28. Ability by which a servant acts in obedience is the same as that by which he disobeys, so the selfsame power is suitable for contrary acts
29. A single knowledge can pertain to two or more objects of knowledge
30. Prophets remain prophets in actuality even after their death
31. The Prophet may act on legal rulings on the basis of revelation or opinion or striving

175 Cf. al-Qārī, *Sharḥ al-Fiqh al-akbar*, Nafā'is ed., p. 76: 'There is no disagreement among *Ahl al-Sunna* over the originated nature of verbal speech (*ḥudūth al-kalām al-lafẓī*).'

32. The imitator's belief is valid even though he is sinning by not seeking to establish proof
33. In proof-based belief it is not necessary to know the rational proof; hadith is sufficient
34. The name is no different than the named and they are one and the same
35. Wisdom is what bodes a good ending while foolishness is the opposite
36. The servant's act is called acquisition (*kasb*), not creation—although this is debatable
37. The act of Allah is called creation, not acquisition
38. The name of 'act' (*al-fiʿl*) includes both of the above without literalness or figurativeness in relation to Allah's creation and the servant's acquisition respectively
39. Whatever occurs without instrument is creation otherwise it is acquisition
40. Perception of something through one of the senses is not knowledge of it but the instrument
41. Maleness is a precondition of Prophethood
42. Whatever pain or fracture follows striking and breaking are not by the servant's act as he cannot acquire what is not within the purview of his power
43. Sound investigation is through both acquisition and creation and not only through the latter
44. The servant's power is effective in his act and it is wrong to say it is ineffective
45. Causes and means such as natural faculties have real effectiveness, not only customary
46. A single object of power (*maqdūr*) may be shared by the power of two potents (*qādirayn*), as stated by some Ashʿarīs
47. Spirits are not a body nor corporeal but matters devoid of materiality
48. Some rulings can be known before prophethood either spontaneously or through thought
49. His attributes remain with a perduring that is the selfsame as the attribute
50. Identicalness can only be by sharing in all characteristics

51. Identicalness is a genus comprising types of resemblance and sameness
52. Ambiguities are interpreted without qualifiers and their details are resigned to Allah
53. The status of ambiguities is that they can never be known in this world
54. The foreordained decree past and future is other than the pre-existent will
55. They stipulated that to say the Prophet knows the unseen is unbelief
56. Not every scholarly striver is right, and truth is one
57. Verbal evidence can convey certitude if mass-transmitted in the absence of objection
58. Divine love is in the sense of high praise, not will, and pertains to obedience exclusively
59. The unbeliever is the recipient of blessings in the world
60. The unbeliever is not tasked with the performance of acts of worship
61. Prophets are immune from the wilful commission of small sins and from major ones in absolute terms
62. The overall leadership of someone who is not the best candidate is valid
63. Death is the corruption of the animal frame, not the non-existence of life, or an accident Allah creates in it
64. Human bodily accidents are not returned i.e. resuscitated [see *Ish* 50]
65. The repentance of the despairer (*tawbat al-ya's*) is accepted
66. What is unjustifiable to annul on grounds of beauty or ugliness is unabrogable[176]
67. Beauty and ugliness are the tokens (*madlūl*) of command and prohibition for whatever can be grasped rationally—some saying in absolute terms—of the wisdom of Allah
68. Affirmation (*iqrār*) is part of belief even, as some said, as a precondition
69. Someone living on an inaccessible mountain whom *daʿwa* did not reach must still believe in the Maker and His attributes insofar as he can infer Him from evidence
70. Reason plays a role in the apprehension of some of the legalities although not in rulings

176 Such as the necessity of belief and the prohibition of unbelief.

71. They affirmed the [indicativeness of] the participial state (*ḥāl)* as discussed in *al-Tawḍīḥ*.[177]
72. The sending forth of messengers is an obligation in the sense of being commensurate with divine wisdom
73. Ability (*istiṭāʿa*) is [concurrent] with the act

Abū ʿAdhaba

Abū ʿAdhaba, al-Ḥasan b. ʿAbd al-Muḥsin. *al-Rawḍat al-bahiyya fī-mā bayna al-Ashāʿira wal-Māturīdiyya*. Hyderabad: Dāʾirat al-Maʿārif al-ʿUthmāniyya, 1322/ 1904.

———. *Ibid.* In al-Jābī, Bassām ʿAbd al-Wahhāb, *al-Masāʾil al-khilāfiyya* (*q.v.*).

———. *Ibid.* In Badeen, *Sunnitische Theologie*. Pp. 133–209 (Arabic).

Little is known about the Ashʿarī master Nūr al-Dīn Ḥasan b. ʿAbd al-Muḥsin, known as Abū al-Ṣalāḥ Zādah and Abū ʿAdhaba (fl. 1172/1758), other than what Ismāʿīl Bāshā and al-Ziriklī gathered up in *Hadiyyat al-ʿārifīn* and *al-Aʿlām* respectively, as summarized by al-Jābī in his recent edition of *al-Rawḍat al-bahiyya*. Abū ʿAdhaba authored *Bahjat Ahl al-Sunna ʿalā ʿaqīdat Ibn al-Shiḥna*; *Sharḥ al-manẓūmat al-bāʾiyya*; *al-Maṭāliʿ al-saʿīda fī sharḥ al-qaṣīdat al-Sanūsiyya*, a commentary on the *ʿAqāʾid* of Muḥammad b. Yūsuf al-Sanūsī (832–895/1428–1490); *Ghāyat al-amālī*, a commentary on a versified doctrinal text by Qāsim al-Qayrawānī al-Ḥaḍramī entitled *Luʾluʾat al-laʾālī*; marginalia on Ibn Ghars's *Sharḥ al-ʿAqāʾid al-Nasafiyya*; and *Natāʾij afkār al-thiqāt fīmā lil-ṣifāt min al-taʿalluqāt* (ed. Saʿīd Fawda at Dār al-Dhakhāʾir, Beirut, 1435/2014). The *Rawḍa* is a reworking of Nūr al-Dīn al-Shīrāzī's commentary on al-Subkī's *Nūniyya* (*q.v.*), a poem on the differences between Ashʿarīs and Māturīdīs which Abū ʿAdhaba counted as thirteen, a number close to Ibn Kamāl Bāsha's (IKB) listing of twelve two centuries prior. The headings of the *Rawḍa* are as follows:

177 See seven notes down.

Exordium

Introduction on the two imams and the differences between Ashʿarīs and Māturīdīs

1. Part One: Issues with terminological differences

    1.1 Exceptionality in *īmān* (adding *in shā Allāh* to the declaration that one is a believer)
    1.2 Can the blissful become wretched and vice versa? (IKB 7, 8)
    1.3 Is the unbeliever a beneficiary of divine favor (*niʿma*) and is the illicit provision (*rizq*)?
    1.4 Does the messengership status of prophets remain after their death?
        1.4.1 Our Prophet is alive in his grave in literal terms (*ḥaqīqatan*)
    1.5 Will is a concomitant of good pleasure but not vice versa
    1.6 Exposition of the imitator's belief and the fact that deeds are not an integral to belief
    1.7 The issue of acquisition (*kasb*) (IKB 12)

2. Part Two: Issues with significant differences

    2.1 The rationally-conceivable possibility of the punishment of obedient servants (IKB 9)
        2.1.1 *Ahl al-Sunna* said: nothing is compulsory for Allah
    2.2 Is knowledge of Allah made obligatory by the sacred law or by reason?
    2.3 Are the [divine] attributes of act without beginning or are they originated?
    2.4 Is it possible for the speech of Allah subsisting in Himself to be heard or not? (IKB 2)
        2.4.1 On the beginningless internal speech (*al-kalām al-nafsī al-qadīm*)
    2.5 On the possibility of tasking servants beyond their capacity (IKB 5)
    2.6 Exposition of the immunity (*ʿiṣma*) of prophets from sins: enormities and small sins

3. Conclusion on the name and the named

4. Is *īmān* created or uncreated?[178]

178 See note 109 on this issue.

THIRTEENTH/NINETEENTH CENTURY

Khālid al-Baghdādī

Khālid al-Baghdādī. *Ḥāshiya ʿalā al-Sayālkūtī ʿalā al-Khayyālī*. With *Risāla fī taḥqīq al-irādat al-juzʾiyya*. Istanbul: s.n., 1259/1843.

———. *Risāla fī taḥqīq masʾalat al-irādat al-juzʾiyya al-mawsūma bil-al-ʿIqd al-jawharī fil-farq bayna kasbay al-Māturīdī wal-Ashʿarī*. In Nizār Abāẓa, *al-Shaykh Khālid al-Naqshbandī al-ʿālim al-mujaddid: ḥayātuh wa-ahamm muʾallafātuh*. Beirut: Dār al-Fikr al-Muʿāṣir; Damascus: Dār al-Fikr, 1994. Rept. 1419/1998. Pp. 32–44.

———. *Risāla fī taḥqīq wa-bayān masʾalat al-irādat al-juzʾiyya wal-musammāt al-ʿIqd al-jawharī fī bayān al-farq bayna kasbay al-Māturīdī wal-Ashʿarī*. In Muḥammad Sharīf al-Ṣawwāf. *Mawlānā al-Shaykh Khālid al-Naqshbandī: ḥayātuh, manhajuh, āthāruh*. Damascus: Bayt al-Ḥikma, 1420/2000. Pp. 133–152.

Abū al-Bahāʾ Ḍiyāʾ al-Dīn Khālid b. Aḥmad b. Ḥusayn al-Kurdī al-ʿUthmānī al-Shahrazūrī al-Shāfiʿī al-Naqshbandī (1193–1242/1779–1827) was chronicled by Muḥammad Sulaymān al-Baghdādī in *al-Ḥadīqat al-nadiyya fil-ṭarīqat al-Naqshbandiyya*, ʿUthmān b. Sanad al-Najdī in *Aṣfā al-mawārid min silsāl aḥwāl al-imām Khālid*, and Muḥammad Jamīl al-Shaṭṭī in *Rawḍ al-bashar fī aʿyān Dimashq fil-qarn al-thālith ʿashar*, on which this entry is largely based. Despite a brief life-span of 49 years Mawlānā Khālid reached mastery in many of the Islamic sciences including hadith, *fiqh*, *kalām*, *uṣūl*, *taṣawwuf*, logic, lexicography, grammar, morphology, prosody, rhetoric, debate, sapience (*ḥikma*), arithmetic (*ḥisāb*) and engineering, astrolabe and astronomy. Among his teachers in Sulaymāniyya were the brothers ʿAbd al-Karīm and ʿAbd al-Raḥīm al-Barzanjī, Mullā Ṣāliḥ, Ibrāhīm al-Bayārī, and ʿAbd Allāh al-Khirbātī. In Kuway he studied under ʿAbd al-Raḥīm al-Zayādī, and he took astronomy and its sciences from Muḥammad Qasīm al-Sanandajī in Sanandaj, after which he succeeded his teacher ʿAbd al-Karīm al-Barzanjī as headmaster in the Sulaymaniyya. On the way to and after pilgrimage in 1220/1805 he visited Damascus where he took *ijāzāt* from Muḥammad al-Kuzbarī and his student Muṣṭafā al-Kurdī. After returning home to Iraq his search for a spiritual guide took him to India through Iran and Afghanistan, where he achieved renown in debating the scholars in various sciences. He then spent a year in Jahān Ābād under the tutelage of Shaykh ʿAbd Allāh al-Dihlawī who conferred on him the Naqshbandi path. He described his journey to visit his shaykh in a long emotional poem in Arabic. He also took *ijāza* from Shāh ʿAbd al-ʿAzīz the son of Shāh Walī Allāh al-Dihlawī. Al-Khānī in *al-Ḥadāʾiq al-wardiyya* (transmitted from his grandfather directly from Mawlānā Khālid) mentions that al-Dihlawī had ordered Mawlānā Khālid 'to meet the author of the *Tuḥfa ithnā ʿashariyya* which is a unique sourcebook for the refutation of the *Rawāfiḍ*, the aged Shaykh Mawlā ʿAbd al-ʿAzīz al-Ḥanafī al-Naqshbandī the son of Shaykh Waliyyullāh.' Upon Shaykh Khālid's departure, Shaykh ʿAbd Allāh stayed with him for four miles, then Shaykh Khālid continued his journey for 50 more days through Shīrāz, Yazd, Aṣfahān, Hamadhān and Sanandaj until he reached Sulaymāniyya in 1226/1811. He then spent five months in Baghdad at the *zāwiya* of Shaykh ʿAbd al-Qādir al-Jīlānī, after which he returned home to settle there, for 12 years, benefitting many people with his erudition, generosity and accessibility, especially the Kurdish community and others from Irbil, Kirkūk, Mosul, ʿImādiyya, al-Jazīra, ʿAyntāb, Aleppo, Damascus, Anatolia, the Hijaz, Basra and Baghdad. He was described, among other praiseful traits, as 'brilliantly eloquent' (*badīʿ al-bayān*) and 'a masterful speaker' (*ṭaliq al-lisān*).

After putting in charge his brother Maḥmūd in Sulaymāniyya, ʿUthmān Sirāj al-Dīn in al-Ṭawīla, and all of Muḥammad al-Jadīd, Mūsā al-Jubūrī and al-Sayyid ʿAbd al-Ghafūr in Baghdad, he moved to Damascus in 1238/1823 where he was received with a grand celebration, accompanied by a large throng of scholars, students and successors including the former mufti of Baghdad ʿUbayd Allāh al-Ḥaydarī, Ismāʿīl al-Anārānī, ʿAbd al-Qādir al-Daylamānī, Ismāʿīl al-Barzanjī, ʿĪsā al-Kurdī, and many others. There, he bought a house which he made into a school and mosque. The plague of 1242 took many people in Damascus, among them his two children ʿAbd al-Raḥmān and Bahāʾ al-Dīn aged 6 and 5 respectively, then himself. Before dying, with his brother-in-law Ismāʿīl al-Ghazzī as witness—he declared his successor as the main spiritual guide to be Ismāʿīl al-Anārānī, then Muḥammad al-Nāṣiḥ, then ʿAbd al-Fattāḥ al-ʿAqrī, then al-Ghazzī himself after them. He authored several works, among them a partial commentary on al-Ḥarīrī's *Maqāmāt*; a treatise on ʿaqīda in Persian entitled *Farāʾid al-fawāʾid* around the hadith of Jibrīl; a detailed epistle on some of the differences between Māturīdīs and Ashʿarīs entitled *al-ʿIqd al-jawharī* which received a commentary by the Ḥanafī Sufi *mutakallim*, logician and poet ʿAbd al-Ḥamīd b. ʿUmar b. Aḥmad al-Nuʿaymī al-Kharbūtī (d. 1320/1902) entitled *al-Simṭ al-ʿabqarī*, published in 1305/1887 in Istanbul;[179] a commentary on the *ʿAqāʾid al-ʿaḍudiyya*; marginalia on Sayālkūtī's marginalia on Khayyālī's marginalia on Taftāzānī's commentary on the *ʿAqāʾid*; a commentary on Zamakhsharī's *Aṭwāq al-dhahab* and its translation into Persian; treatises on the etiquette of *dhikr* in the Naqshbandī path and the etiquette of the *murīd* with his teacher; a treatise on the hadith 'The closest a slave is to his Lord is when in prostration;' a treatise on spiritual connection entitled *Risāla fīl-rābiṭā*; and a long supplicatory text in which he invokes blessings on the Prophet together with all the Names of Allah and the names of the Companions of Badr, entitled *Jāliyat al-akdār wal-sayf al-battār fīl-ṣalāt ʿalā al-Nabī al-mukhtār*. A lot of his correspondence has been preserved as well as a collection of his poetry in Persian and other literary texts in prose.[180] In a letter to one of his students on the life of Prophets in *barzakh* Shaykh Khālid wrote:

> *Adab* requires us not to specify a precise location for the spirits of the Prophets—upon them the blessings of Allah Most High and His greetings of peace, and upon their House and all their Companions. One should never believe there is a single spot in the world of contingencies in the heavens and the earths that is vacant from the expansion *(madad)* of their spiritual presences both generally and specifically *(fa-lā yuʿtaqad anna fī ʿālam al-imkān min al-samāwāt wal-arāḍīn buqʿatan takhlū ʿan madad*

179 https://curiosity.lib.harvard.edu/islamic-heritage-project/catalog/ 40-9901136104502 03941 as of 7 December 2020.

180 Muḥammad Jamīl al-Shaṭṭī, *Aʿyān Dimashq fīl-qarn al-thālith ʿashar wa-nisf al-qarn al-rābiʿ ʿashar* (Damascus: Dār al-Bashāʾir, 1414/1994), pp. 98–103.

> *rūḥāniyyātihim ʿumūman wa-khuṣūṣan)*, and especially the spiritual presence of their liegelord and Seal, upon him and them blessings and peace... The perfect ones [among Prophets] *(al-kummal)* and even some of the *awliyā'* are enabled by Allah Most High to take on form in several images, limited or unlimited; and they may have a single form which fills the universe. It shows through unveiling, at times, that the heavens, the earths, the Throne, and the Footstool are filled with the Messenger of Allah, upon him and his family blessings and peace.[181]

In much of the above works it can be observed that he was a master of the Arabic language and that he called himself 'Khālid al-Mujaddidī' after the Indian branch of his *ṭarīqa*. Among the numerous beneficiaries of his *ijāza* is Kumushkhānawī's teacher, Aḥmad b. Sulaymān al-Arwādī.[182]

The *ʿIqd al-jawharī* shows complete familiarity with some of the foremost authorities of the Māturīdī school and the monikers by which they are known among Ḥanafīs such as *al-Ustāz* (for ʿAbd Allāh b. Muḥammad b. Yaʿqūb al-Subadhmūnī, 258–360/872–971) and *Ṣadr al-Sharīʿa* (see below). It starts with a reference to the Prophetic Sunna as 'the median way (*al-ṭarīqat al-wusṭā*) between determinism (*jabr*) and libertarianism (*qadar*)' to imply that the treatise is a defense against the charge of determinism some people had leveled at the Ashʿarī school. Al-Baghdādī corrects Ibn al-Humām's assertion in the *Musāyara* that the servant 'brings into being his decisive resolve with his own power' (*yūjid al-ʿabd bi-qudratih dhālik al-ʿazm al-muṣammim*), as the servant, by the consensus of Māturīdīs and Ashʿarīs, cannot bring anything into being. He also gives a nuanced affirmation that the Ashʿarīs and Māturīdīs are one and the same on the issue of acquisition (*kasb*) and free choice (*ikhtiyār*), which are both also called 'partial/particular will' (*al-irādat al-juz'iyya*):

> إِعلَمْ أنَ الإرادةَ الجُزْئِيَّةَ ـ الَّتي هي الكَسْبُ عند الماتريديّة ـ صادرةٌ عَنِ العبدِ باختيارِه وَأَثَرٌ لِقُدْرَتِهِ عِندَهُم؛ لأَنَّهم ـ مَعَ مَنْعِهِم أنْ يكُونَ العَبْدُ مُوجِدًا لِشَيءٍ إجماعًا مِنْ مُحَقِّقِيهِم ـ يُجَوِّزُونَ أَنْ يكُونَ لَهُ قُدرَةٌ مَا، تَخْتَلِفُ بِهَا النِّسَبُ والإضافاتُ على وجْهٍ لا يَلْزَمُ منه وجودُ أمرٍ حقيقيٍّ أصلاً، كما صرّح به صدرُ الشريعة في (التوضيح) ونَسَبَهُ

181 In ʿAbd al-Majīd al-Khānī, *al-Kawākib al-durriyya ʿalā al-Ḥadā'iq al-wardiyya fī ajillā' al-sādat al-Naqshubandiyya*, ed. Muḥammad Khālid Kharsa (Damascus: Dār al-Bayrūtī, 1997), pp. 711–713 and ʿIffat Muḥammad ʿAwnī Zakariyyā's 1998 Damascus reedition, pp. 386–387 of the original 1306/1888 edition.

182 Cf. al-Kawtharī, *al-Muntaqā al-mufīd min al-ʿIqd al-farīd fī ʿulūw al-asānīd* (Cairo: al-Maktabat al-Azhariyya lil-Turāth, n.d.).

إلى مشايخ المذهب الماتريدي، وأفاده المولى حَسَنٌ جَلَبيّ في (حاشية شرح المواقف). وهي شرطٌ أو سببٌ عاديٌّ لِخَلْقِ اللهِ ـ تبارك وتعالى ـ الفِعلَ، كما مرّ غيرَ مرّةٍ، وتَتَعَلَّقُ بِوَصْفِ الفِعلِ؛ أَعنِي كَوْنَهُ طاعةً أو مَعْصِيَةً، كَلَطْمِ اليَتِيمِ: إنْ أُرِيدَ بِهِ تَأْدِيبُهُ فَطَاعَةٌ، أو إهَانَتُهُ فَمَعْصِيَةٌ. فَهِيَ أَثَرٌ لِقُدْرَةِ الْعَبْدِ. وَوَصْفُ الفِعْلِ ـ الَّذي هو أيضًا أمرٌ اِعتِبارِيٌّ عَدَمِيٌّ كَما تَدُلُّ عليه الْكُلِّيَّةُ المَارَّةُ عن أهلِ الْحَقِّ، وَصَرَّحَ به غيرُ واحدٍ مِنْ فُضَلاءِ المَذْهَبَينِ ـ أَثَرٌ لَهَا؛ وَأثَرُ الأَثَرِ أَثَرٌ. وَالأَمْرُ العَدَمِيُّ يَجُوزُ أَنْ يَتَوَقَّفَ عليه الأمرُ المَوْجُودُ.

Know that partial will—which is *kasb* for the Māturīdīs—stems from the servant by his free choice and is an effect of his power according to them. For, although they preclude, by consensus of their foremost authorities, that the servant can bring anything into existence, they allow that he possesses some degree of power (*qudrat mā*) whose ascriptions and attributions may differ in a way that does not demand the existence of any actual matter, as explicitly stated by Ṣadr al-Sharīʿa[183] in *al-Tawḍīḥ*; and he said that was the position of the Māturīdī masters.[184] Mawlā Ḥasan Čelebī [Badr al-Dīn Ḥasan Čelebī b. Muḥammad Shāh b. Muḥammad al-Fanārī (d. 886/1481)] expressed the same in *Ḥāshiyat sharḥ al-Mawāqif*.[185] This [partial will] is a customary precondition or cause for the creation by Allah of the act as already mentioned more than once. Furthermore, it pertains to the characterization of the act; I mean whether it is an act of obedience or a sin. For example slapping an orphan: if one intends disciplining him then it is an act of obedience, but if one intends to humiliate him then it is a sin. So it is an effect of the servant's power, and the characterization of the act—which itself is also a nominal, nonactual matter (as indicated

183 ʿUbayd Allāh b. Masʿūd b. Maḥmūd al-Maḥbūbī al-Bukhārī, known as Ṣadr al-Sharīʿa al-Aṣghar (d. 747/1346) to distinguish him from Aḥmad b. ʿUbayd Allāh b. Ibrāhīm al-Maḥbūbī al-Naysābūrī (d. 630/1233), known as Ṣadr al-Sharīʿa al-Akbar, the author of *Talqīḥ al-ʿuqūl fī furūq al-manqūl*.

184 ʿUbayd Allāh al-Maḥbūbī, *Tawḍīḥ maʿa al-Talwīḥ* (Kazan, Russia: al-Maṭbaʿa al-Īmbirāṭūriyya, 1883), p. 296 = al-Taftāzānī, *Sharḥ al-Talwīḥ ʿalā sharḥ al-Tawḍīḥ li-Ṣadr al-Sharīʿa ʿUbayd Allāh ibn Masʿūd al-Bukhārī* with *al-Tawḍīḥ* in the margins, 2 vols. (Cairo: Dār al-Kutub al-ʿArabiyya al-Kubrā, 1327/1909), 1:189 = *Sharḥ al-Talwīḥ ʿalā al-Tawḍīḥ li-matn al-Tanqīḥ fī uṣūl al-fiqh*, ed. Zakariyya ʿUmayrāt, 2 vols. (Beirut: Dār al-Kutub al-ʿIlmiyya, n.d.), 1:353 (*Qism I, Rukn I, Taqsim II: fī istiʿmāl al-lafẓ fil-maʿnā: al-ḥaqīqa wal-majāz wal-murtajal wal-manqūl, Bāb II, Faṣl: fī masāʾil al-jabr wal-qadar, Muqaddima IV*):

فَالْحَاصِلُ: أَنَّ مَشَايِخَنَا ـ رَحِمَهُمُ اللهُ تَعَالَى ـ يَنْفُونَ عَنِ الْعَبْدِ قُدْرَةَ الْإِيجَادِ وَالتَّكْوِينِ؛ فَلَا خَالِقَ وَلَا مُكَوِّنَ إِلَّا اللهُ! لَكِنْ يَقُولُونَ: إِنَّ لِلْعَبْدِ قُدْرَةً مَا، عَلَى وَجْهٍ لَا يَلْزَمُ مِنْهُ وُجُودُ أَمْرٍ حَقِيقِيٍّ لَمْ يَكُنْ؛ بَلْ إِنَّمَا تَخْتَلِفُ بِقُدْرَتِهِ النِّسَبُ وَالْإِضَافَاتُ فَقَطْ؛ كَتَعْيِينِ أَحَدِ الْمُتَسَاوِيَيْنِ وَتَرْجِيحِهِ. هَذَا مَا وَقَفْتُ عَلَيْهِ مِنْ مَسْأَلَةِ الْجَبْرِ وَالْقَدَرِ. وَبِاللهِ التَّوْفِيقُ.

185 Badr al-Dīn Ḥasan Čelebī b. Muḥammad Shāh b. Muḥammad al-Fanārī (d. 886/ 1481).

> by the universal rule spelled out by the People of truth which we mentioned, and this was explicitly stated by several of the eminences of both schools)—is an effect of it [= the partial will]. Now, the effect of the effect is also an effect, and it is permissible for an existent matter to hinge on a non-existent one.[186]

The work carried weight in the latter-time Ashʿarī-Māturīdī debate and earned itself a commentary by an Ottoman Ḥanafī teacher named ʿAbd al-Ḥāmid b. ʿUmar al-Harputi (d. 1320/ 1902)—from Harput (Elazığ) in eastern Anatolia entitled *al-Simt al-ʿabqarī*.

al-Badāyūnī

al-Badāyūnī, Faḍl al-Rasūl. *al-Muʿtaqad al-muntaqad.* With marginalia by Aḥmad Riḍā Khān, *al-Muʿtamad al-mustanad najāt al-abad.* Mubarakpur: al-Majmaʿ al-Islāmī; Mumbai: Raza Academy 1420/1999. Rept. 1422/2001.

Faḍl al-Rasūl b. ʿAbd al-Majīd b. ʿAbd al-Ḥamīd al-ʿUthmānī al-Badāyūnī (1213–1279/1798–1862) was a Ḥanafī jurist who took *fiqh* and *taṣawwuf* from the Indian scholars of his time including his grandfather ʿAbd al-Ḥamīd, and hadith from ʿAbd Allāh Sirāj in Mecca and Muḥammad ʿĀbid al-Sindī in Medina. He authored several works, among them *al-Muʿtaqad al-muntaqad* which, as a manual of Māturīdī doctrine, is proof of the author's mastery of Sunni *kalām*. It doubles as a heresiological treatise aiming to anathemize the Deobandi school, to whom he refers as 'Najdīs' (in reference to the geographical area that was the cradle of Muḥammad b. ʿAbd al-Wahhāb's sect in the present-day area of Riyadh) to show—with mostly accurate insights—that he views Deobandis as ideological inheritors of Wahhābīs in matters related to Godhead and Prophethood, specifically the author of *Taqwiyat al-īmān*, *Īḍāḥ al-ḥaqq*, and *al-Ṣirāṭ al-mustaqīm*—Ismāʿīl b. ʿAbd al-Ghanī al-Dihlawī (1193–1246/1779–1830)—and his followers.[187] Hence, the contents of *al-Muʿtaqad al-muntaqad* go far beyond the traditional chapter-headings of Māturīdī doctrine as shown below:

186 Khālid al-Baghdādī, *Risāla fī taḥqīq masʾalat al-irāda*, Abāẓa ed., p. 37; Ṣawwāf ed., pp. 141–142.

187 See, for example, *al-Muʿtaqad*, pp. 68, 71, 88, 92, 96–97, 107–108, 130, 132, 170, 184, 207–208, etc.

1. Introduction
    1.1 The subdivisions of rulings to ratiocinative, customary, and sacro-legal
    1.2 Subdivisions of ratiocinative rulings to compulsory, possible and precluded
    1.3 Definition of the science of dialectic theology, its subject-matter and its headings
2. TOPICS RELATED TO GODHEAD
    2.1 Acquired knowledge (*ma'rifa*) of Allah is of four types[188]
    2.2 What is the first duty of the legally-liable person?
    2.3 Sixteen necessary attributes of Allah
        2.3.1 Existent
        2.3.2 Without beginning (negatory attribute, *ṣifat salb*)
        2.3.3 Perduring (negatory attribute)
        2.3.4 Unique
        2.3.5 Self-subsistent and self-sufficient
        2.3.6 Unlike anything in essence, attributes and acts, living, all-powerful
        2.3.7 All-living
        2.3.8 All-powerful (*qadīr*)
            2.3.8.1 Divine power (*qudra*) does not pertain to necessities nor to impossibilities
            2.3.8.2 Ibn Ḥazm's misguidance in affirming 'Allah is able to take for Himself a son'
            2.3.8.3 Impossibilities are rational, legal or customary; the former is not under *qudra*
        2.3.9 Hearing and Seeing without instrument
        2.3.10 Speaking with a beginningless speech (*kalām*) subsisting in His essence
            2.3.10.1 The term *kalām* is used for both verbal and internal speech

188 *Ḥaqīqiyya, 'iyāniyya, kashfiyya,* and *burhāniyya*. The author uses the expression *ma'rifat Allāh ta'ālā li-nafsih*, although the expression *ma'rifat Allāh* with Allah as the subject is generally deemed incorrect by the scholars, as distinct from *'ilm*.

2.3.10.2 Things have four types of existence: concrete; conceptual; expressed; and written
2.3.10.3 Heretical sects on the issue of divine speech
2.3.11 Willing with a beginningless will; *irāda* is synonymous with *mashī'a* and near *ikhtiyār*
2.3.12 All-knowing (*'alīm*) with a pre-existent knowledge
2.3.12.1 The affirmation of the attributes is the position of all *Ahl al-Sunna*
2.3.13 Described by attributes of acts
2.3.13.1 Affirming the divine attributes of acts is not an affirmation of 'beginningless entities'
2.3.13.2 Confusions that result from confusing *kalām* with philosophy
2.3.13.3 His attributes are neither originated (*muḥdatha*) nor created (*makhlūqa*)
2.3.14 His foreordained destiny (*qaḍā'* and *qadar*)
2.3.14.1 What is obligatory is acceptance of *qaḍā'*, not of its morally-accountable content
2.3.14.2 They disagreed whether the blissful can become wretched and vice versa
2.3.14.3 Four types of apportionment: knowledge, the Tablet, the womb, timely conveyance
2.3.14.4 Changeable and unchangeable decree
2.3.15 His creation of the acts of servants, so the latter acquire their acts
2.3.16 Allah is seen with the eyes in the hereafter
2.3.16.1 The Prophet's vision of Allah in this world
2.3.16.2 The *awliyā*'s vision of Allah in this world is with their hearts only
2.3.16.3 Most said dream vision [of Allah] is possible but Māturīdī and the Samarqand masters said no
2.4 Impossible attributions to Allah
2.4.1 Lying
2.4.2 Any attribute connoting defectiveness or even lacking perfection

2.4.3 The demonstration of most matters related to Godhead is through transcendence (*tanzīh*)
2.4.4 The unbelief of whoever attributes body to Allah
2.4.5 Is it permissible to derive divine names from what is established as divine attributes?
2.4.6 His transcendence beyond direction
2.4.7 The deviations of Ibn Taymiyya and 'Najdīs' [=Deobandis] from *Ahl al-Sunna*
2.4.8 It is impossible to understand ambiguities according to manifest locutions
2.4.9 'The sacred law is only established through reason' (Ibn Abī al-Sharīf)[189]
2.4.10 It is impossible that something be obligatory for Allah
2.4.11 'Najdīs' went the way of the Muʿtazila in many issues
2.4.12 The mental understanding of 'beauty' and 'ugliness' (*al-ḥusn wal-qubḥ*)
2.4.13 The paining of creatures by Allah without crime or reward is rationally conceivable
2.4.14 Maturidis said tasking beyond capacity is impossible for other reasons than Muʿtazilīs
2.4.15 Likewise regarding the impossibility of punishing the righteous
2.4.16 Rewarding the righteous is through bounty, punishing the unrighteous through justice
2.4.17 Position of the non-Sunni sects regarding the grave sinners

189 This is in line with reason being sufficient as a compelling reason for the obligation of knowing Allah in the Māturīdī and Muʿtazilī schools, although (i) many Māturīdīs took the Ashʿarī position: 'Reason makes knowledge of Allah compulsory for al-Māturīdī and the Samarqandīs, not for al-Ashʿarī and the Māturīdīs of Bukhāra' (al-Pazdawī, *Uṣūl al-dīn*), and 'Reason is but a tool for acquiring knowledge, and the real compeller is Allah' (al-Qārī, *Minaḥ*); and (ii) certain Ashʿarīs took the Māturīdī position, cf. al-Rāzī's interpretation of *the Messenger sent* in al-Isrāʾ 17:15 as the mind (see introduction, 'The construct of Māturīdīs as near to Muʿtazilīs'). Mīrak al-Balkhī (d. 416/1025) stated in *Kitāb al-Iʿtiqād* "Knowledge is superior to reason (*al-ʿilmu afḍal min al-ʿaql)* (cf. also al-Kumushkhānawī, *Jāmiʿ al-mutūn*, p. 28), and whoever says that reason is superior to knowledge is a Muʿtazilī, because knowledge is needed while reason is like the tool for it.'" In Ibn Abī al-Wafā, *al-Jawāhir al-muḍiyya fī ṭabaqāt al-Ḥanafiyya*, ed. ʿAbd al-Fattāḥ Muḥammad al-Ḥilw, 2nd ed., 5 vols. (Giza: Hajr, 1413/1993) 3:308.

2.4.18 Forgiveness for unbelief is legally impossible, and Muʿtazilīs said rationally also
2.4.19 Difference of Māturīdīs with Muʿtazilīs in the matter[190]
2.4.20 Every act of His has wisdoms, but not impelling motives (*ʿilal bāʿitha aw aghrāḍ*)
2.5 What is possible with respect to Allah is the doing of every contingency or leaving it undone

3. TOPICS RELATED TO PROPHETHOOD

3.1 It is a categorical obligation to know what is necessary, possible, or precluded for prophets
3.2 Sending prophets is neither impossible nor obligatory for Allah Most High
3.3 The philosophers' concept of prophethood revolves around heretical beliefs[191]
3.4 Is 'prophet' the same as 'messenger'?
3.5 Anyone that claims revelation is given for other than a prophet is an unbeliever
3.6 Prophethood is not acquirable
3.7 Allowing for the possibility of another prophet after the Prophet is unbelief
3.8 Allowing for the possibility that a prophet loses his mind borders on unbelief; or loses prophethood, constitutes unbelief
3.9 What is necessary for prophets to have
3.9.1 Immunity to sin (*ʿiṣma*), which is exclusive to prophets
3.9.2 Truthfulness (*ṣidq*), a rational necessity for every prophet
3.9.2.1 Whoever allows the possibility of lying for a prophet commits unbelief
3.9.2.2 It is impossible for a staggering miracle to show at the hands of a liar
3.9.3 Trustworthiness (*amāna*)

190 Here the author (p. 90) points out 'al-Nasafī's many errors in this respect in *ʿUmdat al-ʿaqāʾid*, whereby he confused the position of the Māturīdīs with that of the Muʿtazila.... as pointed out in the *Musāyara*.'

191 See Salient Themes, The Maturidi Condemnation of the Philosophers.

- 3.9.4 Conveyance (*tablīgh*) of everything they have been tasked to convey
- 3.9.5 Sagacity (*faṭāna*)
- 3.9.6 Maleness (*dhukūra*)
- 3.9.7 Integrity (*nazāha*) in earning
- 3.9.8 Exemption from any repulsive flaw in his person and lineage
- 3.9.9–10 Being the most perfect of the non-prophet people of his time and most knowledgeable of the sacred law

3.10 Every normal rewardable matter is permissible for them

3.11 One who claims that every species of animal has a prophet is an unbeliever

3.12 Belief in every single prophet by name and collectively is an obligation

3.13 Detailed obligatory beliefs in our Prophet—upon him blessings and peace

- 3.13.1 The universality of his mission to human beings and jinns
- 3.13.2 That he is the Seal of Prophets
  - 3.13.2.1 Claiming a subsequent prophet is possible is inherently false and unbelief
  - 3.13.2.2 The difference between inherently and extrinsically precluded
  - 3.13.2.3 One who claims a Prophet may lie or that a liar may perform a staggering miracle or that a Prophet's perfections may be found in a non-prophet, is an unbeliever
- 3.13.3 That he is the best of all creation
  - 3.13.3.1 Preferring a non-prophet over the Prophet is unbelief
  - 3.13.3.2 al-Qārī said the like of the Prophet is impossible
- 3.13.4 The Night Journey and Heavenly Ascent
- 3.13.5 He is the intercessor whom all will need on the Day of Resurrection including Prophets
  - 3.13.5.1 Typology of the Prophet's various intercessions
  - 3.13.5.2 One must believe in the intercession of other intercessors as well
  - 3.13.5.3 Intercession for the grave sinners is a reality even if they die unrepentant

3.13.5.4 'Najdīs' [=Deobandis] follow Muʿtazilism in their reinterpretation of intercession[192]

3.13.6 His noble body is not subject to decomposition, contrary to the claim of 'Najdīs'

3.14 The obligatory rights owed by all people to the Prophet

3.14.1 The obligation of obeying and loving him

3.14.1.1 Love is either rational or instinctive, and the legally-tasked one is the first

3.14.1.2 The three main causes of loveliness are all found in him

3.14.1.3 The marks of one's love for the Prophet—upon him blessings and peace

3.14.1.3.1 Following him

3.14.1.3.2 Mentioning and remembering him often

3.14.1.3.3 Loving him, his Companions, and Arabs, and hating whoever hates them

3.14.1.3.4 Hating whoever hates him and avoiding the innovator

3.14.1.3.4.1 Magnifying him is obligatory inwardly and outwardly

3.14.1.3.4.2 His sacred status after death is unchanged and just as in his worldly life

3.14.1.3.4.3 Dignifying his family, spouses and companions

3.14.1.3.4.4 Magnifying the places and objects associated with him

3.14.1.3.4.5 Facing him during supplication and the rebuttal of Ibn Taymiyya

3.14.1.3.5 Invoking much blessings and greetings on him—upon him blessings and peace

3.14.1.3.6 Visiting his grave—upon him blessings and peace

3.14.2 The prohibition of disparaging him and the status of whoever does such a thing

3.14.2.1 The various verbal aspects of insult or disparagement

3.14.2.2 Any interpretive attempt for an explicit statement is rejected

192 A reference to Ismāʿīl al-Dihlawī's *Taqwiyat al-īmān* in which is found a comparison of Allah to a king who unable to forgive unless there is some justification: *Muʿtaqad*, p. 130.

3.14.2.2.1 Anything said as disparagement is unbelief even if claimed as accurate[193]

3.14.2.2.2 Disparaging or insulting him unintentionally carries the same status and penalty

3.14.2.2.3 Belying him likewise

3.14.2.2.4 Unclear, ambiguous and interpretable expressions

3.14.2.2.5 Using some of his permissible states in the world as a self-justification

3.14.2.2.5.1 It is impermissible to mention the Prophet's parents in a disparaging manner

3.14.2.2.5.2 The Prophet's *ummiyya* is a staggering miracle for him but a defect for others

3.14.2.2.6 Quoting someone else's disparagement of the Prophet

3.14.2.2.6.1 If one finds the Prophet disparaged in some book he may deface the passage

3.14.2.2.7 Mentioning his possible worldly states in the context of teaching

3.14.2.2.7.1 It is impermissible to refer to ambiguous passages regarding the Prophet[194]

4. TOPICS RELATED TO ESCHATOLOGY

4.1 Doctrines are of three types in relation to apprehension by reason and transmission

4.2 Regathering (*ḥashr*) and resurrection (*nashr*)

4.2.1 Whoever asserts paradise, hell and resurrection then reinterprets them commits unbelief

4.2.2 Is the spirit corporeal so that resurrection is only bodily?

4.3 The questioning of the two angels and the punishment or bliss in the grave

4.3.1 Those who will not be questioned in the grave

193 Such as describing the Prophet as an orphan, or saying 'people should celebrate the descent of the Qur'ān rather than the birth of the Prophet, because before prophethood he was just a boy like our kampong boys' as was mass-reported from the late Nik Azīz (1931–2015) of Malaysia, a Deobandi.

194 I.e., except with authorized knowledge (*'ilm*) together with Godfearingness and utmost courtesy (*adab*).

4.3.2 'Najdīs' adduced the same proofs against the hearing of the dead as Mu'tazilīs did against the punishment and bliss of the grave[195]

4.3.3 *Sharḥ al-Maqāṣid* explicitly states the benefit of visiting graves and using *awliyā*'s help

4.4 The balance of deeds: it does not apply to all

4.5 The Kawthar

4.6 The Bridge [over hellfire]

4.7 Paradise and hell are already created and their respective dwellers will never exit, contrary to Ibn Taymiyya's claim[196]

4.7.1 Ibn al-Qayyim supported the position that hellfire comes to an end, an invalid position

4.8 The preconditions of the Hour

5. TOPICS RELATED TO OVERALL LEADERSHIP

5.1 'Overall leadership' (*imāma*) is the successorship of the Prophet and is an obligation

5.2 Rightful leadership is that of the four rightly-guided caliphs

5.3 Their preferentiality follows the same order as their respective caliphates

5.4 The position of *Ahl al-Sunna* is the affirmation of uprightness for every single Companion

5.5 'Haters' (*Nawāṣib*) are two sects, one hating both 'Uthmān and 'Alī, and one 'Alī only

6. CONCLUSION ON BELIEF

6.1 Explanation of *īmān*, its integrals and its preconditions

6.2 The imitator's belief

195 Denial of the hearing of the dead has been affirmed as the Ḥanafī position by Nu'mān al-Ālūsī in his book *al-Āyāt al-bayyināt fī'adam samā' al-amwāt 'inda al-Ḥanafiyyat al-sādāt*, ed. Muḥammad Nāṣir al-Albānī, 4th ed. (Beirut: al-Maktab al-Islāmī, 1405/1985; Riyadh: Maktabat al-Ma'ārif lil-Nashr wal-Tawzī', 1425/2005). On its rebuttal see Aḥmad Riḍā Khān's *Ḥayāt al-mawāt fī bayān samā' al-amwāt* and *al-Wifāq al-matīn bayna samā' al-dafīn wa-jawāb al-yamīn*.

196 See above, p. 116.

6.3 The latter's precondition is not to alter the object of imitation[197]
6.4 Is the heart's confirmation subsumed under knowledge or speech?
6.5 Are *īmān* and *islām* one and the same?
6.6 Acts are not part of belief: 'Najdīs' [=Deobandis] went the way of Khārijīs in this
6.7 The precise objects of obligatory belief
6.8 The disagreements over the apostatizing of innovators (*mubtadi'īn*)
6.8.1 One who diverges in the foundations of religion is categorically astray (*ḍāll*)
6.8.2 Innovation (*bid'a*) and the status of innovators
6.8.3 Not everything that did not exist in the time of the Companions is an innovation
6.8.4 The difference in interacting with the unbeliever and the innovator—their levels
6.9 Belief neither increases nor decreases
6.10 Is belief created?
6.11 When anything appears confusing, one must believe on the spot whatever Allah deems right

197 For example, those who claim to be imitating the pious *Salaf* in anthropomorphizing, which was never their belief.

Fourteenth/Twentieth Century

al-Qāwuqjī

al-Qāwuqjī, Muḥammad b. Khalīl. *al-Durr al-ghālī ʿalā Badʾ al-amālī*. Shabīn al-Kawm, Egypt: al-Maṭbaʿat al-Naṣriyya, 1317/1900).

———. *al-Iʿtimād fil-iʿtiqād*. Shabīn al-Kawm, Egypt: al-Maṭbaʿat al-Naṣriyya, 1926.

———. *Ibid*. http://www.projectsassociation.org/LibrarySite/aqd/imiq/0imiq.html (internet edition).

———. *Kifāyat al-ṣibyān fi-mā yajib min ʿaqāʾid al-īmān wa-ʿamal al-arkān*. Alexandria: Maṭbaʿat Idārat al-Burhān, [1850?].

———. *Mukhtaṣar al-Iʿtimād fil-iʿtiqād*. Ed. Ziyād Ḥamdān. Beirut: Muʾassasat al-Kutub al-Thaqāfiyya, 1417/1997.

The pious and prolific Ḥasanī Sufi Ḥanafī orator and scholar of hadith, *tafsīr*, Quranic readings, law, theology, sufism, history, genealogy, transmissology, zoology and botany of Tripoli, Lebanon, famed and feted in Egypt and buried in Mecca, Abū al-Maḥāsin Muḥammad b. Khalīl al-Qāwuqjī al-Azharī (1224–1305/1809–1888) was hailed by ʿAbd al-Ḥay al-Kattānī as ʻthe transmissologist (*musnid*) of Syro-Palestine (al-Shām) lands at the start of this century on whose transmission chains everyone today revolves in most of the lands of Egypt, Syro-Palestine and Hijaz.ʼ[198] He descended, on his father's side, from Muḥammad al-Quṣaybātī the son of ʿAbd al-Salām b. Mashīsh—to whom he liked to

198 Muḥammad ʿAbd al-Ḥay al-Kattānī, *Fahras al-fahāris*, ed. Iḥsān ʿAbbās, 2nd ed., 3 vols. (Beirut Dār al-Gharb al-Islāmī, 1402/1982), 1:105.

ascribe himself by calling himself al-Mashīshī—and from ʿUmar b. al-Khaṭṭāb on his mother's side. His name is derived from the hat-making trade of one of his ancestors in Levantine Tripoli, after the Ottoman *kavuk* (lit. 'hollow'), a large tubular hat (similar to that worn today by Maronite prelates) on top of which a turban is tied.[199] After memorizing the Qur'ān in his childhood he moved to al-Azhar at age 15 to pursue his studies and lived in Egypt for 27 years. He studied under Ibrāhīm al-Bājūrī, Muḥammad b. Aḥmad al-Khalīlī al-Tamīmī the mufti of Ḥanafis, Muḥammad b. Aḥmad al-Bahī (his highest chain of transmission), Muḥammad ʿĀbid al-Sindī, Muḥammad Ṣāliḥ al-Sibāʿī al-Adwī, Aḥmad al-Ṣaʿīdī al-Mālikī and others, whom he names in his still-manuscript 57-folio *thabat* entitled *Maʿdin al-laʾālī fil-asānīd al-ʿawālī*. Among his many other unpublished works (kept mostly in Dār al-Kutub al-Miṣriyya) is a commentary on the *ʿAqāʾid* entitled *al-Durr al-ṣafi ʿalā ʿaqīdat al-Nasafī*. In *al-Iʿtimād fil-iʿtiqād* he restated the well-known position of Māturīdīs on exclusive divine arch-effectiveness (*faʿʿāliyya*) in rebuttal of the ultra-libertarian (Qadarī) claim that people possess autonomous power and create their own destiny in the following terms:

> It is impossible for anyone or anything in existence to effect or create any act together with Allah.... Whoever believes that eating satiates in itself, or fire burns in itself, or knives cut in themselves without Allah creating that, is an unbeliever.... and whoever believes that a human being creates his act with a power which Allah created in him is an unbeliever, because he deems that Allah is in need of an intermediary in certain acts.[200]

Among Abū al-Maḥāsin al-Qāwuqjī's noteworthy students were his son Abū al-Naṣr, Aḥmad b. Muḥammad al-Dalbashānī, Ṣāliḥ b. ʿAbd Allāh al-ʿAbbāsī, Muḥammad b. Maḥmūd Khafāja al-Dimyāṭī, Ḥabīb al-Raḥmān al-Kāẓimī al-Hindī, Abū al-Ḥasan ʿAlī al-Watarī al-Madanī, Ḥasan al-Saqqā al-Faraghlī al-Azharī, ʿAbd al-Fattāḥ al-Zughbī al-Ṭarābulusī, Aḥmad al-ʿAṭṭār, ʿAbd al-Raḥmān al-Ḥūt the *Naqīb al-ashrāf* of Beirut, Basyūnī al-Qarnashāwī, Salīm al-Musūtī al-Dimashqī, etc. After his shaykh the mufti of Jaffa Ḥusayn

199 See Rajab ʿAbd al-Jawād Ibrāhīm, *al-Muʿjam al-ʿarabī li-asmāʾ al-malābis fiḍawʾ al-maʿā-jim wal-nuṣūṣ al-muwaththaqa min al-Jāhiliyya ḥattā al-ʿaṣr al-ḥadīth* (Cairo: Dār al-Āfāq al-ʿArabiyya, 1423/2002), pp. 371–372.

200 al-Qāwuqjī, *Mukhtaṣar al-Iʿtimād fil-iʿtiqād*, ed. Ziyād Ḥamdān (Beirut: Mu'assasat al-Kutub al-Thaqāfiyya, 1417/1997), pp. 11–12.

al-Dajjānī informed him that he would die in the sacred lands he completed *ʿumra* and died of a fever shortly thereafter, facing the Kaʿba. He was buried in al-Muʿallāt between the graves of Khadīja and Āmina—may Allah be well-pleased with them.[201]

al-Kumushkhānawī

al-Kumushkhānawī Aḥmad Ḍiyāʾ al-Dīn b. Muṣṭafā. *Jāmiʿ al-mutūn fī ḥaqq anwāʿ al-ṣifāt al-ilāhiyya wal-ʿaqāʾid al-Māturīdiyya wa-alfāẓ al-kufr wa-taṣḥīḥ al-aʿmāl al-ʿajībiyya.* [Istanbul:] Dār al-Ṭibāʿat al-ʿĀmira, 1273/1857.

Ahmed Ziyâeddin Gümüşhanevi (1228–1311/1813–1894) was a hadith scholar and Sufi master whom al-Kawtharī called the *mujaddid* of Ottoman lands at the turn of the 14th Islamic century. He authored many books on hadith, doctrine, supplications and sufism. Born in Gümüşhane (in the Black Sea region of Turkey) he moved to Trebizon with his father who was a merchant, then to Istanbul where he studied under the Kurdish Naqshbandi Shaykh ʿAbd al-Raḥmān al-Harputi after memorizing the Qur'ān in his childhood. Among his teachers in later life was the *musnid* of Tripoli Aḥmad al-Arwādī, who gave him *ijāza*. Among al-Kumushkhānawī's students were Zaynulla Rasulev and two of al-Kawtharī's teachers: his father Ḥasan Ḥilmī b. ʿAlī and Ḥasan b. ʿAbd Allāh al-Qasṭamūnī (d. 1329/1911), who also narrates from al-Arwādī directly.[202] His magnum opus is his source index entitled *Rāmūz al-aḥādīth* (Ocean of hadiths)[203] published in Istanbul in 1275 (which al-Kawtharī read in full in the dedicated Istanbul gatherings to that effect) and its large five-volume commentary, *Sharḥ Rāmūz al-aḥādīth al-muttasam Lawāmiʿ al-ʿuqūl* (Gleams of minds), published in Cairo at Maktab al-Ṣanāyiʿ in 1294 and at al-Ṭibāʿat al-ʿĀmira in 1291–1295. The *Rāmūz* has received many editions

201 See ʿAbd al-Qādir b. ʿAbd al-Qādir b. ʿAlī al-Ad-hamī, *Tarjamat quṭb al-wāṣilīn wa-ghawth al-sālkīn al-ʿārif bil-Lāh taʿālā sayyidī Shams al-Dīn Muḥammad Abī al-Maḥāsin al-Qāwuqjī* (Beirut: al-Maṭbaʿat al-Adabiyya, 1306/1889), pp. 6–9, 14–20.

202 al-Kawtharī, *al-Taḥrīr al-wajīz fi-mā yabtaghīh al-mustajīz*, ed. ʿAbd al-Fattāḥ Abū Ghudda (Aleppo: Maktab al-Maṭbūʿāt al-Islāmiyya, 1413/1993), pp. 47–51 and *al-Muntaqā al-mufīd*, pp. 20–21.

203 The word *rāmūz* escaped the notice of Lane, Dozy, and Wehr among Western Arabic lexicographers, but Kasimirski did document it in his 1860 *Dictionnaire Arabe-Français.*

in Turkey but no critical edition as of yet. In his *Jāmiʿ al-mutūn* he lists the chapter-headings of the Māturīdī creed as follows:[204]

1. All legally-liable persons must know what is incumbent or impossible or possible with regard to Allah
2. Belief has two sides: *tawfiq*, guidance and love from Allah, in which case it is uncreated; affirmation and confirmation from the slave, in which case it is created
3. Allah's essential attributes are neither He nor other than Him
4. Allah has at least 220 transcendental attributes (*ṣifāt tanzīhiyya*)
5. The modality of the Throne and the minutiae of the science of *kalām*
6. There are eight agreed-upon affirmatory (*thubūtiyya*) attributes: *al-ḥayāt, al-qudra, al-ʿilm, al-irāda, al-samʿ, al-baṣar, al-kalām, al-takwīn/al-takhlīq*.[205]
7. The attributes of acts are beyond count
8. The significatory (*maʿnawiyya*) Attributes correspond to the affirmatory ones and are *al-Ḥayy, al-Qādir, al-Murīd, al-Samīʿ, al-Baṣīr, al-Mutakallim, al-Mukawwin*.
9. The essential (*dhātiyya*) Attributes are six: existence (*al-wujūd*), beginninglessness (*al-qidam*), perdurance (*al-baqāʾ*), unicity (*al-waḥdāniyya*), self-subsistence (*al-qiyām bi-nafsih*), and alterity/otherness than all originated things (*al-mukhālafa lil-ḥawādith*)
10. What is impossible to claim with regard to Allah is the contrary of all the above attributes
11. What is possible with regard to Allah
12. What is necessary with regard to prophets
13. What is impossible with regard to prophets
14. What is possible with regard to prophets
15. What is necessary with regard to angels
16. What is impossible with regard to angels
17. What is possible with regard to angels

204 *Jāmiʿ al-mutūn*, p. 145.

205 Shīʿīs drop out *al-samʿ*, *al-baṣar* and *al-takwīn*, and they add *al-idrāk*, *al-ṣidq*, and *al-sarmadiyya*. See Naṣīr al-Dīn al-Ṭūsī, *Tajrīd al-ʿaqāʾid*, ed. ʿAbbās Muḥammad Ḥasan Sulaymān (Alexandria: Dār al-Maʿrifa al-Jāmiʿiyya, 1996), pp. 117–118; cf. http://www.erfan.ir/arabic/9985.html.

18. Detailed creed of the Māturīdīs
19. All Quranic verses are equal in greatness but some have merit both in the mention and the subject-matter (e.g. *āyat al-kursī*) while others have merit in the mention only (e.g. unbelievers)
20. Seeing Allah
21. Partial will (*al-irāda al-juz'iyya*)
22. That nothing is obligatory for Allah
23. Ability (*istiṭā'a*)
24. Nothing other than Allah effects anything
25. The firm course of the custom of Allah
26. Exposition of 'divinely-granted success' (*tawfiq*), 'lifespan' (*ajal*) and 'provision' (*rizq*)
27. Exposition of the grave and its interrogation
28. Exposition of the states of resurrection
29. Paradise and hell
30. The ascent to heaven
31. Detailing of the preconditions of the Hour
32. The major sin does not expel one from the pale of belief
33. The harm of sins
34. Allah forgives all that is less than polytheism
35. Self-display cancels out reward
36. Talion punishment on the Day of Resurrection
37. The acceptance of supplication
38. The punishment of the unbelievers of the jinns
39. Satan has a certain freedom to act (*taṣarruf*)
40. *Īmān* and *islām*
41. *Tawḥīd* and *ma'rifa*
42. The wretched and the blissful
43. The wisdom behind the sending of messengers
44. The unabrogability of our Law
45. Preferentiality between angels and human beings as well as among the Companions
46. The miraculous gifts of the friends of Allah
47. The beguiling of enemies [of Allah]
48. Those specifically promised paradise

49. Sultanate and kingdom
50. The state of *Ahl al-qibla*
51. Supplication possesses effectiveness (*lil-duʿāʾ taʾthīr*)
52. The pre-excellence of places
53. Knowledge (*ʿilm*) is superior to reason (*ʿaql*), furthermore, the latter has levels
54. Reason is the tool for acquired knowledge (*maʿrifa*) but it is Allah Who really necessitates it
55. The name is other than the named
56. *Qurʾān* is a name denoting both the compositional structure (*naẓm*) and the meaning (*maʿnā*)
57. Belief at the time of despairing from life (*īmān al-yaʾs*) is not accepted
58. No Muslim may be cursed
59. The belief of the imitator is valid
60. Fear for one's status at the time of death
61. The children of polytheists
62. The reality of witchcraft and the evil eye
63. Texts are understood according to their manifest locutions
64. A slave is liable on the basis of his intent
65. The pauper is better than the rich man
66. Prophets are not subject to reckoning or scrutiny[206]
67. The affairs of people on earth are not related to the stars
68. The calamus and preordainment is the secret of Allah
69. The command to do good and the acceptance of repentance

Ibrāhīm al-Wafī

al-Wafī, Ibrāhīm Ḥilmī b. Ḥusayn. *Salām al-aḥkam ʿalā sawād al-aʿẓam.* Āsitāna: Dār Saʿādat, 1313/1895. 224 p.

A recapitulation of the articles of the Māturīdī creed together with various *fiqh* rulings, explanations of certain suras, fatwas and moral teachings. The work expands on *al-Sawād al-aʿẓam* by the qadi Abū al-Qāsim Isḥāq b.

206 Cf. al-Badāyūnī, *Muʿtaqad*, p. 184: والأصح أن الأنبياء لا يُسألون... وكذا أطفال المؤمنين، واختُلف في سؤال أطفال المشركين وفي دخولهم الجنة والنار

Muḥammad, known as al-Ḥakīm al-Samarqandī (*q.v.*). Among other benefits, the author states that the doctrine of the reality of the punishment of the grave musters the consensus of all *Ahl al-Sunna wal-Jamāʿa*.

Bājahjī Zādah

Bājahjī Zādah, ʿAbd al-Raḥmān Bayk. *al-Fāriq bayna al-makhlūq wal-Khāliq*. With al-Qarāfī's *al-Ajwibat al-fākhira ʿan al-asʾilat al-fājira* and Ibn al-Qayyim's *Hidāyat al-ḥayārā min al-Yahūd wal-Naṣārā*. 2 vols. in 1. Cairo: Maṭbaʿat al-Taqaddum, 1322/1904. 408 p. + 120 p.

This heresiological reference-work by the Iraqi Ḥanafī master ʿAbd al-Raḥmān b. Salīm b. ʿAbd al-Raḥmān Bājahjī Zādah (1248–1330/1832–1911) contains a chapter-by-chapter Muslim reading of the Gospels of Mark and Matthew establishing the humanity of the Messiah, followed by a recension of all the Biblical references to the person of the Prophet Muḥammad—upon him blessings and peace. It is not a Māturīdī creed but deserves mention as the foremost Ḥanafī contribution to the Ghazālian-Rāzian tradition of systematic refutation of the Scripture-based claims of Trinitarian Christology, of which an earlier extensive treatment was given by the Mālikī master Shihāb al-Dīn al-Qarāfī (628–684/1228–1285) in his *Ajwiba*, published along with it.

Muḥammad Wahbī al-Khādimī

al-Khādimī, Muḥammad Wahbī b. Ḥusayn Afandī. *al-ʿAqāʾid al-khayriyya fī taḥrīr madhhab al-firqat al-nājiya wa-hum Ahl al-Sunnati wal-Jamāʿa, wal-radd ʿalā mukhālifīhim*. [Cairo:] Dār Iḥyāʾ al-Kutub al-ʿArabiyya, [1349/1930?]. 136 p.

Muḥammad Wahbī b. Ḥusayn Afandī al-Khādimī (Mehmet Vehbi Hadimli Çelik 1861–1949) is known for authoring a four-volume commentary on the Qurʾān in Turkish entitled *Khulāsat al-bayān fī tafsīr al-Qurʾān* and another commentary, *al-Aḥkām al-Qurʾāniyya*, devoted to the verses denoting legal rulings. In his colophon to *al-ʿAqāʾid al-khayriyya* he said he authored the latter in a month (from 13 Jumādā al-Ākhar to 16 Rajab 1334/April-May

1916). It is a doctrinal guidebook in which he covered the headings of the Māturīdī creed while addressing the atheistic, materialistic and anti-religious trends of his time (e.g. objections to the *ḥijāb* and to polygyny pp. 88–93). He showed leaning towards certain Ashʿarī positions (p. 18) and asserted that 'the dispute in dialectic theology (*kalām*) between the Muʿtazila and *Ahl al-Sunna* is terminological, not real' (p. 43).

al-Kawtharī

al-Kawtharī, Muḥammad Zāhid b. al-Ḥasan. *al-Istibṣār fil-taḥadduth ʿan al-jabr wal-ikhtiyār.* Cairo: [?], 1370/1951. 2nd ed. Cairo: al-Maktabat al-Azhariyya lil-Turāth, 2005.

———. *Maqālāt al-Kawtharī.* Cairo: Dār al-Salām, 1998.

———. *Maqālāt al-Kawtharī.* Cairo: Dār al-Tawfīq al-Namūdhajiyya lil-Ṭibāʿa; al-Maktabat al-Azhariyya lil-Turāth, 1414/1994.

———. *Maqālāt al-Kawtharī.* Riyadh: Dār al-Aḥnāf, 1414/1993.

———. *Maqālāt al-Kawtharī.* [Damascus?:] Rātib Ḥākimi, [1968].

———. *Maqālāt al-Kawtharī.* Karachi: H.M. Company, 1372/1953.

———. *al-Taḥrīr al-wajīz fi-mā yabtaghīh al-mustajīz.* [Cairo:] Maṭbaʿat al-Anwār, 1360/1941.

———. *al-Taḥrīr al-wajīz fi-mā yabtaghīh al-mustajīz.* Ed. ʿAbd al-Fattāḥ Abū Ghudda (Aleppo: Maktab al-Maṭbūʿāt al-Islāmiyya, 1413/1993

Muḥammad Zāhid b. Ḥasan Ḥilmī b. ʿAlī al-Kawtharī (1296–1371/1879–1952) was a Ḥanafī jurist, theorist of law, hadith scholar, Sufi, theologian, manuscriptologist, rhetorician and grammarian in Turkish and Persian as well as Arabic, debater and historian whose contribution to the Māturīdī school and the general defense of Sunni tenets against many modern trends and heresies is unsurpassed in the last hundred years, with incalculable influence on the Sunnis of the world, particularly Ḥanafīs in the Arab world, Turkey, and the Indian subcontinent. His writings form a diagnosis of the state of the post-Ottoman Sunni world and the demise of al-Azhar. He did not author or edit a specific work on Māturīdī creed other than the brief *al-Istibṣār fil-taḥadduth ʿan al-jabr wal-ikhtiyār* (Insights in discussing determinism and free choice), but his monographs and articles, his introductions, editions and notes to countless books bear testimony to his status as a pre-eminent contemporary Māturīdī authority, whose effective marginalization by Wahhābī authors and publications over the last fifty years is perhaps the most successful blow dealt against the Māturīdī school to date.

Al-Kawtharī wrote *al-Istibṣār* in 1951 (one year before his death) in defense of the concepts of 'partial will' (*al-irādat al-juz'iyya*) and of the servant's God-sanctioned power (*qudrat al-ʿabd bi-idhn Allāh*) as held in the Māturīdī school, as a belated rebuttal of a 1352/1933 book by the last Shaykh al-Islām of the Ottoman Caliphate Muṣṭafā Ṣabrī Bāshā (1286–1373/1869–1954)—of which he was the deputy (*wakīl*)[207]—entitled *Mawqif al-bashar taḥta sulṭān al-qadar*, which he had already criticized in veiled terms in the introduction to his 1367/1948 edition of Imām al-Ḥaramayn's *al-Risāla al-Niẓāmiyya*. Al-Kawtharī had detected in the *Mawqif* what he deemed the outright determinism (*jabr*) of the Ashʿarī position on the chapter of 'acquisition' (*kasb*) and the divine creation of the acts of human beings—which some have called, in defense of Ashʿarīs, 'soft' determinism (*jabr mutawassiṭ*). He notably asserted that *al-irādat al-juz'iyya* was also the position of al-Ashʿarī in the *Lumaʿ*, Imām al-Ḥaramayn, and al-Ālūsī who defended the latter in *al-Ajwiba al-ʿirāqiyya*.

Al-Kawtharī was a major Ḥanafī jurist praised by the imam of al-Azhar Muḥammad Abū Zahra as 'one of the renewers *(mujaddidīn)* in the true sense of renewal' for the fourteenth Islamic century.[208] He studied under his father as well as the scholar of Qur'ān and Hadith Ibrāhīm Ḥaqqī (d. 1345/1927), Zayn al-ʿĀbidīn al-Alaṣūnī (d. 1336/1918), Muḥammad Khāliṣ al-Shirwānī, al-Ḥasan al-Aztuwā'ī, and others whom he chronicled in his catalogue of teachers (*thabat*) entitled *al-Taḥrīr al-wajīz*. When the Ottoman Caliphate fell he moved to Cairo, then Syria, then Cairo again until his death, where the

207 For al-Kawtharī's explanation of the history and function of the *wikālat mashyakhat al-Islām* see his *al-Taḥrīr al-wajīz*, pp. 45–47.

208 In Abū Zahra's preface to al-Kawtharī's *Maqālāt* and *Muqaddimāt.*

late shaykhs ʿAbd al-Fattāḥ Abū Ghudda, ʿAbd Allāh al-Ghumārī and Wahbī Sulaymān Ghawjī—our teacher—became his students. Among his many prestigious chains of transmission al-Kawtharī received the Islamic sciences from his father Ḥasan Ḥilmī b. ʿAlī and Ḥasan b. ʿAbd Allāh al-Qasṭamūnī, both of them from Aḥmad Ḍyāʾ al-Dīn b. Muṣṭafā al-Kumushkhānawī, from Sayyid Aḥmad b. Sulaymān al-Arwādī (d. 1275/1859)—al-Qasṭamūnī also narrates directly from al-Arwādī—from Muḥammad Amīn ʿĀbidīn (d. 1252/1836), with his chain to Ibn Ḥajar al-ʿAsqalānī, from Shams al-Dīn al-Qurashī, from ʿAbd Allāh al-Kashgharī, from Ḥusām al-Dīn Ḥusayn b. ʿAlī al-Sighnāqī, from Ḥāfiẓ al-Dīn al-Nasafī al-Kabīr with the chain described in Tables 3 and 5 below.[209] A tireless scholar, there is apparently no field of the Islamic sciences in which he did not have a well-founded claim to authority. He edited and brought back into circulation countless classical books of *fiqh*, hadith, and legal theory after he moved to Cairo. A staunch Māturīdī, he held a harshly critical view of literalists and considered Ibn Taymiyya an outright anthropomorphist. Due to this position among many others, he has endured as the *bête noire* of ʿSalafīs' and Wahhābīs of yesterday and today.

Among the books al-Kawtharī authored:

- *Bulūgh al-amānī fī sīrat al-imām Muḥammad ibn al-Ḥasan al-Shaybānī*, a biography of the foremost Ḥanafī authority after Abū Ḥanīfa.
- *al-Farāʾid al-wāfiya* (or *al-Fawāʾid al-kāfiya*) *fī ʿilmay al-ʿarūḍ wal-qāfiya* (The abundant rarities in the two arts of prosody and rhyme), published without the name of the author.
- *Fiqh ahl al-ʿIraq* (Jurisprudence of the Iraqi scholars), less than a hundred pages in length and meticulously edited and commented by ʿAbd al-Fattāḥ Abū Ghudda, it is a useful work on the remarkable character of Ḥanafī *fiqh* and its school and contains useful definitions of key concepts such as analogy *(qiyās)*, scholarly exertion *(ijtihād)*, perspicuity (*raʾy*), discretionary rulings *(istiḥsān)* as well as biographical notices on the most eminent figures of the school. Among his observations: (in praise of al-Zaylaʿī) ʻIf students of *fiqh* find

209 Cf. *Thabat Ibn ʿĀbidīn*, pp. 433–434.

one among the hadith masters who is profoundly learned and truly insightful without being taken over by vain lusts, let them hold onto him tooth and nail, for such a type is, among them, as rare as red sulphur.' 'There is no jurisprudence without juridical opinion' *(lā fiqha bi-dūni ra'y).*

- *Ḥanīn al-mutafajji' wa-anīn al-mutawajji'*, a poem on the horrors of the first world war.
- *al-Ḥāwī fī sīrat al-imām Abī Ja'far al-Ṭaḥāwī*, a biography of one of the foremost authorities in the early Ḥanafī school.
- *Ḥusn al-taqāḍī fī sīrat al-imām Abī Yūsuf al-qāḍī*, a biography of the second foremost Ḥanafī authority after Abū Ḥanīfa.
- *Ibdā' wujūh al-ta'addī fī Kāmil Ibn 'Adī* (Showing the rampant enmity found in Ibn 'Adī's *al-Kāmil fī ḍu'afā' al-rijāl)* in which al-Kawtharī demonstrated the flaws of the reports adduced by Ibn 'Adī whereby Abū Ḥanīfa was purportedly criticized by Sufyān al-Thawrī, Mālik, and Ibn Ma'īn. Al-Kawtharī did the same counter-critique in his *Ta'nīb al-Khaṭīb, al-Imtā' bi-sīrat al-Imāmayn*, his introduction to *Naṣb al-rāya* and in *Fiqh ahl al-'Irāq*. In the latter two he states, 'Among the defects of Ibn 'Adī's *Kāmil* is his relentless criticism of Abū Ḥanīfa with reports that are all narrated by Abā' b. Ja'far al-Nājirāmī, one of Ibn 'Adī's shaykhs, and the latter tries to foist what al-Nājirāmī has on Abū Ḥanīfa, and this is injustice and enmity, as is the rest of his criticism. The way to expose such cases is through the chain of transmission.'
- *al-Ifṣāḥ 'an ḥukm al-ikrāh fil-ṭalāq wal-nikāḥ* (Elucidation of rulings concerning forced divorce or marriage).
- *Iḥqāq al-ḥaqq bi-ibṭāl al-bāṭil fī Mughīth al-khalq*, a refutation of Imām al-Ḥaramayn's pamphlet entitled *Mughīth al-khalq fī tarjīḥ al-qawl al-ḥaqq* to the superiority of the Shāfi'ī school over the Ḥanafī and Mālikī schools. He followed it up with a tract entitled *Aqwam al-masālik fī baḥth riwāyat Mālik 'an Abī Ḥanīfa wa-riwāyat Abī Ḥanīfa 'an Mālik* in which he adduced narrations purporting to show that Mālik had narrated from Abū Ḥanīfa and vice versa.

- *al-Imtāʿ bi-sīrat al-imāmayn al-Ḥasan ibn Ziyād* (al-Lu'lu'ī d. 204/819) *wa-ṣāḥibihi Muḥammad ibn Shujāʿ* (al-Thaljī d. 266/880), a biography of two great figures of the early Ḥanafī school.
- *Irghām al-marīd fī sharḥ al-naẓm al-ʿatīd li-tawassul al-murīd bi-rijāl al-ṭarīqat al-Naqshbandiyya al-Ḍiyā'iyya al-Khālidiyya qaddasa Allāhu asrārahum al-ʿaliyya* (Confounding the rebel: commentary on the poem on intercessory means sought by students through the men of the Naqshbandī path of Ḍiyā' al-Dīn Khālid [al-Baghdādī]) in which he said:

> I saw a book by one of the shaykhs of our time in which he objected that forty-day seclusions (*arbaʿīnāt*) were not in usage among Naqshbandī masters and that using such seclusions was therefore a deviation from their method. He means by this to object to Mawlānā Shaykh Khālid who chose that practice, considered it extremely useful, and made it one of the pillars of his path. I shall just reply with something that shall convince him in this chapter and say that Mawlānā al-Akhsīktī in *al-Maqāmāt al-kāsāniyya* said that Mawlānā al-qāḍī Muḥammad al-Samarqandī, one of the great caliphs of Khwājā [ʿUbaydullāh] Aḥrār, used to sit in forty-day seclusions although they were not in usage among the Naqshbandī masters. They asked Shaykh Shams al-Dīn Aḥmad al-Kāsānī about this and he replied: 'The path of the Naqshbandī masters is a comprehensive replica (*nuskhatun jāmiʿa*) of all the paths of the *awliyā'*. Therefore it [the forty-day seclusion] is not confined to a single path. It follows that they let it appear in every age according to whatever the spiritual wellsprings of the people of that time require. In so doing they employ whatever they wish of the pillars of the paths. No wonder at all! Some of the Khwājagān [e.g., Sayyid Amīr Kulāl] used to focus on loud *dhikr* although it was not their usage. Hence, it [loud *dhikr*] is not considered a deviation from the path of the Khwājagān in any way whatsoever.' In another place of that book he reported from his teacher, al-Kāsānī, that he used to say: 'In truth, if I were to expose all the different kinds of paths of which no ears have heard nor anyone imagines, that this [Naqshbandī] path enfolds, they would exceed one thousand.' He also said: 'Whoever thinks that the path of the Khwājagān is confined to the mountain of secrecy *(ṭūr al-ikhfā')* [i.e. in *dhikr*] has committed a huge mistake,

thrown himself into destruction, and deprived himself of the felicity of this assembly.'[210]

- *Is'ād al-rāqī 'alā al-Marāqi* on Ḥanafī *fiqh*, in which he documented the hadiths of al-Shurunbulālī's *Marāqī al-falāḥ*.[211]
- *Al-Ishfāq 'alā Aḥkām al-ṭalāq fil-radd 'alā Niẓām al-ṭalāq al-ladhī aṣdarah Aḥmad Shākir al-qāḍī* (thus published in 1900) which doubles as a refutation of Ibn Taymiyya's position on divorce in which the latter dissented from the consensus of the Sunni schools. In it al-Kawtharī wrote of the Egyptian scholar Aḥmad Shākir:

  Singling oneself out with a certain opinion among the people of learning and saying something no one ever said before are two indices of mental deficiency. We narrated as part of *Faḍā'il Abī Ḥanīfa wa-aṣḥābih* by the *ḥāfiẓ* Ibn Abī al-'Awwām with his chain to Ẓufar b. al-Hudhayl that the latter said something to this effect: 'Truly I do not debate anyone until he falls silent but until he becomes mad.' They asked how so? He said, 'He says something no one ever said.' And I consider it my religious obligation to recommend to him—if erring continues to replace intelligence for him—that he abandon writing on *fiqh* and hadith as it has become incontrovertibly clear from his writings that they are not his expertise; and the intelligent man leaves alone what he cannot excel in. A poet said, 'Allah has created certain men for wars and other men for dishes of *tharīd*.' Mistakes in *fiqh* and hadith are mistakes in the core of the religion, and mindlessness in them spells destruction here and hereafter.[212]

  The book is also known as *al-Ishfāq 'alā aḥkām al-ṭalāq fil-radd 'alā man yaqūl inna al-thalāthata wāḥida*.

210 al-Kawtharī, *Irghām al-marīd* (Cairo: [?,] 1328/1910; rept. Cairo: al-Maktabat al-Azhariyya, 2000), pp. 63–64.

211 See also Muḥammad 'Adnān Darwīsh, *Hidāyat al-Fattāḥ fī dhikr adillat* Nūr al-idāḥ (Damascus: Dār al-Majd, 1994), a complete documentation of the hadiths of *Nūr al-iḍāḥ*.

212 Thus cited in Abū Ghudda's *al-'Ulamā' al-'uzzāb* and thence in Bakr Abū Zayd's *al-Naẓā'ir*, 2nd ed. (Riyadh: Dār al-'Āṣima, 1423/2002) in which the latter viciously attacks both al-Kawtharī and Abū Ghudda, as he does in other writings of his.

- *al-Istibṣār fil-taḥadduth 'an al-jabr wal-ikhtiyār* (Insights in discussing determinism and free choice). See above.
- *Izāḥat shubhat al-mu'ammam 'an 'ibārat al-Muḥarram*, resolving the ambiguity of a certain expression used by a shaykh named al-Muḥarram in his supercommentary on al-Jāmī's commentary on Ibn al-Ḥājib's *Kāfiya* in Arabic grammar.
- *al-Jawāb al-wāfī fil-radd 'alā al-wā'iẓ al-awfī*. This is an extemporaneous 20-page reply to a preacher from the town of Awf (on the shore of the Black Sea) who had attacked Sufis.
- *Lamaḥāt al-naẓar fī sīrat al-imām Ẓufar*, a biography of the third foremost Ḥanafī authority after Abū Ḥanīfa.
- *Maqālāt al-Kawtharī*, a 600-page collection of important articles written in Egypt in the 1930s and 40s on a variety of contemporary issues and ranging from two to twenty pages each. These articles are seminal in representing the besieged state of *Ahl al-Sunna wal-Jamā'a* doctrines in the world following the fall of the Ottoman caliphate, the corrupting of al-Azhar, and the rise of modernism, secularism and purism in the *Ummah*, to the undying chagrin of Saudi critics.[213] Among these articles:
  - *Bid'at al-ṣawtiyya ḥawl al-Qur'ān* (The innovation of asserting pre-existence for the recitation of Qur'ān) in which he states: 'It is a fact that the Qur'ān as found on the Tablet, on Jibrīl's tongue and that of the Prophet, as well as the tongue of all those who recite it, their hearts, and their tablets, is created, originated, and necessarily brought to be. Whoever denies this is a sophist who is unworthy of being heard. The pre-existent is only the concept that subsists in Allah in the sense of Allah's own self-discourse

213 See, for example, Muḥammad b. Māni', *Ta'līqāt al-'allāma Muḥammad ibn Māni' 'alā* Maqālāt *al-Kawtharī wa-ba'ḍ kutubih*, ed. Sulaymān al-Kharāshī (Riyadh: Dār al-Ṣumay'ī, 1435/2014), and the vituperative literature listed in note 20.

(al-kalām al-nafsī) within His knowledge, as expressed by Aḥmad ibn Ḥanbal and Ibn Ḥazm.'[214]

- *Ḥadīth 'Man tashabbaha bi-qawm fa-huwa minhum'* (The hadith 'Whoever outwardly imitates a people, he is one of them')[215] in which he says: 'This hadith is one of the pithy statements of the Prophet. Al-Najm al-Ghazzī—one of the great Shāfiʿī scholars of the eleventh century—authored a large volume titled *Ḥusn al-tanabbuh li-aḥkām al-tashabbuh* (Awakening to the rulings that pertain to outward imitation) in which he examines at length the rulings inferred from this hadith. This volume is in the Damascus Ẓāhiriyya library and deserves to be published.'[216] In the corollary article entitled *Mansha' ilzām ahl al-dhimma bi-shiʿār khāṣṣ wa-ḥukm talabbus al-muslim bih ʿinda al-fuqahā'* (Origin of the imposition of a distinctive vestimentary sign on covenantee citizens and the legal ruling of a Muslim donning it), written in response to Muḥammad ʿAbduh's fatwa permitting the donning of fedoras and top hats by Muslims, he cites the hadith of the Prophet: 'Dye your white hair and do not imitate the Jews'[217] and mentions that Ibn Taymiyya adduced it as evidence that the forbidden *tashabbuh* may well take place

214 al-Kawtharī, *Maqālāt*, Azhariyya ed., p. 123. Cf. Ibn ʿAbd al-Salām's *al-Mulḥa fī iʿtiqād ahl al-ḥaqq*, translated in full as *The Belief of the People of Truth*, transl. Gibril Fouad Haddad (Fenton, MI: As-Sunna Foundation of America, 1999).

215 Narrated by Abū Dāwūd, Aḥmad and Ibn Abī Shayba with a sound chain according to al-ʿIrāqī as stated by al-ʿAjlūnī in *Kashf al-khafā* and Ibn Ḥajar in *Fatḥ al-Bārī* while Ibn Taymiyya in his *Iqtiḍā' al-ṣirāṭ al-mustaqīm* calls Abū Dāwūd's and Aḥmad's chain 'a good chain,' cf. Ibn Kathīr in his *Tafsīr*. Al-Bazzār also relates it through Ḥudhayfa and Abū Hurayra; Abū Nuʿaym through Anas, and al-Quḍāʿī relates it through Ṭāwūs, a chain which Ibn Ḥibbān declared sound in his *Ṣaḥīḥ*. It is confirmed by the hadith 'He is not one of us who outwardly imitates other than us' *(laysa minnā man tashabbaha bi-ghayrinā)*, narrated from ʿAbd Allāh b. ʿAmr by al-Tirmidhī who declared its chain weak.

216 al-Kawtharī, *Maqālāt*, Azhariyya ed., p. 164. See al-Ghazzī, *Ḥusn al-tanabbuh li-mā warada fil-tashabbuh*, ed. Nūr al-Dīn Ṭālib et al., 12 vols. (Damascus: Dār al-Nawādir, 1432/2011). This book is the ultimate word on the subject and its author took 40 years to complete it.

217 Narrated from Abū Hurayra by al-Tirmidhī *(ḥasan ṣaḥīḥ)* and Aḥmad, from Ibn ʿUmar and al-Zubayr by al-Nasā'ī, and from al-Zubayr and Anas by Aḥmad. Ubay ibn Kaʿb was an exception among the Companions in the fact that he left his white hair undyed.

passively on our part and without forming a specific intention.[218] This is a proof against beardless Muslims that follow Western fashion 'without intending to imitate non-Muslims' let alone those who do.

- *Ḥijāb al-mar'a* (Woman's veil).
- *Khuṭūrat al-qawl bil-jiha* (The gravity of the doctrine that attributes direction [to Allah]).
- *al-Lāmadhhabiyya qanṭarat al-lādīniyya* (No-madhhabism is the archway of atheism).[219]
- *Laylat al-niṣf min Shaʿbān* (The night of mid-Shaʿbān) in which he cites the hadith whereby the Prophet said: 'The night of mid-Shaʿbān let all of you spend in prayer and its day in fasting, for Allah descends to the nearest heaven during that night beginning with sunset and says: Is there no one asking forgiveness that I may forgive them? Is there no one asking sustenance that I may grant them sustenance? Is there no one under duress that I may relieve them? Is there not such-and-such, is there not such-and-such, and so forth until dawn rises.'[220] Al-Kawtharī commented:

218 al-Kawtharī, *Maqālāt*, Azhariyya ed., p. 323.

219 al-Kawtharī, *Maqālāt*, Azhariyya ed., p. 219–228. This article has been translated into English and published.

220 Narrated from ʿAlī by Aḥmad and Ibn Mājah with a chain containing Ibn Abī Sabra who is very weak, but it is corroborated by the hadith whereby ʿĀ'isha said: 'I missed the Prophet one night so I went out to al-Baqīʿ [and found him there]. He said: "Were you afraid that Allah would wrong you and that His Prophet would wrong you?" I said: "Messenger of Allah, I thought that you might have gone to visit one of your wives." He said: "Allāh descends to the nearest heaven on the night of mid-Shaʿbān and He forgives to more people than the number of hairs on the hides of the sheep of the tribes of Kalb."' Narrated by Aḥmad, Ibn Mājah, and al-Tirmidhī who said that he had heard al-Bukhārī grading this hadith as weak because some of the sub-narrators did not narrate directly from each other. In a similar hadith the Prophet said: 'Allah looks at His creation in the night of mid-Shaʿbān and He forgives all His creation except for the idolater and the one bent on hatred.' Narrated by Ibn Ḥibbān in his *Ṣaḥīḥ* with a sound chain and by al-Ṭabarānī with a chain of *Ṣaḥīḥ* narrators.

> The meaning of 'descent' is His opening the gate of response to His servants, and this is true Arabic usage. As for explaining it as His displacement from top to bottom, it is ignorance of what is permissible and impermissible to apply to Allah! Therefore, one has to explain it metaphorically as Allah's sending down a herald sounding out this call, as indicated by Nasā'ī's narration; or also metaphorically as His 'turning toward' *(yuqbilu 'alā)* those who ask forgiveness etc. as related from Ḥammād b. Zayd and others. Also, sunset and the last third of the night differ for each region, so both go on continuously according to each different region of the world. It cannot be imagined that a sensory descending is meant in all the formulations of the hadith of descent, and the hadith of mid-Shaʿbān is in the same category.[221]

- *Mā hiya al-aḥruf al-sabʿa?* (What are the seven wordings [of Qur'ān]?) in which he expressed the positions that the *aḥruf al-sabʿa* were not dialects but synonyms, most of which were either abrogated or retained in their known current form.[222]
- *Maḥq al-taqawwul fī mas'alat al-tawassul* (Eradication of gossip concerning the use of intermediaries), a seminal article on the question in refutation of those who deny the validity of using the Prophet and the righteous as means in supplicating Allah[223] in which he states:

> Those who deny [*tawassul*] have the Book of Allah, the Sunna, the continued practice of the Umma, and reason as a proof against them! As for the Book of Allah, this includes His saying, *And seek the means (wasīla) to Him* (al-Mā'ida 5:35). *Wasīla* in its general indication includes *tawassul* both by persons and through actions. Actually, the apparent meaning of *tawassul* in the sacred law is both this and that, despite the claims of those who lie and deceive. The distinction [made by some] between the living and

221 al-Kawtharī, *Maqālāt*, Azhariyya ed., p. 145.
222 al-Kawtharī, *Maqālāt*, Azhariyya ed., p. 121.
223 al-Kawtharī, *Maqālāt*, Azhariyya ed., p. 450–468. Re-published with notes by Wahbī Sulaymān Ghāwjī ([Beirut:] n.p., 1417/1997) and again together with Muḥammad 'Ābid al-Sindī's *Ḥawl al-tawassul wal-istighātha* and Ghāwjī's own *Kalima 'ilmiyya hādiya fil-bidʿa wa-aḥkāmihā*, ed. Wahbī Sulaymān Ghāwjī (Damascus: Dār al-Bashā'ir, 1424/2004).

the dead in this matter can only come from one who believes in the perishing of souls [upon death]—which leads to denying Resurrection—and claims that the soul's ability to discern particulars ends when it leaves the body, which is a denial of the primary evidence affirming that.[224]

- *Taḥdhīr al-umma min du'āt al-wathaniyya* (Warning the community of those who call to idol-worship), written in 1942, in which he lambasts al-Azhar for allowing the publication of 'Uthmān b. Sa'īd al-Dārimī's *al-Radd 'alā al-Jahmiyya* which contains phrases like '[Allah] moves if He wishes, descends and ascends if He wishes... stands and sits if He wishes,' 'Allah has a limit... and His place also has a limit, as He is on His Throne above His heavens, and these are two limits,' 'if He wished, He would have settled on the back of a gnat' and other enormities.[225] This is identical to Ibn Karrām's doctrine whereby 'Allah has a body unlike bodies, and a limit.'[226] Yet Ibn Taymiyya ardently defends al-Dārimī's views,[227] citing them time and again in *al-Ta'sīs radd Asās al-taqdīs*[228] (an all-out attack on Fakhr al-Dīn al-Rāzī's refutation of anthropomorphism titled *Asās al-taqdīs*) including the gnat remark,[229] even claiming that Imām

224 Shaykh Wahbī Ghāwjī in his footnotes quoted Fakhr al-Dīn al-Rāzī as saying, 'Souls remain after the perishing of bodies. This is a matter agreed upon by Prophets, *awliyā'*, and sages.' In Rāzī, *Ma'ālim uṣūl al-dīn* (Bāb 8, Mas'ala 6). Then he quoted Ibn al-Qayyim from his book *al-Rūḥ* in support of this. *Maḥq al-taqawwul* (1997 ed. pp. 102–104; 2004 ed. pp. 99–101).

225 al-Kawtharī, *Maqālāt*, Azhariyya ed., pp. 378–383, cf. 361–367, 391–406, 420.

226 See 'Abd al-Qāhir al-Baghdādī, *al-Farq bayna al-firaq*, pp. 203, 217.

227 Ibn al-Qayyim in *Ijtimā' al-juyūsh* (p. 88=p. 143) revealed that Ibn Taymiyya 'praised and recommended al-Dārimī's two books [*Naqd al-Jahmiyya* and *al-Radd 'alā Bishr al-Marrīsī*] most strenuously.'

228 The *Ta'sīs* is a refutation of al-Rāzī's *Asās al-taqdīs*, itself in refutation of anthropomorphism. The *Ta'sīs* was newly printed under the made-up title of *Bayān talbīs al-Jahmiyya fī ta'sīs bida'ihim al-kalamiyya*, ed. Muḥammad b. 'Abd al-Raḥīm b. Qāsim, 2 vols. (Mecca: Maṭba'at al-Ḥukūma, 1972). Cf. *Bayān talbīs al-Jahmiyya*, 1:426–427, 1:433, 1:443–444, 2:111, 2:157–160, 2:494–495.

229 *Bayān talbīs*, 1:568, 2:160.

Aḥmad upheld the doctrine of that Allah possesses a limit.[230] At the same time he admits that *Ahl al-Sunna* did hold the opposite view: 'The position that He is above the Throne but has no limit *(ḥadd)* nor dimension nor body is that of many of the upholders of the divine attributes *(al-ṣifātiyya)* among the followers of Ibn Kullāb and the Ashʿarī imams including their early authorities and whoever agrees with them among the jurists,... the hadith scholars, and the Sufis... among them Abū Ḥātim, Ibn Ḥibbān, and Abū Sulaymān al-Khaṭṭābī.'[231] Then he states: 'The Qadi [Abū Yaʿlā] said that Aḥmad asserted in absolute terms that Allah had a limit but he negated it in Ḥanbal's narration, saying: "We believe Allah is on the Throne in the manner He wishes and however He wishes, without limit nor description anyone could give or define Him by." So he negated the limit that pertains to the description he mentioned, meaning the limit known by creatures... And that is the meaning of Aḥmad's statement: "Allah has a limit that only He knows."'[232] The latter is in blatant contradiction of what is authentically reported from Imam Aḥmad by the major authorities of this school.[233]

230 Ibn Taymiyya, *Taʾsīs* = *Bayān talbīs al-Jahmiyya*, 1:445 and 2:162: 'The Book and the Sunna definitely show that concept [that Allah exists and is separate from His creation and firmly established to be real] as already mentioned of Imām Aḥmad's adducing as proof for this what the Qur'ān says, which indicates that *Allāh has a limit* by which He distinguishes Himself from creatures, and that there is a chasm *(infiṣāl)* and a separation *(mubāyana)* between Him and creation, so it is true that matters ascend and rise up to Him, and it is true that He comes and arrives.' 'Al-Khallāl said: Muḥammad b. ʿAlī al-Warrāq narrated to us: Abū Bakr al-Athram narrated to us: Muḥammad b. Ibrāhīm al-Qaysī narrated to me: I said to Aḥmad b. Ḥanbal that it is said that Ibn al-Mubārak was asked: How do we know our Lord? and he replied: "In the seventh heaven on His Throne, with a limit." Aḥmad said: "That is what we say also."' Cf. from Isḥāq b. Rāhūyah and Ibn al-Mubārak in al-Harawī, *Dhamm al-kalām* (4:337–338). On the actual status of such narrations see our published edition of Ibn Jahbal, *Refutation of Him [Ibn Taymiyya] Who Attributes a Direction to Allah.*

231 Ibn Taymiyya, *Bayān talbīs*, 1:548, 1:600, 2:169.

232 Ibn Taymiyya, *Bayān talbīs*, 2:173.

233 See the narrations from al-Khallāl, Ḥanbal, and Abū al-Faḍl al-Tamīmī in our edition of Ibn Jahbal.

- *al-Muntaqā al-mufīd min al-ʿIqd al-farīd fī ʿulūw al-asānīd*, his abridgment of his great-grandshaykh al-Arwādī's *thabat*.[234]
- *Muqaddimāt al-Kawtharī* is a compilation of all the scholarly introductions penned by al-Kawtharī for the books he edited and manuscripts he published.[235]
- *Naqd Kitāb al-ḍuʿafāʾ līl-ʿUqaylī* (Rebuttal of al-ʿUqaylī's *Ḍuʿafāʾ*), in which al-Kawtharī denounced the Ḥanbalī al-ʿUqaylī's excessive anti-Ḥanafī bias in his book of discredited narrators titled *Kitāb al-Ḍuʿafāʾ*. Possibly the most fanatic and least reliable of narrator-criticism authorities, his notice on Abū Ḥanīfa is a collection of weak and fabricated reports but he also attacked the likes of Thābit al-Bunānī, Ibn al-Madīnī, al-Bukhārī, ʿAbd al-Razzāq, Ibn Abī Shayba, ʿAffān b. Muslim and others, for which he earned al-Dhahabī's strong reprimand.[236] Al-Kawtharī said: 'We find in al-ʿUqaylī's *Ḍuʿafāʾ* and Ibn ʿAdī's *Kāmil* much idle talk against our masters, the imams of jurisprudence, because of the former's anthropomorphist creed and the latter's bias for his [Shāfiʿī] school, together with his questionable creed.'[237]
- *al-Naqd al-tāmmī ʿalā al-ʿiqd al-nāmī ʿalā sharḥ al-Jāmī*, a supercommentary on the Turkish Muḥammad Raḥmī al-Akīnī's commentary titled *al-ʿIqd al-nāmī* on ʿAbd al-Raḥmān al-Jāmī's *al-Fawāʾid al-ḍiyāʾiyya sharḥ al-Kāfiya* in grammar.
- *al-Naẓm al-ʿatīd li-tawassul al-murīd* and its commentary entitled *Irghām al-murīd fī sharḥ al-Naẓm al-ʿatīd*, already discussed above.

234 See above, note 182.

235 *Muqaddimāt al-imām al-Kawtharī* (Damascus and Beirut: Dār al-Thurayyā, 1418/1997).

236 'Have you no *ʿaql*, ʿUqaylī? Do you know whom you are speaking about? The only reason we mention what you say about them is in order to repel from them the statements made about them—as if you did not know that each one of those you target is several times more trustworthy than you! Nay, more trustworthy than many trustworthy narrators whom you did not even cite once in your book... If the hadith of these narrators were to be abandoned, then shut the gates, cease all speech, let hadith transmission die, put the free-thinkers in office, and let the antichrists come out!' al-Dhahabī, *Mīzān al-iʿtidāl*, 2:230, 3:140.

237 al-Kawtharī, *Fiqh ahl al-ʿIraq*, p. 83.

- *Naẓm ʿawāmil al-iʿrāb* (Poem on declensions), in Persian, his first work.
- *Naẓra ʿābira fī mazāʿim man yunkir nuzūl ʿĪsā ʿalyh al-salām qabla al-ākhira* (A glimpse at the claims of those who deny ʿĪsā's descent before the next life), a 67-page treatise which inspired ʿAbd Allāh al-Ghumārī's subsequent *ʿAqīdat ahl al-Islām fī nuzūl ʿĪsā ʿalayhi al-salām* (Creed of the Muslims concerning the descent of ʿĪsā) which lists all the authentic evidence to that effect and which al-Kawtharī prefaced. Both works were written in refutation of a strange fatwa by Shaykh al-Azhar Maḥmūd Shalṭūt in which he apparently followed Muḥammad ʿAbduh's and Rashīd Riḍā's precedent in questioning the mass-transmitted, obligatory Muslim creed in the forthcoming descent of ʿĪsā—upon him peace.[238]
- *al-Nukat al-ṭarīfa fil-taḥadduth ʿan rudūd Ibn Abī Shayba ʿalā Abī Ḥanīfa*, a rebuttal of Ibn Abī Shayba's attacks on Abū Ḥanīfa in his *Muṣannaf*.
- *Qawāʿid ʿaqāʾid al-Bāṭiniyya* (Foundations of the doctrines of the Esoterics).
- *Qurrat al-nawāẓir fī ādāb al-munāẓir*, a treatise on debate translated from the original Turkish of Jawdat Bāshā.
- *Rafʿ al-ishtibāh ʿan ḥukm kashf al-raʾs wa-labs al-niʿāl fil-ṣalāt* (Removal of doubt concerning the status of praying bare-headed and wearing shoes), a fatwa—also included in the *Maqālāt*—which denounces the then new 'Salafī' tendency of praying 'in the appearance of the lowborn.'[239]

238 See *al-Manār*, January 1928 issue, and *Tafsīr al-Manār*, 3:317 where they claim there is no mass transmission. See also the compilation of reports establishing mass transmission of the prophesy of the descent of ʿĪsā by Anwar Shāh Kashmīrī, edited and published by Abū Ghudda.

239 Cf. al-Kawtharī, *Maqālāt* (Riyadh ed., pp. 201–218 = Azhariyya ed., pp. 258–273). See the translated excerpts in the *Encyclopedia of Islamic Doctrine*, 6:128–130.

- *al-Ṣuḥuf al-munshara fī sharḥ al-uṣūl al-ʿashara li-Najm al-Dīn Kubrā*, an explanation of the Ten Principles by the Central Asian Sufi master Najm al-Dīn Kubrā.
- *Tadrīb al-ṭullāb ʿalā qawāʿid al-iʿrāb*, a manual for training in parsing.
- *Tadrīb al-waṣīf ʿalā qawāʿid al-taṣrīf*, on morphology
- *Tafrīḥ al-bāl bi-ḥall Tārīkh Ibn al-Kamāl*, on the way to solve the riddles contained in the history of the Ottomans entitled *Tārīkh Āl ʿUthmān* by Shams al-Dīn Aḥmad b. Sulaymān b. Kamāl Bāshā (873–940/1469–1534).
- *al-Taḥrīr al-wajīz fī-mā yabtaghīh al-mustajīz*, his catalogue of shaykhs.
- *Taʾnīb al-Khaṭīb ʿalā mā sāqahu fī tarjamat Abī Ḥanīfa min al-akādhīb* (Rebuking al-Khaṭīb for citing lies in his biographical notice on Abū Ḥanīfa) to which the 'Salafī' scholar ʿAbd al-Raḥmān b. Yaḥyā al-Muʿallamī al-Yamānī (1313–1386/1895–1966) responded with a two-volume work entitled *al-Tankīl li-mā warada fī* Taʾnīb *al-Kawtharī min al-abāṭīl* (Repelling the falsehoods cited in al-Kawtharī's *Taʾnīb*). The *Tankīl* contains an attack on the early Ḥanafī school engulfing Ashʿarīs and giving free vent to the author's anti-*madhhabī* and anthropomorphist views, to the point that he states: 'To negate [from Allah] the corporeality that is necessarily forbidden, some said that Allah has a body unlike bodies.'[240] Al-Kawtharī countered with *al-Tarḥīb bi-naqd al-Taʾnīb*[241] in which he revealed that the publication of al-Muʿallamī's critique was financed by Muḥammad Naṣīf, the same wealthy Jeddah patron who had financed (i) the printing of al-Qārī's hapless fatwa that the parents of the Prophet were in hellfire; (ii) the dissemination in India of the derogatory part of al-Khaṭīb's biography of Abū Ḥanīfa with an Urdu translation;[242] and (iii) the publication of the rankly anthropomorphist *Kitāb al-Sunna*

240 al-Muʿallamī, *al-Tankīl*, 2:371.

241 The *Taʾnīb* and the *Tarḥīb* were reprinted together in 1990 without mention of place nor publisher, and in Egypt at al-Maktabat al-Azhariyya līl-Turāth in 1998.

242 Cf. also *Maqālāt*, Azhariyya ed., p. 416.

attributed to ʿAbd Allāh b. Aḥmad b. Ḥanbal, concerning which book Shuʿayb al-Arnāʾūṭ said that 'at least 50 percent of the hadiths in it are weak or outright forgeries.'[243] Al-Kawtharī also revealed that al-Muʿallamī's editor, Muḥammad ʿAbd al-Razzāq Ḥamza, collaborated on the publication of ʿUthmān b. Saʿīd al-Dārimī's *Naqd al-Jahmiyya*, which contains similar Israelite reports, anthropomorphist forgeries and other enormities.

- *Tarwīḍ al-qāriḥa bi-mawāzīn al-fikr al-ṣaḥīḥa*, a treatise on logic translated from the original Turkish of Jawdat Bāshā.

Among the books al-Kawtharī edited or foreworded:

- al-Bayāḍī's (*q.v.*) *Ishārāt al-marām min ʿibārāt al-Imām*, on Abū Ḥanīfa's *Fiqh al-absaṭ*, his positions in *kalām*, the terminologies he used and the Māturīdīs' differences with the Ashʿarīs.
- al-Bayhaqī's *al-Asmāʾ wal-ṣifāt*.[244]
- al-Ghaznawī's (d. 773/1372) *al-Ghurra al-munīfa fī taḥqīq baʿḍ masāʾil al-Imām Abī Ḥanīfa*, a work of comparative *fiqh* between the Ḥanafī and Shāfiʿī schools similar to al-Bayhaqī's *Khilāfiyyāt*, written by request of the scholarly emir Ṣirghatmīsh al-Miṣrī in refutation of al-Rāzī's *al-Ṭarīqa al-bahāʾiyya fīl-khilāf*, a treatise on the differences of the jurists advocating the supremacy of the Shāfiʿī school. Al-Ghaznawī translated al-Rāzī's work into Arabic from the original Persian in the process.
- Ibn ʿAsākir's *Tabyīn kadhib al-muftarī ʿalā Abī al-Ḥasan al-Ashʿarī*, a biography of the imam of *Ahl al-Sunna wal-Jamāʿa* containing a

243 As cited by Nuh Keller in his translation of Ibn al-Naqīb al-Miṣrī's *ʿUmdat al-sālik* entitled *Reliance of the Traveller*.

244 The 'Salafī' editor of the two-volume edition of this work in Riyadh, ʿAbd Allāh al-Ḥāshidī, openly states in his preface that his purpose was to fulfill his shaykh's wish that 'someone should refute al-Kawtharī's heretical positions in his edition of *al-Asmāʾ wal-ṣifāt*.' A refutation of al-Ḥāshidī's own heretical positions can be found in our published translation and commentary of excerpts from al-Bayhaqī's work published at as-Sunna Foundation of America in 1999.

statement of his doctrine and a refutation of positions falsely attributed to him.

- Ibn Quṭayba's *al-Ikhtilāf fil lafẓ wal-radd 'alā al-Jahmiyya wal-Mushabbiha* (The disagreement concerning pronunciation [of Qur'ān] and the refutation of the Jahmīs and anthropomorphists).[245]
- Ibn Quṭlūbaghā's (d. 879/1474) *Munyat al-alma'ī fi-mā fāta min takhrīj aḥādīth al-Hidāya lil-Zayla'ī*, a continuation of al-Zayla'ī's *Naṣb al-rāya* in the documentation of al-Marghīnānī's *al-Hidāya* in Ḥanafī *fiqh*.
- al-Nābulusī's (d. 1143/1731) *Kashf al-satr 'an farḍiyyat al-watr* (Disclosure of the obligatory nature of the *witr* prayer), in which the author adduces the proofs of the Ḥanafī school on this topic. Al-Kawtharī mentioned in his introduction the sayings of the authorities on this prayer, notably the rejection of the legal testimony of one who did not pray *witr* by Mālik and Aḥmad, and the saying of al-Shāfi'ī in *al-Umm*: 'Whoever leaves the Sunna of *fajr* or *ṣalāt al-witr* is in a worse state than if he had left all the supererogatory prayers.'[246]
- al-Qaysarānī's *Shurūṭ al-a'immat al-sitta* (The criteria [of hadith authentication] according to the six imams: al-Bukhārī, Muslim, Abū Dāwūd, al-Tirmidhī, al-Nasā'ī, and Ibn Mājah) together with al-Ḥāzimī's *Shurūṭ al-a'imma al-khamsa* (The criteria [of hadith authentication] according to the five imams: al-Bukhārī, Muslim, Abū Dāwūd, al-Tirmidhī, and al-Nasā'ī).
- al-Shāfi'ī's *Musnad* and his *Aḥkām al-Qur'ān*.
- Sibṭ Ibn al-Jawzī's *al-Intiṣār wal-tarjīḥ lil-madhhab al-ṣaḥīḥ* (The defense and advocacy of the true school of law) in praise of Abū Ḥanīfa and his school.
- al-Ṭaḥāwī's *'Aqīda*.

245 The fact that Ibn Qutayba made a scathing attack on Abū Ḥanīfa in his *Ta'wīl mukhtalif al-Ḥadīth* shows that al-Kawtharī placed the necessity of refuting the anthropomorphist heresy above his *madhhab* affiliation.

246 Narrated from al-Rabī' in *al-Umm*, 1:142.

- Ibn al-Jawzī's *Dafʿ shubah al-tashbīh* (The repelling of the insinuations of anthropomorphism at the hands of divine transcendence) in which al-Kawtharī collected many of the most insightful explanations of the Sunni scholars on the verses and hadiths misquoted by the anthropomorphists to support their ideas.
- *Tabdīd al-ẓalām*, Kawtharī's commentary on al-Subkī's refutation of Ibn al-Qayyim entitled *al-Sayf al-ṣaqīl fil-radd ʿalā Ibn Zafīl* in which he said: 'The *Ibāna* was authored at the first of [Ashʿarī's] return from Muʿtazilī thought and was by way of trying to induce al-Barbahārī to embrace the tenets of faith of *Ahl al-Sunna*. Whoever believes it to be the last of his books believes something that is patently false. Moreover, pen after pen of the anthropomorphists has had free disposal of the text, particularly after the strife that took place in Baghdad,[247] so that what is in the work that contradicts the explicit positions transmitted from al-Ashʿarī by his own disciples and their disciples, cannot be relied upon.'[248]

A sharp reader and unparalleled expert in rare books and manuscripts, al-Kawtharī revealed that the printed version of Maḥmūd b. ʿAbd Allāh al-Ālūsī's (1217–1270/1802–1854) commentary on Qur'ān entitled *Rūḥ al-maʿānī* published by his 'Salafi' son Nuʿmān al-Ālūsī in Bulaq (Egypt) in 1301/1884 (then again twice by the Damascene 'Salafi' Munīr ʿAbduh Āghā at his Muniriyya Press in Egypt) contained alterations and foreign accretions, responsibility for which al-Kawtharī laid squarely at the feet of Nuʿmān: 'He cannot be trusted over the publication of his father's commentary, and if someone were to compare it [the latter edition] with the [autograph] manuscript kept today at the Rāghib Bāshā library in Istanbul, which is the manuscript gifted by the author to the Sultan ʿAbd al-Majīd Khān, one would certainly find in it what will make him certain of that.'[249] In his 1968 372-page book

247 After 323/935, when the disciples of al-Barbahārī gained the upper hand in Baghdad, Shāfiʿīs were beaten and anthropomorphism became the creed of the day as chronicled by Ibn al-Athīr, *al-Kāmil fil-tārikh*, 7:114.

248 al-Kawtharī, notes on al-Subkī's *al-Sayf al-ṣaqīl*, p. 108. As for the claim by Ibn ʿImād in *Shadharāt al-dhahab*, 1:303, that the *Ibāna* was al-Ashʿarī's last book, he gave no proof and is alone in claiming this.

249 al-Kawthari, *Maqālāt*, p. 344, and marginalia on al-Subkī's *al-Radd ʿalā* al-Nūniyya, p. 108.

al-Ālūsī Mufassiran, Muḥsin ʿAbd al-Ḥamīd[250] denied the charge that there had been any tampering with *Rūḥ al-maʿānī* as 'a bizarre fiction,' claiming he had compared the manuscript kept at Baghdad's general Awqāf library and found no discrepancies, and that he consulted with [the 'Salafi'] Muḥammad Bahjat [al-Bayṭār] and Munīr al-Qāḍī who were of one mind with him. However, in an internet communication on February 26, 2006 the Riyadh genealogist and historian of scholarship Muḥammad b. ʿAbd Allāh Āl Rashīd mentioned all the above and commented:

> This claim [by Muḥsin ʿAbd al-Ḥamīd] avails us nothing, since al- Kawtharī very precisely referred to the autograph manuscript and its location. In the Ḥajj of the year that just passed (1426/2005) I met the researcher and teacher Aḥmad b. ʿAbd al-Karīm al-ʿĀnī who told me that the Imām al-Aʿẓam faculty in the city of Baghdad had tasked thirty Master's candidate students to prepare a critical edition of al-Ālūsī's commentary, *Rūḥ al-Maʿānī*, Ustādh al-ʿĀnī being one of those students... and they were basing themselves on the manuscript indicated by Shaykh al-Kawtharī. He told me that the printed version was indeed filled with alterations, tamperings, gaps and suppressions in many places, which confirms the words of Shaykh al-Kawtharī that the printed version which is in circulation contains tamperings and suppressions.[251]

Al-Kawtharī was criticized for what is perceived by some as excessive bias for the Ḥanafi school and a contentious style in refuting or attacking opponents. ʿAbd Allāh b. Muḥammad b. al-Ṣiddīq al-Ghumārī (1328–1413/1910–1993) wrote:

> We admired al-Kawtharī for his knowledge, wide reading, and modesty, just as we hated his bias for the Ḥanafīs. This bias of his exceeded al-Zamakhsharī's bias for the Muʿtazilī school to the point that my brother, the hadith master Abū al-Fayḍ [Aḥmad b. Muḥammad b. al-Ṣiddīq al-Ghumārī] used to call him 'Abū Ḥanīfa's madman" *(majnūn Abī Ḥanīfa).*

250 Muḥsin ʿAbd al-Ḥamīd also authored the 1983 book in defense of al-Afghānī entitled *Jamāl al-Dīn al-Afghānī: al-muṣliḥ al-muftarā ʿalayh.*

251 http://cb.rayaheen.net/showthread.php?tid=11817 as of 22 October 2017. Muḥ. Zāhid Abū Ghudda confirmed in a November 2013 post that the issue would not be settled until the actual Rāghib Bāshā autograph manuscript was verifiably perused and published: https://islamsyria.com/site/show_articles/11777 as of 3 December 2020 and http://zahidabdulfattah.blogspot.com/2013/11/ as of the same date.

When he gave me his treatise entitled *Iḥqāq al-ḥaqq* [*bi-Ibṭāl al-bāṭil fī* Mughīth al-khalq] (Letting truth prevail in exposing the falsehoods of *Mughīth al-khalq*), a refutation of Imām al-Ḥaramayn's [Abū al-Ma'ālī 'Abd al-Malik b. 'Abd Allāh b. al-Juwaynī] (419–478/1028–1085) epistle on the superiority of the Shāfi'ī school [entitled *Mughīth al-khalq fī tarjīḥ al-qawl al-ḥaqq* in which the Imam attacked the Ḥanafī and Mālikī schools], I found him casting aspersions [cf. *Iḥqāq*, p. 19–20] on the [Qurayshī] lineage of Imam al-Shāfi'ī, citing [the trustworthy hadith master Zakariyyā b. Yaḥyā b. Dāwūd] al-Sājī's statement [in his book *Manāqib al-Shāfi'ī*].[252] I criticized him for this aspersion and said to him: 'Questioning lineage does not make a scholarly refutation.' He replied, 'A sectarian rebutting a sectarian!' He said this verbatim, so he acknowledges his sectarianism.

I visited him in his house once, together with the noble Sherif, Sayyid Muḥammad al-Bāqir al-Kattānī, and as we discussed certain scholarly issues the name of the hadith master Ibn Ḥajar came up. Sayyid al-Bāqir expressed his admiration of Ibn Ḥajar's memorization and his commentary on al-Bukhārī, and I echoed his opinion. Whereupon he deprecated that commentary and said, 'Ibn Ḥajar used to depend upon hadith indexes *(al-aṭrāf)* when collating the different routes of the hadith,' which is untrue. Then he said that he—Ibn Ḥajar—used to follow women in the street and make passes at them, at one time following a woman thinking that she was beautiful, until she arrived at her house with him in her tracks; when she removed her face-veil *(burqu')*, she turned out to be an ugly black woman, so he turned back, frustrated. Now, the reason behind this attack, is that al-Ḥāfiẓ used to assail some of the Ḥanafīs in his books of biography, such as *al-Durar al-kāmina* and *Raf' al-iṣr* ['*an quḍāt Miṣr*].[253] He said of the Ḥanafī al-'Aynī that he used to take the manuscript pages of *Fatḥ al-Bārī* from one of his students and use them in his commentary [on *Ṣaḥīḥ al-Bukhārī*, entitled '*Umdat al-qārī*]. When al-Ḥāfiz. found out, he prevented the distribution of these pages to students.

252 Al-Sājī is not alone in narrating this lineage, as shown by Ibn Ḥajar's narration of an identical report from al-Za'farānī through Abū Nu'aym in *Tawālī al-ta'nīs*, p. 34.

253 As recognized by his student al-Sakhāwī in *al-Ḍaw' al-lāmi'*, cf. al-Kawtharī, *al-Ḥāwī*, pp. 28–30.

Worse than this, al-Kawtharī imputed senility to Anas bin Mālik for relating a hadith that contradicts the school of Abū Ḥanīfa![254] Worse yet is his attempt to pass a fabricated hadith as authentic because it might imply the tidings of Abū Ḥanīfa, namely, the hadith: 'Were knowledge *('ilm)* to be found at the Pleiades, certain men from among the Persians would go there to obtain it.' The hadith is in the two *Ṣaḥīḥ*s with the word 'belief' [Were belief *(īmān)* to be found at the Pleiades, a man from those people would go there to obtain

254 The charge that al-Kawtharī imputed senility to Anas is true, since he himself said in *Ta'nīb al-Khaṭīb* (orig. ed., p. 80 = 1990 ed., pp. 158–159 = 1998 ed., p. 129): 'The narration of the braining [of the young girl by a Jewish robber who was then brained in requital] is related [by al-Bukhārī and Muslim] from Anas alone in the time of his senility (*fī 'ahdi haramih*), just as he is alone to relate the drinking of the urine of the camels in Qatāda's narration [in *Ṣaḥīḥ Muslim*] and the account of the punishment of the *'Uraniyyīn* [by mutilation and blinding in *Ṣaḥīḥ Muslim*].' This imputation of senility specifically to Anas is unprecedented–as pointed out by Mu'allamī in *al-Tankīl*, 1:63–64–but not baseless, and the latter's reaction seems overdone and disingenuous. Al-Khaṭīb narrated in his *Jāmi' li-akhlāq al-rāwī*, 2:474 no. 1999, chapter 46 entitled 'Quitting hadith narration in old age lest memory is affected and the mind becomes confused': 'Abū Muḥammad al-Ḥasan b. 'Abd al-Raḥmān b. Khallād said "If the hadith scholar lives a long life, I find it preferable that he stop transmitting narrations at the age of eighty, for it is the period of senility."' Abū Ḥanīfa did narrate from Anas–who died at the age of 103–a full twenty hadiths in his *Musnad* according to al-Qārī in *Sharḥ Musnad Abī Ḥanīfa* through the following *Tābi'īn*: Ḥammād b. Abī Sulaymān (1), al-Zuhrī (3), Muḥammad b. al-Munkadir (1), Yaḥyā b. Sa'īd (2), al-Haytham and Rabī'a (1), Ibrāhīm al-Nakha'ī (2), Yazīd b. 'Abd al-Raḥmān (2), Sufyān b. Ṭalḥa (1), 'Abd al-Karīm b. Umayya (1), al-Haytham b. Ḥabīb (1), Muslim b. Kaysān (2), 'Abd al-Raḥmān b. Ḥazm (1), and al-Qāsim b. 'Abd al-Raḥmān (2). However, as Kawtharī said in his response to *al-Tankīl* entitled *al-Tarḥīb bi-naqd* al-Ta'nīb (1990 ed., p. 415=1998 ed., pp. 337–338): 'All I did concerning Anas was convey the method of Abū Ḥanīfa in selecting some of his narrations [*i.e.* those which he is not alone to narrate]. This is well-known in the books of the people of learning, and does not constitute an aspersion against Anas.' So the real reason for al-Kawtharī's remark on Anas is not 'for relating a hadith that contradicts the school of Abū Ḥanīfa' as claimed by al-Ghumārī, but because the method of Abū Ḥanīfa in hadith narrators was primarily precaution *(iḥtiyāṭ)*. Furthermore, Anas's narration of the braining conveys a ruling *(ḥukm)* that is contradicted by the sound hadith '[Let there be] no capital requital except by the sword' *(lā qawad illā bil-sayf)* narrated from five Companions–Abū Bakrah, al-Nu'mān b. Bashīr, Ibn Mas'ūd, Abū Hurayra, and 'Alī b. Abī Ṭālib–so that the ruling of retributive braining not only 'contradicts the school of Abū Ḥanīfa' but also that of al-Sha'bī, al-Nakha'ī, al-Ḥasan al-Baṣrī, and Sufyān al-Thawrī as pointed out by al-'Aynī in in his commentary on al-Bukhārī's *Ṣaḥīḥ* entitled *'Umdat al-qārī*, 9:597–598 *(Kitāb al-ṭalāq, bāb al-ishāra fil-ṭalāq)*.

it'[255]], and when the Prophet said it he put his hand on the shoulder of Salmān al-Fārisī. Some forger then changed the word 'belief' to 'knowledge' as pointed out by my brother the hadith master Abū al-Fayḍ in *al-Mathnawī wal-battār.*[256] He added: 'Even if it were authentic there would not be in it any reference to Abū Ḥanīfa but to the hadith masters who came out of Persia, such as Abū al-Shaykh and Abū Nuʿaym, for *ʿilm* in the terminology of Islamic law means the Book and the Sunna, not juridical opinion *(raʾy)* and analogy *(qiyās)*!'[257] Al-Kawtharī took him to task in *Taʾnīb al-Khaṭīb* for saying this and replied to him with some harsh words, whereupon my brother wrote a reply to him in

255 Narrated from Abū Hurayra by al-Bukhārī, Muslim, and al-Tirmidhī.

256 Aḥmad al-Ghumārī was referring to the narration 'Were knowledge *(ʿilm)* hanging at the Pleiades, people—or: a man—from Persia would go there to obtain it' which, far from being a forgery, is narrated from Abū Hurayra by Aḥmad with a good chain through Shahr ibn Ḥawshab cf. al-Haythamī, *Majmaʿ al-zawāʾid*, 10:64 and others. Ibn Ḥazm in *al-Iḥkām*, 6:288, declared this wording '*ṣaḥīḥ* without the slightest doubt' but within a discussion where his purpose is to discredit the narration predicting Mālik. The upshot is that, contrary to the claim of the Ghumārīs, the narration of 'knowledge at the Pleiades' is not forged but authentic. Furthermore, a confirmatory narration states that Abū Hurayra used to pay special attention to the Persians and say to them: 'Draw near, Banū Farrūkh! For if knowledge were hanging at the Pleiades, there would be among you one/those who would take it.' Narrated by Abū Khaythama in *al-ʿIlm*, p. 21 no. 82) with a sound chain per the criterion of the *Ṣaḥīḥayn*. Yet another version states 'the religion' *(al-dīn)*. Narrated from Ibn Masʿūd by al-Ṭabarānī in *al-Kabīr*, 10:204 no. 10470.

257 Al-Qārī and countless hadith scholars before him saw tidings of Abū Ḥanīfa in the hadith of the Pleiades and there is no doubt that their vast majority consider him an foremost authority of *ʿilm* in the Book and the Sunna whose stature excels that of Abū al-Shaykh and Abū Nuʿaym. Furthermore, *ʿilm* as defined in the Qurʾān and *mutawātir* narrations means the *fiqh* of the religion exactly as Abū Ḥanīfa exemplifies it. In fairness, the Ghumārīs' aspersions against him are offensive to say the least, and more aberrant yet is Aḥmad al-Ghumārī's own declaration in *al-Mughīr ʿalā al-aḥ ādīth al-mawḍūʿa fil-Jāmiʿ al-ṣaghīr*, pp. 102–104, that al-Bukhārī and Muslim's *Ṣaḥīḥ*s contain fabricated narrations. The great *Tābiʿī* Ibrāhīm ibn Abī 'Abla (d. 152/769) said: 'Whoever learns the aberrations of knowledge learns a great evil.' Narrated by al-Khaṭīb in *al-Kifāya*, al-Mizzī in *Tahdhīb* al-Kamāl, 2:144, and al-Dhahabī in the *Siyar*, Dār al-Fikr ed. 6:486 = Risāla ed. 6:324, while al-Awzāʿī warned, 'Whoever holds on to the rare and unusual positions of the scholars has left Islam.' At any rate, the ulema recommend discarding the mutual aspersions related from contemporaries, cf. Ibn 'Abd al-Barr, *Jāmiʿ bayān al-ʿilm*, 2:1087–1119, al-Dhahabī, introduction to *Mīzān al-iʿtidāl*, and Ibn al-Subkī, *Qāʿida fil-jarḥ wal-taʿdīl*. For example: inter-*Ṣaḥābī* divisions; al-Shaʿbī and 'Ikrima; Mālik and Ibn Isḥāq; Muḥāsibī and Aḥmad b. Ḥanbal; Ibn Mandah and Abū Nuʿaym; al-Sakhāwī and al-Suyūṭī; Allāh have mercy on them and us.

which he collected his scholarly blunders and the self-contradictions caused by his odious fanaticism, with some harshness, at the same time acknowledging his knowledge and learning. That reply was not submitted for publication out of deference for their friendship.[258] The difference of opinion between two scholars does not break up their friendship and, like two lawyers differing in a court of justice, they meet as friends outside of it.... May Allah have mercy on my brother and on al-Kawtharī, the two major scholars of their time without contest, and may Allah gather us with them in the Abode of His Mercy.[259]

The former friend and student of Aḥmad al-Ghumārī, Muḥammad Abū Khubza, called al-Kawtharī 'a paragon of *shu'ūbiyya* and hatred of the Arabs' in his brief, rabidly anti-*madhhabī* book *Naẓarāt fī tārīkh al-madhāhib al-Islāmiyya*. In his anti-Ḥanafī and anti-Māturīdī book *'Adā' al-Māturīdiyya lil-'aqīdat al-salafiyya*, also known as *al-Māturīdiyya wa-wawqifuhum min tawḥīd al-asmā' wal-ṣifāt*, originally a three-volume Master's thesis at the University of Medina, the late Shams al-Dīn al-Afghānī culled Aḥmad al-Ghumārī's book against al-Kawtharī (from which al-Ghumārī reportedly repented and which he never published but which the Wahhābī writer 'Alī al-Ḥalabī obtained and published in full) for hundreds of cut-and-paste, carefully decontextualized nuggets intended to show al-Kawtharī in a less than flattering light. As usual, it did not bother the author, his sponsors, and his present-day promoters and translators that such excerpts have mostly nothing to do with doctrine or Māturīdism but carry value only as fodder for calumny of the ulema. There was intense rivalry between Aḥmad al-Ghumārī and al-Kawtharī in the sciences, particularly *fiqh* and hadith as well as competitiveness in erudition. It is truly hard to say which possessed a more prolific output than the other or more proficiency in manuscripts, narrators, and the paths of narration as both were prodigious in those fields. Al-Ghumārī emerges as the one who specialized in hadith and its documentation.[260] Both defended *Ahl al-Sunna* against its detractors, but al-Kawtharī shone more in the defense of Sunni doctrine while al-Ghumārī's Shī'ī lean-

258 This voluminous (360 pages) full-fledged, venomous attack on the Ḥanafī school by Aḥmad al-Ghumārī entitled *Bayān talbīs al-muftarī Muḥammad Zāhid al-Kawtharī* was published at Riyadh's Dār al-Ṣumay'ī in 1993 by none other than the Wahhābī enemy of the Ghumārīs themselves, 'Alī al-Ḥalabī.

259 'Abd Allāh al-Ghumārī, *Bida' al-tafāsīr*, pp. 179–181.

260 He also wrote on legal theory but his followers have not focused so much on publishing his *uṣūl* texts.

ings are well-known. Nor did the latter benefit from as brilliant a servant of his legacy as al-Kawtharī did in the person of ʿAbd al-Fattāḥ Abū Ghudda who painstakingly edited and published much of his work and was himself a jurist and hadith scholar, although he failed to illustrate his teacher's proficiency in theology and sufism. Al-Ghumārī's attack on al-Kawtharī is also an attack on the Ḥanafī school and Abū Ḥanīfa. He calls not only al-Kawtharī but Mullā ʿAlī al-Qārī 'rabid anti-Arabs' and attributes what he calls 'squalid bases' (*uṣūl khabītha*) to the entire Ḥanafī school. More importantly, when one looks at his virtual *takfīr* and apoplectic insults of al-Kawtharī on the one hand, then goes back to check the *fiqh*-imbued context of the latter's discussions in his *Taʾnīb* and *Nukat* for example, one realizes that al-Ghumārī was of a lesser standing in knowledge and morals than al-Kawtharī.

Following is Muḥammad Abū Zahra's funeral eulogy of al-Kawtharī:

> Islam has lost one of the imams of the Muslims, one who worked alone far from the trifles of this life, devoting himself to knowledge with the devotion of a believer to the worship of his Lord. That is because he knew that knowledge is part of the acts of worship whereby the scholar seeks the pleasure of Allah and none besides Him; he does not seek thereby a lofty station on earth, or corruption, or influence on account of distinction and reputation; nor does he seek any of the fleeting things of this world. He seeks only to make truth victorious in order to please the True One. Such was Imam al-Kawtharī. May Allah grant him pleasure for his resting place, may He be pleased with him and make him pleased! I do not know of any scholar who has departed and left his position vacant these past years such as the position Imam al-Kawtharī has left behind. He was the remnant of the pious predecessors, who did not take knowledge as a source of income, nor as a stepping-stone to a worldly goal. He was—may Allah be well-pleased with him!—a scholar of learning who personified the transmitted report, 'The Ulema are the inheritors of the Prophets.'[261] He did not consider this inheritance a mere title of honor by which to pride himself and dominate others. Rather, he considered it a jihad for the purpose of proclaiming Islam, showing its truths, and banishing the illusions that conceal its essence. He would show it to people pristine and radiant so that they rose to its light and were well-directed by its guidance. He considered such an inheritance a demand on the scholar that he strive just as the

261 Narrated in al-Bukhārī and the *Sunan* from Abū Saʿīd al-Khudrī.

Prophets strove, standing firm against hardships and tribulations just as they did, remaining patient like them when faced by the stubbornness of those he summoned to truth and guidance. Such inheritance is not an honor except to those who practice the means that lead to it, give it its due rights, and know the duties that come with it. Imam al-Kawtharī did all of the above. That distinguished imam was not an adherent of a new school of thought; nor was he someone inviting others to a novel matter with no precedent; nor was he one of those whom people label nowadays as 'reformers.' Nay! He used to shy away from that, for he was strictly a follower *(muttabiʿ)* and not an innovator. Yet, in spite of that, I say that he was one of the renewers *(mujaddidīn)* in the true sense of renewal. For renewal is not what people today commonly think, namely, casting off the noose and a return to the beginnings of Prophecy. Rather, it consists in giving back to the religion its splendor and dispelling the confusions that were cast over it, so that it will be shown to people in the purity of its essence and in its original pristine state. Renewal consists in giving life to the Sunna, causing innovation to die, and for the pillar of religion to stand tall among mankind. That is real and true renewal and, indeed, Imam al-Kawtharī undertook the revival of the Prophetic Sunna. He uncovered what had lain hidden in the alcoves of history out of the books of the Sunna; clarified the methods of its narrators; and made known to the people the Sunna of the Prophet in its sayings, its deeds and its tacit rulings through his treatises and books. Then he devoted himself entirely to the efforts of the past ulema who upheld the Sunna and gave it its due right. He published the books in which they compiled their works for the purpose of reviving the Sunna at a time when souls were imbued with love of the religion, hearts had not yet been corrupted, and the scholars were not swayed by the world away from the hereafter nor spent time at the beck and call of rulers. Imam al-Kawtharī was a true scholar. The scholars knew his knowledge. I knew him years before meeting him. I knew him through his writings in which the light of truth shone forth. I knew him through his commentaries on manuscripts which he undertook to publish. By Allah! My amazement at the manuscript did not match my amazement at the commentary of the editor. Even when the original manuscript was a brief epistle, yet the Imam's commentary on it would turn it into a major work that should be read. Truly one's insight and wide erudition show plainly in such commentaries. All this he did with an elegant style, subtle allusions, forceful analysis, accomplished accuracy, and total mastery over his own thought and writing technique. It could not occur to the mind of the reader that he was a non-Arab writer and not patently Arab. … Yet it is not really astonishing, for he was Turkish in ancestry, education, and everyday life at the time he lived in Istanbul but his scholarly life was purely Arabic, for he read nothing but Arabic, and nothing filled his head but the shining light of Muḥammadan Arabic. … He hailed from a family in the Caucasus, as reflected in his vigor, strength, handsome body and spirit, and the quality and depth of his thought. His father moved to Istanbul where he was born in surroundings of guidance and truth. He studied the Islamic sciences until he attained the highest rank in them at around twenty-eight years of age. Then he ascended the ladder of teaching positions until he reached their highest level quite early. He reached the point when he was confronted by those who wanted to separate the world from religion in order to rule the world by other than what Allah has revealed, but he stood in ambush for them despite the fact that he was yet without experience, with everything that a young man at the beginning of his career could hope for. But he chose his religion over their world. He chose to defend what was still left of Islam rather than have a pleasant life. He preferred to face continuous enmity while obtaining the good pleasure of Allah rather than pleasure and comfort amidst people's approval and the good pleasure of those who held the keys of the lower world. Obtaining the good pleasure of Allah is truly the goal of faith. He fought the promoters of atheism (*al-ilḥādiyyīn*) who were in power when they tried to shorten the period of study for the religious curriculum; he realized that to shorten it would jeopardize its preliminary and final parts, so he left no stone unturned until he did away with their agenda and even lengthened the period that they were trying to cut short, so that students would be able to absorb and digest all the disciplines they needed, especially for non-natives learning in a patent Arabic tongue. … He strove with all his might and effort—may Allah be well-pleased with him—on the loftiest paths until he became deputy of the office of Shaykh al-Islām in [Ottoman] Turkey. He was among those known to give such a post its due. He never exceeded bounds so as to please someone high-placed, no matter how great their power was over him, eventually preferring to be expelled from his position for the sake of upholding the public good. It is better to be expelled for the sake of truth than to implement falsehood. … Then the lofty-minded, abnegating, Godwary scholar was put to the severest test when he saw his dear country—the great land of Islam, the pivot of his strength, the locus of hopes for Muslims—overshadowed by atheism and taken over by those who do not wish any honor for this religion. The one who clings to his

> religion in such a place soon becomes like one clasping a burning coal. Then he finds himself targeted by persecution so that, unless he escaped, he would be thrown into some forlorn prisons and blocked from all that is knowledge and teaching. At that point, the imam faced three choices: either to remain a prisoner in chains, his knowledge buried in the deep gaol—a harsh fate for a scholar of learning accustomed to teach and guide others, extracting the treasures of the religion and bringing them to light for the benefit of humankind; or grovel and flatter and kowtow, short of which he would remain in fetters or even risk losing his life; or emigrate—and vast are the lands of Allah. He remembered the saying of Allāh, *Was not the earth of Allāh spacious that you could have migrated therein?* (al-Mā'ida 4:97). So he emigrated to Egypt then moved to Syria, then returned to Cairo, then went back to Damascus again, until he finally settled in Cairo. During his trips to Sham and his residence in Cairo he was a beacon of light. His residence expanded into a school to which flocked the students of true knowledge–not the students of schoolish knowledge. Those students were guided to the sources of knowledge through the books that were written when the marketplace of the Islamic sciences was vibrant and the souls of the Ulema were thriving with Islam. He coached the minds of those searching students with those sources and directed them to them. At the same time he would explain whatever they found obscure and pour out the abundance of his learning and share the fruits of his thought. ... I bear witness that I have heard the praise of eminent personalities and scholars, but I never prided myself with any of it as much as I prided myself with the praise of this magnificent shaykh–for such is a scholarly badge from someone who is truly able to give it. ... That noble man who suffered many trials and overcame them, was also afflicted with the loss of loved ones, for he lost his children during his own lifetime, death taking them one after the other. By virtue of his knowledge, he was able to be patient, uttering the statement of the Prophet Yaʿqūb, *Patience is beautiful, and the help of Allāh must be entreated* (Yūsuf 12:18).... He passed on to his Lord, patient, thankful and praiseful, as the sincere and righteous pass on. May Allah be pleased with him and make him pleased![262]

Al-Kawtharī himself recognized the charge that he was a fanatic Ḥanafī. This admission of guilt is paramount to understand the rationale of his attacks on such as Imām al-Ḥaramayn and Ibn Ḥajar which critics harped on.

262 Muḥammad Abū Zahra, preface to al-Kawtharī's *Maqālāt* and his edition of Ibn al-Jawzī's *Daf' shubah al-tashbīh.*

They themselves quoted him as responding, 'a fanatic rebutting a fanatic.' The latter is a rhetorical tit-for-tat 'discoursing with the opponent's tongue' even to extremes. Thus, because al-Kawtharī considered Ibn Ḥajar's disparagement of al-Ḥasan b. Ziyād al-Lu'lu'ī in *Lisān al-mīzān* went beyond the bounds of propriety, he himself went beyond them in his disparagement of Ibn Ḥajar; and because he thought Imām al-Ḥaramayn had gone too far in reviling Abū Ḥanīfa and his school in *Mughīth al-khalq*, he himself went too far in reviling al-Shāfiʿī in *Iḥqāq al-ḥaqq*. This is not to say that such a method is correct or appropriate, but it is a rhetorical repayment for the disparager's act in his own currency without ultimately claiming that such currency was ever valid, as proven by al-Kawtharī's immense respect and love for both Ibn Ḥajar and al-Shāfiʿī everywhere other than in the context of those disputes. Allah knows best.

al-Ṣaʿīdī

al-Ṣaʿīdī, ʿAbd al-Mutaʿāl. *Kitāb zubad al-ʿaqāʾid al-Nasafiyya.* Cairo: al-Maṭbaʿat al-Raḥmāniyya, [1930?].

Famed as an Azharī reformer who authored more than forty books, ʿAbd al-Mutaʿāl al-Ṣaʿīdī (1311–1386/1894–1966) said he wrote the *Zubad* out of class notes summarizing all his readings of the marginalia and commentaries on the Nasafī creed, organized with a revisionist twist under the following headings:

1. Preamble
2. Introduction: The reality of existent things is firmly established and their knowledge is verifiable
3. Knowledge and its paths
4. The world: its definition and its subdivisions
5. Is the world originated or without beginning?
6. The Initiator of existents
7. The reality of the Initiator is unfathomable
8. The attributes of the Initiator are undefinable
9. The necessity of His existence
10. Unicity

11. Beginninglessness
12. Divine alterity/otherness apart from all originated things (*al-mukhālafa lil-ḥawādith*)
13. Knowledge
14. Power
15. Life, hearing and sight
16. Speech
17. The issue of the createdness of the Qur'ān
18. Existentiation
19. Will
20. Is attribute other than essence or the very same?
21. Vision of Allah
22. The creation of acts and their being according to His will
23. Tasking of something impossible
24. The pairing of power with the act
25. The one murdered dies by virtue of his lifespan
26. Provision
27. Guidance and misguidance
28. The question of that which is fitting and fittest
29. The states of the grave and resurrection
30. The balance of deeds
31. The record of deeds, the questioning, the basin and the bridge
32. Paradise and hellfire
33. Allah forgives sins
34. Intercession
35. Belief
36. Belief neither increases nor decreases
37. Saying *in shā' Allah* in belief
38. *Islām*
39. The wisdom of sending messengers
40. The prophethood of Adam
41. The prophethood of Muḥammad and the number of prophets
42. What is obligatory concerning prophets and what is impossible
43. Angels and paradise
44. Preferentiality between humans and angels

45. The miraculous gifts of the friends of Allah
46. The night journey and heavenly ascent
47. Overall leadership
48. Conclusion on miscellaneous issues

Contemporary Literature (in Order of Publication)

Devenny, Joseph Austin. *Al-Maturidi's Sharh al-Fiqh al-Akbar and his Quranic Argument for Qadr*. Unpubl. diss. Cambridge, Mass.: Harvard University, 1954. 273 p.

Madelung, Wilferd. "The spread of Māturīdism and the Turks." In *Actas do IV Congresso de Estudos Árabes e Islâmicos, Coimbra-Lisboa 1968*. Leiden: E.J. Brill, 1971. Rept. In Wilferd Madelung, *Religious Schools and Sects in Medieval Islam*. London: Variorum Reprints, 1985.

al-Ghālī, Balqāsim. *Abū Manṣūr al-Māturīdī: ḥayātuh wa-ārā'uh al-ʿaqadiyya*. Tunis: Dār al-Turkī lil-Nashr, 1989.

Lewinstein, Keith. 'Notes on Eatern Ḥanafite Heresiography.' *Journal of the American Oriental Society*. Vol. 114 no. 4 (Oct.-Dec. 1994), pp. 583–598.

Cerić, Mustafa. *Roots of Synthetic Theology in Islām: A Study of the Theology of Abū Manṣūr al-Māturīdī*. Kuala Lumpur: International Institute of Islamic Thought and Civilization, 1995.

Farfūr, Muḥammad Ṣāliḥ (1901–1986). *al-Risālat al-nāfiʿa wal-ḥujjat al-qāṭiʿa*. Damascus: Dār al-Farfūr, 1421/2001. English Translation: *The Beneficial Message and the Definitive Proof in the Study of Theology*. Transl. Wesam Charkawi. [Auburn, Australia:] Wesam Charkawi, 2010.

Zysow, Aron. "Muʿtazilism and Maturidism in Hanafi Legal Theory." In *Studies in Islamic Legal Theory*. Ed. Bernard G. Weiss. Leiden and Boston: Brill, 2002. Studies in Islamic law and society, vol. 15.

Jābī, Bassām ʿAbd al-Wahhāb, ed. *al-Masāʾil al-khilāfiyya bayna al-Ashāʿira wal-Māturīdiyya.* Beirut: Dār Ibn Ḥazm, 1424/2003. Comprising Tāj al-Dīn al-Subkī, *al-Qaṣīdat al-nūniyya fil-khilāf bayna al-Ashāʿira wal-Māturīdiyya*; Abū ʿAdhaba, *al-Rawḍat al-bahiyya fī mā bayna al-Ashāʿira wal-Māturīdiyya* (*q.v.*); [pseudo-] Shaykh Zadah, ʿAbd al-Raḥīm b. ʿAlī, *Naẓm al-farāʾid wa-jamʿ al-fawāʾid fī bayān al-masāʾil al-latī waqaʿa fīhā al-ikhtilāf bayna al-Māturīdiyya wal-Ashāʿira fil-ʿaqāʾid* (*q.v.*).

Kutlu, Sönmez. *İmam Mâturidi ve Maturidilik: tarihi arka plan, hayatı, eserleri, fikirleri ve Maturidilik mezhebi.* Ankara: Kitâbiyat, 2003.

Er al-Mīrānī, Muḥammad Amīn. *ʿAwn al-Raʾūf fī ʿilm uṣūl al-dīn.* In his *Jāmiʿ al-Mutūn al-Dirāsiyya.* Damascus: Dār al-Thaqāfa wal-Turāth, 2007. Pp. 411–415.

A brief treatise by the Naqshbandi Kurdish master Mullā Muḥammad Amīn Er b. Dhūl-Kifl b. ʿAlī b. Aḥmad al-Mīrānī (1332–1434/ 1914–2013), one of many he authored on various topics, recapitulating the themes of Māturīdī doctrine with several pithy definitions (e.g. 'the *muʿjiza* is a breach of custom coupled with a challenge and devoid of opposition'; '*īmān* is confirmation by the heart… and *islām* is the declaration [of the two testimonies of faith]') and several choices of his own such as the interdiction (*manʿ*) of imitative belief; the possibility of seeing Allah in this life; refraining from declaring as an unbeliever any of the People of the Qibla; and the validity of saying 'I am a *muʾmin in shāʾ Allāh*' not out of doubt.

al-Ḥāḍirī, ʿAbd al-ʿAzīz ʿAbd al-Jabbār. *Tanzīh al-Ḥaqq al-maʿbūd ʿan al-ḥayyiz wal-ḥudūd.* [The declaration that the Real Who is worshipped is transcendent beyond dimension and limits.] Damascus: Maktabat al-Yusr, 1428/2007. 500 p.

This is a major work in the reaffirmation of the Sunni foundations of the creed with regard to the divine transcendence and the invalidation of anthropomorphism, written by a Damascene Hanafi who also authored a major refutation of Ibn al-Qayyim's anthropomorphist manifesto *Ijtimāʿ al-juyūsh al-Islāmiyya* entitled *al-Naqḍ al-kabīr ʿalā Ijtimāʿ al-juyūsh al-Islāmiyya.* The book received forewords by Shaykh Adīb Kallās and Shaykh ʿAbd al-Hādī Kharsa among others. Its subtitle is, 'A word on al-Ṭaḥāwī's creed *He – Most High – is exalted beyond boundaries and confines* and the extent to which Ibn Taymiyya is in violation of it.' It contains (pp. 200–204) a valuable list of the Sunni authorities who declared the attribution of the anthropomorphist *Risālat al-istiwā'* to Abū Muḥammad al-Juwaynī a forgery.

Ak, Ahmet. *Büyük Türk âlimi Mâturîdî ve Mâturîdîlik*. A. Ak, 2008.

Badeen, Edward. *Sunnitische Theologie in osmanischer Zeit*. Würzburg: Ergon Verlag, 2008.

al-Maghribī, ʿAbd al-Fattāḥ. *Imām Ahl al-Sunna wal-Jamāʿā Abū Manṣūr al-Māturīdī wa-ārāʾuh al-kalāmiyya*. Cairo: Maktabat Wahba, 1430/2009. 455 p.

Başaran, Yasin Ramazan. 'The Idea of Subjective Faith in al-Maturidi's Theology.' *Journal of Islamic Research*. Vol. 4 no. 2 (2011). Pp. 48–54.

Lange, Christian. 'Sin, Expiation and Non-rationality in Ḥanafī and Shāfiʿī *Fiqh*.' In *Islamic Law in Theory*. Ed. A. Kevin Reinhart and Robert Gleave. Leiden and Boston: Brill, 2014. Pp. 143–175.

Brodersen, Angelika. *Der Unbekannte Kalām: Theologische Positionen der Frühen Māturīdīya am Beispiel der Attributenlehre*. Berlin: Lit, [2014].[263]

Rudolph, Ulrich. *al-Māturīdī and the Development of Sunnī Theology in Samarqand*. Transl. Rodrigo Adem. Leiden and Boston: Brill, 2015. First published as *al-Māturīdī und die Sunnitische Theologie in Samarkand*. Leiden, New York, Cologne: E.J. Brill, 1997.

———. "Ḥanafī theological tradition and Māturīdism." In *The Oxford Handbook of Islamic Theology*. Ed. Sabine Schmidtke. Oxford, UK: Oxford University Press, 2016.

263 See also https://www.academia.edu/13832577/The_Divine_Will_in_the_Conception_of_al-Māturīdī_and_his_Successors

Berger, Lutz. "Interpretations of Ash'arism and Māturīdism in Mamluk and Ottoman times." In *The Oxford Handbook of Islamic Theology*. Ed. Sabine Schmidtke. Oxford, UK: Oxford University Press, 2016.

Haida, Yahya Raad. *The Debates between Ash'arism and Māturīdism in Ottoman Religious Scholarship: A Historical and Bibliographical Study*. Unpubl. Diss. Australian National University, March 2016. 228 p.

Chaker, Aref. 'The Life of Abū Manṣūr al-Māturīdī and the Socio-Political and Theological Context of Central Asia in the Tenth Century.' *Australian Journal of Islamic Studies*. Vol. 1, Issue 1, 2016. Pp. 39–64.

Aldosari, Ayedh S. *Hanafi Maturidism: Trajectories of a Theological Legacy. With a Study and Critical Edition of al-Khabbazi's* Kitab al-Hadi. Sheffield, UK and Bristol, CT Equinox Publishing, 2017.

Darwīsh, 'Ādil. *al-Ashā'ira wal-Māturīdiyya nash'atan wa-fikran*. [Cairo:] Maktabat al-Īmān lil-Ṭibā'a wal-Tawzī', 2017.

Sālim, 'Awwād Maḥmūd 'Awwād. *al-Ta'rīf bil-madrasat al-Māturīdiyya tārīkhān wa-manhajan wa-'aqīda*. Cairo: Dār al-Imām al-Rāzī, 2017. 124 p.

al-Damanhūrī, Aḥmad Sa'd. *Sadd al-thughūr bi-sīrat 'Alam al-hudā Abī Manṣūr al-Imām al-Māturīdī*. Amman: Dār al-Nūr al-Mubīn, 2018.

Brodersen, Angelika. "The Divine Will in the Conception of al-Māturīdī and his Successors." In *International Symposium on Maturidism (past, present and future): Papers*. Ankara: Ahmet Yesevi Üniversitesi, 2018. https://www.academia.edu/13832577/The_Divine_Will_in_the_Conception_of_al_Māturīdī_and_his_Successors

Harvey, Ramon. "Al-Māturīdī on the Abrogation of the *Sharī'a* in the Qur'an and Previous Scriptures." In *İmâm Mâtürîdî ve Te'vîlâtü'l-Kur'ân*. Ed. Hatice K. Arpaguş, Mehmet Ümit and Bilal Kır. Istanbul: M.Ü. İlâhiyat Fakültesi Vakfı Yayınları, 2019.

SUPPLEMENTS: CHAINS OF TRANSMISSION OF SOME OF THE MĀTURĪDĪ MASTERS

Table 3
al-Ṭaḥāwī, al-Māturīdī, al-Ṣābūnī and the Nasafīs[264]

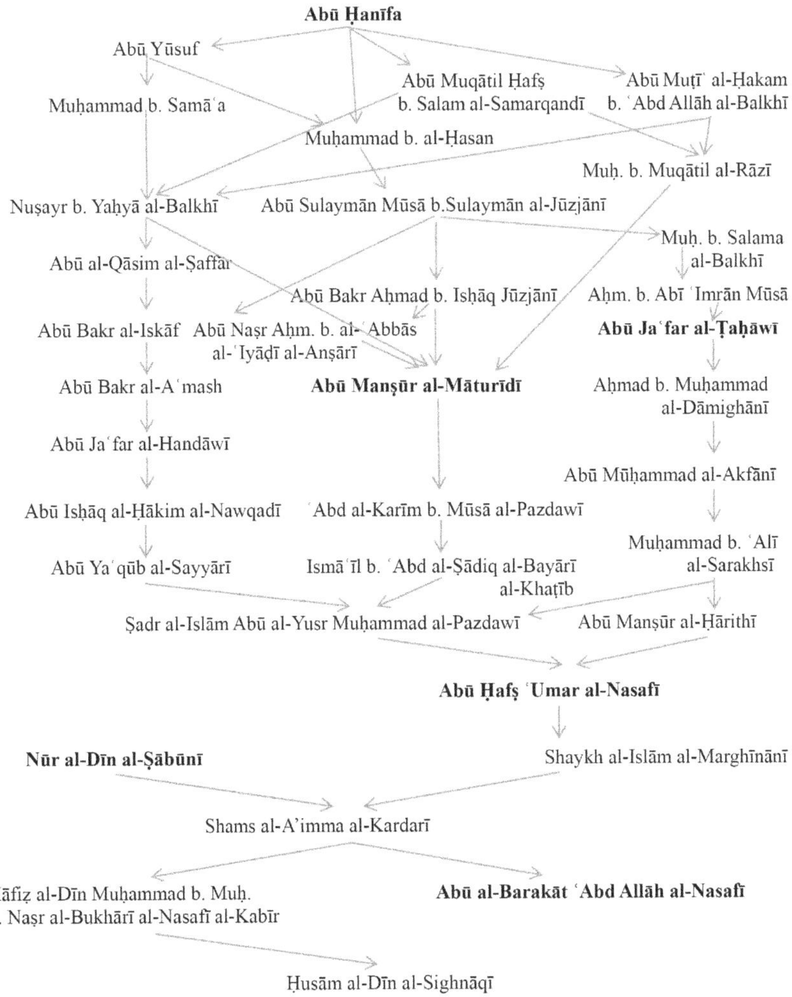

264 'Ubayd Allāh al-Sindī, *Tamhīd*, pp. 210, 217

Table 4
The Pazdawīs, the Samarqandīs and the Nasafīs[265]

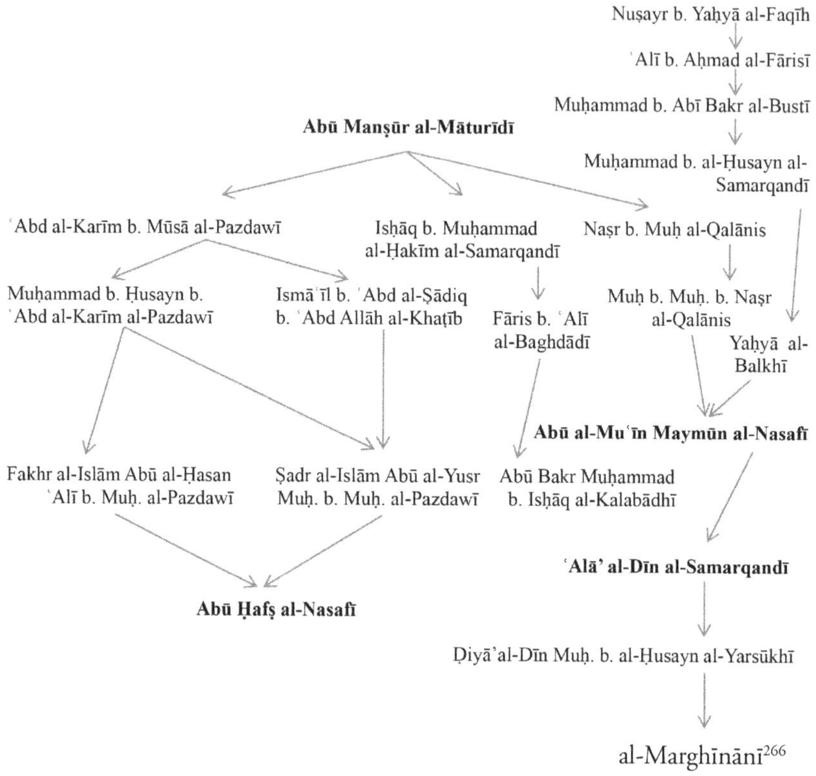

265 ʿUbayd Allāh al-Sindī, *Tamhīd*, pp. 217, 290–291; ʿAbd al-Fattāḥ Abū Ghudda, *Namādhij min rasā'il al-a'immat al-salaf wa-adabihim al-ʿilmī* (Aleppo: Maktab al-Maṭbūʿāt al-Islāmiyya, 1417/1996), p. 21.

266 See also Ulrich Rudolph, *al-Māturīdī und die Sunnitische Theologie in Samarkand* (Leiden, New York, Cologne: E.J. Brill, 1997), p. 161. English: *al-Māturīdī and the Development of Sunnī Theology in Samarqand.* Transl. Rodrigo Adem. Leiden and Boston: Brill, 2015. Note, however, that contrary to what Rudolph suggests in his lineage tree of al-Māturīdī's teachers and students, Abū Muṭīʿ al-Balkhī does *not* narrate from Abū Muqātil al-Samarqandī.

Table 5
Kawtharī's *Isnāds* in Ash'arī *Kalām* (I–II), Māturīdī *Kalām* and Ḥanafī Fiqh/*Uṣūl* (III), Qur'ān and Hadith (IV–V)[267]

I. Muḥammad Zāhid b. Ḥasan Ḥilmī b. ʿAlī al-Kawtharī (1296–1371/1879–1952) narrates from Ibrāhīm Ḥaqqī b. Ismāʿīl b. ʿUmar al-Akīnī (d. 1318/1900) and

II. Abū al-Ikhlāṣ ʿAlī Zayn al-ʿĀbidīn b. al-Ḥasan b. Mūsā al-Alaṣūnī (d. 1336/1918), both of them from Aḥmad Shākir b. Khalīl Istanbūlī (d. 1315/1897), from Muḥammad Ghālib b. Muḥammad al-Amīn al-Istanbūlī (d. 1286/1869), from Sulaymān b. Ḥasan al-Kirīdī (d. 1258?/1842?), from Ibrāhīm b. Muḥammad al-Isbīrī[268] al-Arḍrūmī (d. 1255/1840), from ʿAlī al-Fikrī b. Muḥammad Ṣāliḥ al-Akhiskhawkhī (d. 1236/1821), from (i) the Ottoman Ḥanafī jurist, qadi, exegete, logician, mathematician, astronomer, and doctrinologist Abū al-Fatḥ Ismāʿīl b. Muṣṭafā b. Maḥmūd al-Kalanbawī (d. 1205/1791); (ii) Muḥammad Amīn b. Yūsuf al-Āyāqlī al-Anṭālī, known as Muftī Zādah al-Kabīr and as Āyāqlī Kutubkhānah [walking library] (1112–1212/1700–1797), from Abū Saʿīd al-Khādimī (*q.v.*); and (iii) Muḥammad Munīb al-ʿAynatābī (d. 1238/1823) author of marginalia on Shaybānī's *al-Siyar al-kabīr*, the latter from Ismāʿīl b. Muḥammad al-Qūnawī (d. 1195/1781) author of the major supercommentary on *Anwār al-tanzīl*, from ʿAbd al-Karīm al-Qūnawī al-Āmidī (d. 1150/1737), from ʿUthmān al-Diwrikī al-Qayṣarī, from ʿAlī al-Natharī al-Qayṣarī, from Rajab b. Aḥmad al-Āmidī al-Qayṣarī, from ʿAbd al-Raḥmān al-Āmidī, from Muḥammad b. ʿAlī—known as Mullā Čelebī al-Āmidī—and Muḥyī al-Dīn al-Jazarī, both of them from Muḥammad Amīn al-Shirwānī, from al-Ḥusayn al-Khalkhālī and Aḥmad al-Mujalī,

267 See al-Kawtharī's *Taḥrīr al-wajīz*, pp. 10, 16–22, 41 and his *ijāza* to the first Mufti of Eritrea Ibrāhīm al-Mukhtār Aḥmad ʿUmar al-Jabartī al-Zaylaʿī (1909–1969) posted with many misspellings at http://www.azahera.net/showthread.php?t=3506 and http://mukhtar.ca/نص-إجازتي-الشيخ-البنا-الساعاتي-و-الشيخ/. Also see Abū al-Muʿīn al-Nasafī, *Tabṣira*, ʿĪsā ed., 1:26–28.

268 From present-day İspir in Erzurum, Eastern Anatolia.

both of them from Ḥabīb Allāh Mīrzājān, from Jamāl al-Dīn Maḥmūd al-Shīrāzī, from Jalāl al-Dīn Muhammad b. Asʿad al-Dawwānī, from his father, from al-Sayyid al-Sharīf al-Jurjānī, from Muḥammad Mubārak Shāh al-Manṭiqī, from Quṭb al-Dīn al-Rāzī, from Quṭb al-Dīn al-Shīrāzī and Najm al-Dīn ʿAlī b. ʿUmar al-Kātib al-Qazwīnī, both of them from al-Naṣīr Muḥammad b. Muḥammad b. al-Ḥasan al-Ṭūsī, from Quṭb al-Dīn Ibrāhīm b. ʿAlī al-Miṣrī, from Fakhr al-Dīn al-Rāzī, from Majd al-Dīn al-Jīlī, from Muḥammad b. Yaḥyā al-Naysābūrī, from Abū Ḥāmid al-Ghazālī.

III. Both Ḥaqqī al-Akīnī and al-Alaṣūnī with their chain to ʿAbd al-Karīm al-Qūnawī al-Āmidī, from Muḥammad al-Yamānī al-Azharī (d. 1135/1723), from ʿAbd al-Ḥayy al-Shurunbulālī, from Abū al-Ikhlāṣ al-Ḥasan al-Shurunbulālī (d. 1069/1659), from ʿAbd Allāh b. Muḥammad al-Niḥrīrī and Shams al-Dīn Muḥammad al-Muḥibbī al-Qāhirī (d. 1041/1632), both of them from from ʿAlī al-Maqdisī (d. 1004/1596), from Aḥmad b. Yūnus al-Shalabī (d. 948/1541), from ʿAbd al-Barr Ibn al-Shiḥna (851–921/1447–1515), from al-Kamāl b. al-Humām al-Sakandarī (790–861/1388–1457), from Sirāj al-Dīn ʿUmar b. ʿAlī b. Fāris al-Kinānī al-Qāhirī *qāri' al-Hidāya* (d. 829/1426), who took *fiqh* **(1)** from ʿAlā' al-Dīn al-Sīrāmī (d. 790/1388), from Jalāl al-Dīn b. Shams al-Dīn al-Khwārizmī al-Karlānī, from ʿAlā' al-Dīn ʿAbd al-ʿAzīz b. Aḥmad b. Muḥammad al-Bukhārī (d. 730) the author of *Kashf al-asrār* (a commentary on Pazdawī's *Uṣūl)*, from Ḥāfiẓ al-Dīn Abū al-Barakāt ʿAbd Allāh b. Aḥmad b. Maḥmud al-Nasafī (d. 710/1310) (*q.v.*), author of *Madārik al-tanzīl*, from *Shams al-a'imma* Muḥammad b. ʿAbd al-Sattār al-Kardarī (d. 642/1244); and **(2)** from Akmal al-Dīn Muḥammad b. Muḥammad b. Maḥmūd al-Bābirtī (714–786/1314–1384) author of *al-ʿInāya*, from Qiwām al-Dīn Muḥammad al-Kākī (d. 749/1348) author of *Miʿrāj al-Dirāya*, from Ḥusām al-Dīn al-Ḥusayn b. ʿAlī b. al-Ḥajjāj al-Sighnāqī (d. 710/1310) (*q.v.*), author of *al-Nihāya*, from Ḥafiẓ al-Dīn al-Kabīr Muḥammad b. Muḥammad b. Naṣr al-Bukhārī (d. 693/1294), from al-Kardarī, from Shaykh al-Islām Burhān al-Dīn Abū al-Ḥasan ʿAlī b. Abī Bakr b. ʿAbd al-Jalīl al-Marghīnānī (d. 593/1197) author of *al-Muntaqā*, *Nashr al-madhhab*, and *al-Hidāya*, from **(i)** Ḍiyā' al-Dīn Muḥammad b. al-Ḥusayn

b. Nāṣir al-Yarsūkhī, from ʿAlā' al-Dīn Abū Bakr [b.] Muḥammad b. Aḥmad al-Samarqandī author of *Mīzān al-uṣūl fī natā'ij al-ʿuqūl*, from Abū al-Muʿīn al-Nasafī (*q.v.*) with the chain cited above; and from **(ii)** Najm al-Dīn Abū Ḥafṣ al-Nasafī (*q.v*), from the two Pazdawī brothers Fakhr al-Islām (d. 482/1089) and Ṣadr al-Islām (d. 493/1100), the first of whom took *fiqh* from *Shams al-a'imma* al-Sarakhsī (d. 483/1090) author of the *Mabsūṭ*, from *Shams al-a'imma* al-Ḥulwānī (d. 448/1056), from al-Ḥusayn b. Khaḍir al-Nasāfī (d. 423/1032), from Muḥammad b. al-Faḍl al-Bukhārī (d. 381/991), from ʿAbd Allāh b. Muḥammad al-Ḥārithī (d. 340/951), from Muḥammad b. Aḥmad b. Ḥafṣ (d. 264/878), from his father Abū Ḥafṣ al-Kabīr (d. 217/832), from Muḥammad b. al-Ḥasan al-Shaybānī (d. 189/805); while Ṣadr al-Islām took *fiqh* from Ismāʿīl b. ʿAbd al-Ṣādiq, from ʿAbd al-Karīm al-Pazdawī (d. 390/1000) (*q.v.*), from *Imām al-hudā* Abū Manṣūr al-Māturīdī (d. 333/945) (*q.v.*), from Abū Bakr al-Jūjzānī, from Abū Sulaymān Mūsā b. Sulaymān al-Jūjzānī, from Muḥammad b. al-Ḥasan al-Shaybānī, from Abū Ḥanīfa.

IV. al-Kawtharī also narrates from his father and

V. al-Ḥasan b. ʿAbd Allāh al-Qasṭamūnī, both of them from Ḍiyā' al-Dīn al-Kumushkhānawī (*q.v.*), from ʿAbd al-Raḥmān b. ʿAbd Allah Afandī al-Kurdī al-Kharbūtī (d. 1270/1854), from al-Ḥusayn al-Īlghīnī, from Muḥammad Ṣādiq b. ʿAbd al-Raḥīm b. Sulaymān al-Arzanjāni known as Muftī Zādah al-Ṣaghīr (d. 1223/1808), from ʿAbd al-Raḥmān al-Quyūjaghī, from Muftī Zādah al-Kabīr and al-ʿAynatābī.[269] (ح) al-Kumushkhānawī also narrated from Aḥmad b. Sulaymān al-Arwādī, from Khālid al-Baghdādī, from Shāh ʿAbd al-ʿAzīz b. Aḥmad b. ʿAbd al-Raḥīm al-Dihlawī, from his father Aḥmad b. ʿAbd al-Raḥīm known as Shāh Walī Allāh al-Dihlawī, from Ibn ʿAqīla, from al-ʿUjaymī, from Muḥammad Ḥusayn al-Khāfī the author of *al-Ṭarīqat al-Muḥammadiyya fī bayān al-ṭarīqat al-Naqshbandiyya*, from ʿAbd al-Ḥaqq al-Dihlawī, from ʿAlī al-Muttaqī al-Hindī, from Mullā ʿAlī al-Qārī. (ح) Shāh Walī Allāh also narrated from Tāj al-Dīn al-Qalʿī who represents the highest chain among his teachers, from Khālid b. Aḥmad

269 *al-Taḥrīr al-wajīz*, p. 61.

al-Jaʿfarī al-Mālikī al-Makkī, from Shams al-Dīn Muḥammad al-Ramlī, from Shaykh al-Islām Zakariyyā al-Anṣārī with his chains.

Theme-to-Source Index

Milton Keynes UK
Ingram Content Group UK Ltd.
UKHW041418121224
3633UKWH00043B/294

9 781912 356720